Communication and Latin American Society

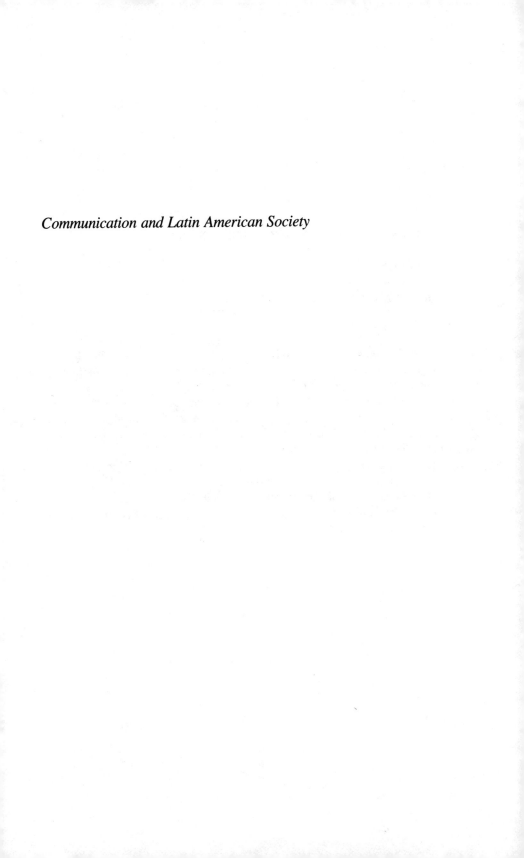

Studies in Communication and Society

A series edited by

Vincent Mosco and Janet Wasko

Studies in Communication and Society is a series of books covering the wide range of substantive and theoretical issues in the relationship of communications to social structure. The series is connected by a commitment to challenge established perspectives in communications research, identify the connections between communication practices and the wider social and historical setting, and advance the use of media and information technologies as instruments of democratic social change.

The series represents the diversity and richness of recent critical communications scholarship. The contributions by critical scholars to the field involve a wide range of research endeavors, including the historical analysis of communications/information policies, the political economy of communications, cultural studies, and the study of ideology.

Communication and Latin American Society

Trends in Critical Research, 1960–1985

Edited by

Rita Atwood and Emile G. McAnany

THE UNIVERSITY OF WISCONSIN PRESS

Published 1986

The University of Wisconsin Press
114 North Murray Street
Madison, Wisconsin 53715

The University of Wisconsin Press, Ltd.
1 Gower Street
London WC1E 6HA, England

First printing

Printed in the United States of America

For LC CIP information see the colophon

ISBN 0-299-10720-5

This book is dedicated to the pioneers of critical communication research in Latin America: Luis Ramiro Beltrán, Armand Mattelart, Antonio Pasquali, and Eliseo Veron. This book is also dedicated to Paulo Freire, whose efforts on behalf of oppressed people have had universal influence in communication, education, and many related fields.

Contents

Part IV. Alternatives for Latin American Cultures

Acknowledgments

We would like to express our appreciation to the College of Communication and the Institute of Latin American Studies at the University of Texas, Austin, for sponsoring the conference on Transnational Communication and Culture in June 1982, that provided impetus and much of the material for this book. We would like to thank the Instituto Latinoamericano de Estudios Transnacionales for support and specially mention Rafael Roncagliolo and Noreene Janus who helped initiate contacts with Latin American scholars attending this conference. We appreciate the participation of those Latin American scholars, and the graduate students and faculty from the United States who attended.

The Department of Radio-Television-Film at the University of Texas assisted with support for this manuscript. We would also like to thank the editors of this series, Janet Wasko and Vincent Mosco, and the staff of the University of Wisconsin Press with whom we have worked, particularly Jack Kirshbaum and Gordon Lester-Massman. Jane Barry did an excellent job as copy editor for this volume.

On a more personal note, we are grateful to Evelyn Atwood, Rosemary Elmer, and Austin McAnany for their encouragement. Finally, we appreciate the efforts of those individuals who contributed chapters to this book and helped us realize the completion of this project.

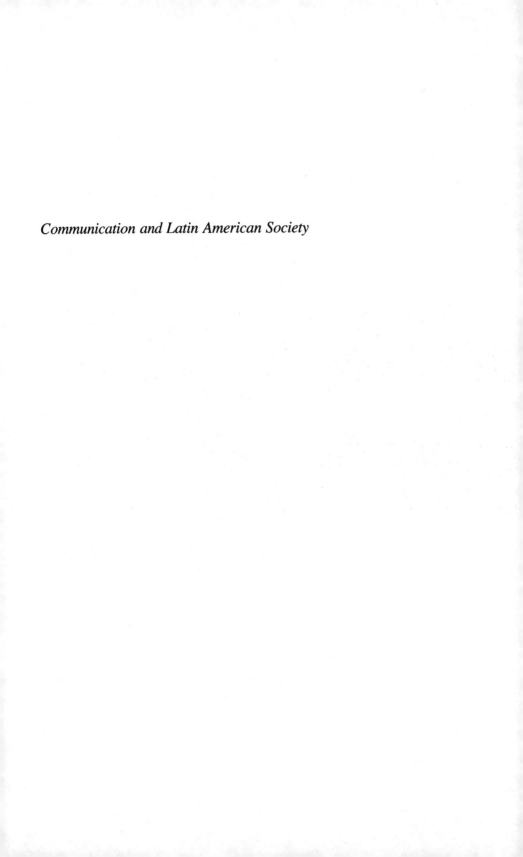

Communication and Latin American Society

Janet Wasko

Overview

Although critical communications research continues to expand in the United States, there are still noticeable gaps in our knowledge of similar traditions in other parts of the world. There seems to be increased awareness of Western European scholarship. However, relatively less seems to be known about critical communications research from Latin America.

Critical communication scholars and practitioners in the U.S. are now confronted by a number of challenges relating to Latin America. As U.S. military and economic activities in the area intensify, there is an urgent need not only to become more cognizant, but involved in struggles relating to communication.

Since communication and information issues have become key factors in U.S. foreign policy, it is even more urgent for critical researchers and activists to participate in and contribute to policy debates.

In addition, the dramatic growth of the Hispanic population in the U.S. should prompt immediate attention to Latin American issues.

Thus, not only geography, but history, as well, compels us to overcome our ethnocentric biases and our ignorance of Latin American research and practice. This collection is an effort to bridge this gap and contribute to a better understanding of communications and society in Latin America.

An Introduction to Latin American Critical Research

Rita Atwood states in the first introductory chapter: "the main objectives of this volume are to contribute to an expanded awareness of Latin American critical communication literature and to encourage an intensified South–North dialogue among communication scholars and practitioners." In discussing the various constraints that have inhibited a South–North flow of critical communication research, Atwood notes that most communication research in or about Latin America by U.S. scholars has suffered from "ethnocentric rigidity, mercantile or imperialistic motives, and methodological inadequacy." She argues that the most productive way to begin a dialogue between critical

3

communicators from these regions is to identify research issues from both traditions so that research issues and controversies in North America can be contrasted with Latin American approaches.

Although there are economic, social, and political differences between researchers in Latin America and North America, Atwood observes that U.S. scholars have lessons to learn from the contributions of their Latin American counterparts. The importance of linking theory with practice, for instance, is given far more prominence in Latin American work, and Atwood concludes that "this element of praxis in mass communication inquiry may turn out to be the most durable lesson from Latin America."

Emile McAnany provides an overview of critical literature from Latin America during the last two decades, relating the various themes to concerns facing colleagues in the United States and Western Europe. The first theme, transnationalization, is not a new one for scholars in the United States and Canada, for much critical work has been done to document this phenomenon, as McAnany's list of references confirms. However, he calls for further analysis of this long-term trend from "inside the belly of the beast." He reviews the literature on the theme of cultural imperialism and dependency, identifying three traditions that have contributed to this discussion. He names Canada as a traditional ally of Latin America in this type of analysis, but suggests areas where U.S. researchers could also contribute. In his discussion of a closely related theme, McAnany suggests that a better understanding of Latin American Marxist and neo-Marxist analysis could promote a more complete cultural analysis by North American researchers.

Latin American scholars also raise questions about communication technology and its impact, many of which are applicable to North America and to other societies. McAnany notes that the answers to these questions could be applied to the problem of the uneven distribution of information technology in industrialized countries. Another area of concern for critical researchers is alternative communication. Latin Americans insights in this area are especially interesting, as efforts to democratize communication and build a "culture of opposition" are often identified as fundamental weaknesses in critical work in the United States. Finally, McAnany discusses efforts to build an indigenous communication model in Latin America. Although North American and other researchers may not be able to contribute directly to such efforts, it is still important to remain aware of these developments.

In the final introductory chapter, Cristina Schwarz and Oscar Jaramillo offer a more in-depth view of indigenous critical communication research in Hispanic America, arguing that such work represents a consistent and coherent set of theoretical propositions. They locate the critical approach within the concrete historical reality of Latin America. Four pioneers of critical research are featured, indicating the diversity of approaches to communications in Latin America, as opposed to the dominance of the functionalist tendency in U.S. research.

Schwarz and Jaramillo then discuss the arguments that formed the initial concerns of the critical tradition, tracing them to their present expression. They begin with the influence of developmentalism in the 1950s and 1960s, noting that "the incongruity between local reality and the developmentalist model . . . increased in the 1970s to the point where a systematic expression of that incongruity began to emerge in Hispanic American critical communication scholarship."

These authors identify technology transfer as a fundamental concern of Latin American researchers, who have focused on such areas as information flow, national sovereignty, and national communication policies. Research on transnationalization is given credit for bringing empirical evidence to bear on otherwise abstract arguments. The authors also discuss recent important work on national communication policies and examine the influence of European theories—particularly Marxist analysis and Europe's structuralist and semiotic traditions—on Hispanic America's analysis of capitalism.

Finally, Schwarz and Jaramillo discuss the search for communication alternatives, noting that the social reality of Hispanic America has prompted researchers to investigate the active role of audiences who receive mass-mediated messages: "Researchers are thus driven to participate, in a non-manipulative way, in the people's communication processes." They emphasize the importance of integrating theory with the material conditions that generated it, reminding us that "it is people—not theories—who make change possible."

Critical Theory, Transnational Communication and Culture

The remaining chapters in the volume were selected from the papers presented at a conference on U.S. and Latin American communication research at the University of Texas at Austin in 1982. These essays, which address many of the issues and concerns discussed in the introductory chapters, are representative of current Latin American critical communication work.

Rafael Roncagliolo presents an overview and analysis of communication research conducted by Latin Americans during the past decade, particularly work done by communication scholars associated with the Instituto Latinoamericano de Estudios Transnacionales (ILET). More specifically, Roncagliolo assesses research concerning international news flows, the transnationalization of the mass media, the expansion of new information technologies, and alternative approaches to democratic communication. He provides several propositions summarizing research findings and conclusions in these areas, offering suggestions for future directions.

Carlos Eduardo Lins da Silva analyzes both communication and cultural phenomena in the light of insights from Gramsci's theories, as well as those of various Latin American scholars. He deals explicitly with the theoretical assumptions guiding the study of the values and beliefs transmitted through communication media in Latin America and particularly in Brazil. Lins da Silva provides a summary account of the foreign influences on Brazilian culture, including a description of the communication mechanisms through which that culture has been formed, maintained, and sometimes altered.

In another theoretical essay, Javier Esteinou Madrid focuses on the tendency of the contemporary capitalist state to transform and dominate societal structures. Such domination, according to Esteinou Madrid, takes place through the creation of cultural support systems that assist the growth of multinational corporations and their related information apparatuses. Thus, mass media systems become vehicles for the legitimation of dominant ideologies and exercise great power in controlling opinion and destabilizing antiestablishment social movements.

The Effects of Transnationals on Culture

Latin American participants at the University of Texas conference agreed that it is important for U.S. researchers to provide knowledge about transnational communication from a U.S. perspective, since the phenomenon is a cross-cultural one that will only be understood and confronted if both sides work together. The first article in this section represents such an effort. Noreene Janus presents a study of international advertising in the context of transnational economic expansion from the U.S. outward and its impact on peripheral countries, especially those of Latin America. Her analysis includes the economic context of expanded transnational advertising and the consequent transnationalization of local mass media and consumption patterns. She also discusses the social, political, and cultural consequences of advertising growth, plus the efforts of peripheral groups to protect themselves in the face of this expansion.

In the next article, Alberto Montoya Martín del Campo and María Antonieta Rebeil Corella examine the thesis that commercial television is an important part of the informal educational sector among Mexico's youth. Their study looks at lower-class secondary school students who are involved in an educational television project. Satellite technology will expand this type of educational work throughout the country, but, the authors fear, will bring about a similar expansion of commercial television.

Montoya Martín del Campo and Rebeil Corella provide content and institutional analyses of commercial television in Mexico and, against this background, report on their study of 528 lower-class secondary school students in the Telesecundaria project. They found three areas where commercial television influences students' attitudes and values: opinions about U.S. and Mexican societies, ideas about social reality, as presented on soap operas, and knowledge and understanding of important international events affecting Mexico and Latin America, including the U.S. role in those events. The empirical results of their study fit the theoretical framework outlined at the beginning of the paper and show the power of commercial television to "Americanize" Mexican youths.

Alternatives for Latin American Cultures

As noted previously, work on alternative communications is an important contribution of critical communication researchers from Latin America. Maximo Simpson Grinberg begins his chapter on this subject with a brief analysis of the relationship between communication systems and other global economic and political structures. He ties this relationship to the dominant themes in Latin American communication research, delineating the points of agreement and controversy. Specific definitions of alternative communication in Latin American research are explored. The author concludes by urging the promotion of communication processes that reinforce basic societal and humanistic objectives as the only means of ensuring democratic and participatory systems in Latin America.

In the final chapter, Fernando Reyes Matta challenges models of communication processes that have been rooted in capitalist expansion and distinguishes between the strategy and the tactics necessary to develop alternative forms of communication. Reyes Matta argues that an analysis of alternative communication should not be limited to a communication perspective, but should situate communication phenomena within global economic, political, and cultural contexts. In an attempt to accomplish this objective, he traces the role of historical factors in the evolution of alternative communication concepts and practices in Latin America, describing a wide spectrum of alternative communication processes. This chapter, like those that precede it, provides a useful basis for increased South-North dialogue about communication issues of mutual concern.

I. AN INTRODUCTION TO
   LATIN AMERICAN CRITICAL
   COMMUNICATION RESEARCH

1 *Rita Atwood*

Assessing Critical Mass Communication Scholarship in the Americas: The Relationship of Theory and Practice

For decades North American mass communication research has been dominated by a restricted set of theoretical tenets and a correspondingly limited repertoire of rules for collecting and analyzing evidence. The boundaries of mass communication scholarship in the United States have been created, in part, as a response to the needs of government and industry and maintained to ensure research funding and academic security in university settings not particularly conducive to challenges directed toward established institutions (Fish, 1984; Gitlin, 1978; Thayer, 1983).

Exceptions to this pattern have emerged at various junctures in the evolution of North American mass communication research, but substantive departures from prevalent assumptions and methodologies have proliferated noticeably only in recent years. Among those diverging from mainstream mass communication research approaches are scholars whose work could be classified as belonging to the "critical" tradition of social science inquiry. Although many of these critical scholars acknowledge their debt to such North American researchers as Herb Schiller and Dallas Smythe, they often cite European scholars as providing the theoretical and methodological bases for critical inquiry. Certainly, the impact of European thought merits recognition. However, a review of North American critical communication literature might leave one with the mistaken impression that researchers in the Northern hemisphere have an exclusive claim to critical approaches to mass communication study.

11

To the contrary, a rich body of critical communication scholarship generated by Latin Americans during the past twenty years shares some of the fundamental concerns of U.S. research. The approaches even have similar historical origins. It is somewhat puzzling, then, that North American mass communication publications are almost uniformly devoid of reference to these Latin America writings when North American scholars in other disciplines are paying considerable attention to the work of their Latin American colleagues (Tulchin, 1983). This lack of attention is even more baffling when one considers that the most significant issues and problems covered by critical communication inquiry impinge directly on Third World nations.

Thus, the main objectives of this volume are to contribute to an expanded awareness of Latin American critical communication literature and to encourage an intensified South-North dialogue among communication scholars and practitioners. Consistent with these objectives, this chapter contains: (1) a description of the various factors that have inhibited a "South-North" flow of critical communication research; (2) an analysis of the basic components of critical communication approaches in the United States and Latin America; and (3) a summary of the contributions that Latin American critical communication literature has to offer to North American scholarship.

The Top-Down Flow of Mass Communication Research in the Americas

Among the most obvious reasons for the dearth of attention to Latin American writings in North American mass communication literature is the fact that few U.S. scholars read Spanish or Portuguese proficiently and translated materials are rare. However, North American linguistic deficiencies do not adequately explain the lack of scholarly attention to Latin American work, nor do they account for the historical dominance of the U.S. communication research models exported to Latin America. Imperialistic intentions and ethnocentricity have been attributed to many of the North American social scientists whose influence has been experienced in Latin America (Carter, 1983; Fuenzalida, 1983; Horowitz, 1967). Increasingly, U.S. social science approaches are being seen in Latin America as significant components of scientific or cultural imperialism (Capriles, 1980; Fals Borda, 1980, 1985).

Focusing on mass communication inquiry, Beltrán (1975, 1976) argues that U.S. researchers working in Latin America have consistently emphasized the effects of media messages in order to enhance persuasion techniques aimed at desired consumer markets. Other scholars contend that communication research conducted in Third World countries by North Americans has been guided by the agendas of the U.S. government and multinational business concerns (Rota, 1980; Schiller, 1979; Smythe, 1979). Diaz Bordenave (1976) suggests that the ethnocentric assumptions, as well as the marketing goals, of scholars from industrialized nations have misdirected foreign communication research activities in Latin America. Atwood (1980) provides evidence that ethnocentric bias has permeated U.S. communication literature regarding Latin America for the past fifty years, in contexts ranging from evaluations of press freedom to studies of "cognitive modernity" and the effects of innovation diffusion.

Numerous researchers have questioned the validity of concepts and data collection methods employed by U.S. communication investigators in Latin America and other developing regions (Dervin, 1980; Golding, 1974; Halloran, 1981; Hedebro, 1982; Hur, 1982; McAnany, 1980; McAnany, Schnitman, and Janus, 1981; Mattelart, 1979; Nordenstreng and Varis, 1974; Roling, Ascroft, and Chege, 1976). Marques de Melo (1975) identifies the major flaw of traditional U.S. communication research as a preoccupation with theory testing as opposed to a concern with solving the problems confronting the citizens of Latin American countries. Rogers (1976) admits that work on the diffusion of innovations failed to yield much useful data from Latin America because the model was neither theoretically nor culturally appropriate. White (1984) criticizes the authoritarian concepts inherent in North American mass communication approaches and suggests that researchers involved in Latin American communication must alter both their ideas and their allegiances.

It appears that the track record of most mass communication research conducted in or exported to Latin America by U.S. scholars lends credence to charges of ethnocentric rigidity, mercantile or imperialistic motives, and methodological inadequacy. Further, these factors have assisted in creating a historical situation in which readers of North American communication literature learn about Latin America almost exclusively through the often distorted perceptions of U.S. scholars.

One should not be surprised, then, to find that many critical communication researchers from Latin America have expressed skepticism regarding the existence of common grounds for discussion with their North American colleagues. Beltrán (1975, p. 192) was prompted a decade ago to stress the wide breach between U.S. and Latin American communication scholars, proposing that the latter might have to opt for "ideologically conservative and methodologically rigorous research" or risk accusations of "unrigorous radicalism." Martín Barbero (1982, p. 101) explains that Latin American communication scholars from both ends of the political spectrum are wary of the importance attached to "theory construction"—those on the right see theory as the proper domain of scholars from industrialized countries, those on the left believe that Latin America's problems dictate immediate, energetic action. Yet Martín Barbero goes on to say that the real crux of dependency is not assuming theories imposed by foreign scholars but accepting external conceptions of science, scientific work, and the role of science in society.

Challenges to the epistemological foundations of social science are not unique to Latin American scholars. As Marsal says:

The crisis of social science is not a crisis stemming from the curious mentality of the "thinkers" in Latin America. Nor is it, as is thought nowadays, a sociology of the Southern hemisphere against one of the Northern hemisphere. . . . It is because the political circumstances and the ideological crises in Europe and the United States have an extraordinary resemblance to those we have suffered for decades in Latin America [that] the ideological questioning of the social sciences has spread throughout the world. (1970, p. 91, my translation)

Such questioning resides at the core of critical communication inquiry in both the United States and Latin America. As the intellectual horizons of mass communication scholarship in North America have expanded to include departures from mainstream paradigms, the need for sharing with and learning from Latin American critical thinkers has become more apparent. The ignorance of Latin American research endeavors evident among many North American scholars suggests that the most meaningful efforts to stimulate dialogue might involve identifying and defining basic assumptions and orientations.

Other serious impediments to a productive South-North discourse are semantic differences and diverse perspectives on the relation of theory to practice in communication inquiry. Therefore, whereas other authors more thoroughly treat the sociology of communication scholarship in North America (Fish, 1984; Katzen, 1975; McQuail, 1984) and Latin America (Correl, 1982; Marques de Melo, 1984; Martín Barbero, 1982), the following section compares critical communication approaches in both regions.

Critical Communication Research Issues: Definitions and Debates

Critical communication research has been the target of attacks from scholars defending more traditional, mainstream models. These denunciations usually charge that critical researchers are unscientific radicals who substitute political propaganda and ideological rhetoric for sound research practices (Lindsay, 1980; Pool, 1982; Stevenson, 1983). Most of these critics defend the ideals of positivist science while ignoring the fact that value-free positivism has been widely discredited in other scientific disciplines and the arena of the philosophy of science for some time (Capra, 1982; Gouldner, 1970; Lewontin, Rose, and Kamin, 1984; Melendez, 1970; Myrdal, 1969; Rose and Rose, 1976). Not only has positivism been challenged on metascientific grounds, but it has been accused of having inextricable links to capitalist modes of material production, knowledge being the produced commodity in this case.

Smythe (1979) rejects the notion that science can be value-free or apolitical and asserts that positivist science provides a model ideologically consistent with free-enterprise capitalism. Further, he says:

any commitment of resources, whether material or personal, in the context of the real world obviously has a dialectical political consequence—either in some fashion to support or to change the ongoing social system, or to clarify or obfuscate political issues. . . . Behaviorism and logical positivism have provided a rationale for conservative, conformist, and escapist (scientific) activity. (p. 104)

Despite the myopic nature of most arguments against critical communication theory, challengers have pointed out several genuine weaknesses. For example, Lang and Lang (1983, p. 132) emphasize the ambiguity of its terminology and suggest that critical scholars are "open to seduction by big words with global meanings but vague referents." More respectfully, but with no less concern, critical communication scholars from the United States and Latin America have voiced dissatisfaction with the lack of conceptual clarity and definitional specificity in pockets of their respective literatures (Marques de Melo, 1984; Martín Barbero, 1982; Smythe and Van Dinh, 1983).

U.S. Critical Communication Controversies

In North American critical communication writings, scholars have often categorized mass communication research as either administrative or critical, adhering to a distinction introduced by Lazarsfeld (Real, 1980). However, some U.S. and European authors claim that this distinction does not provide a useful basis for talking about epistemological differences between critical research and other orientations (Carey, 1982; Curran, Gurevitch, and Woollacott, 1983). Hamelink (1983, p. 76) shuns the dichotomy of administrative and critical research because it does not adequately reflect philosophical underpinnings; nor does it "recognize the empirical work done by many researchers who see themselves as belonging to the critical tradition." Slack and Allor (1983, p. 208) summarize the confusion over terminology:

Recent attempts to define just exactly what it means to do critical research oversimplify the differences between critical research approaches and other research. These oversimplifications have led to the characterization of the differences in terms of a series of simple dichotomies: empirical versus critical; administrative versus critical; repressive science versus emancipatory science. These dichotomies are insensitive to the diverse range of critical approaches, while at the same time mystifying the complex political and epistemological commitments that underlie and link that diversity.

In addition to equating empiricism with administrative research, critical scholars have treated both terms as synonymous with positivism, and have mixed in quantification, objectivity, determinism, and behaviorism as part of the same epistemic package. Although a thorough and detailed sorting out of these various concepts is beyond the scope of this endeavor, a few examples may suffice to establish the need for such a task.

Empiricism, for instance, means verification through sensory observation rather than metaphysical experience or pure rationalism (Kaplan, 1964). Melody and Mansell (1983, p. 107) say that the problems faced by communication researchers do not revolve around the validity of empirical evidence, but have more to do with the nature, collection, interpretation, and use of evidence. They argue that reliance on empirical data is often necessary for comprehending political, economic, and cultural processes in their historical context, and that reliance on reason is "required for the integration of empirical evidence in a systematic way." Mosco (1983) also says that it is not support of or opposition to empirical evidence that distinguishes a critical perspective from a positivist one, but the commitment to human emancipation.

A related tendency among critical communication researchers is to relegate all quantitative elements of inquiry to the positivist camp. Although it cannot be denied that positivist approaches have often justified their knowledge claims on the basis of statistically significant results rather than the validity of ideas, it is a mistake to assume that the use of numbers or the process of counting is inherently positivist. Smythe (1979, p. 104) states that advocating critical scholarship does not categorically imply a rejection of mathematical and statistical tools, but he cautions that these tools must be used to address questions that are posed critically in relation to policy issues.

It has been suggested that North American critical mass communication research questions should be derived from an ideological dedication to social change and should focus on social inequalities, rather than on individual behavior or the effects of media on individuals. The research practices advocated as most appropriate for examining such questions are aligned with political economy, history, anthropology, and linguistics (Carey, 1982; Guback, 1969; Haight, 1983; Mosco, 1982; Schiller, 1982; Tuchman, 1979).

Despite an increasing number of valuable studies critically examining, for example, the historical development of mass media institutions within their political and economic milieus, questions remain about the boundaries, purposes, and actual effects of critical mass communication research in the United States. Blumler (1983) suggests that rejecting the liberal-pluralist idea of democracy undermines the ability of critical researchers to make realistic policy contributions that could enable communication systems to implement a vision of human beings as active, purposeful media consumers. Tuchman (1983), however, asserts that some U.S. scholars have adopted European perspectives on communication, culture, and consciousness, but have not adapted such views to North American realities, often disdaining the lower socioeconomic classes of people who use the mass media. She argues that this disdain has resulted in work that divorces the media from the context of U.S. society. Melody and Mansell (1983, p. 110) claim that much critical communication research has been too "reactive" in making administrative research its major target, rather than the problems of society and media structures. The result, they say, is that critical communication scholarship "usually does not provide a clear idea of how these structures should, could, or would be realistically changed to alternative institutional structures that research has shown are better." Several other scholars have argued that focusing on structural change alone is not sufficient for an effective critical communication paradigm and that new concepts of how individuals create meaning from their message environments are needed (Atwood and Mattos, 1982; Dervin, 1980; Halloran, 1981; Sarti, 1981).

These are merely some of the controversies surrounding U.S. critical mass communication inquiry. Some of these concerns are also being discussed by Latin American critical communication scholars, although they have somewhat distinct vantage points and use different ideas and terminology.

Critical Communication Approaches in Latin America
Like their U.S. colleagues, some Latin American critical scholars have denounced empiricism and quantitative data collection methods, equating them with positivist approaches originated in industrialized countries. But critical communication writers in Latin America rarely use the term "administrative" to denote positivist kinds of inquiry. Instead, the most prevalent dichotomy discussed by Latin Americans is one that associates positivism with "functionalism" and critical orientations with "structuralism." This distinction reflects the ways similar European influences have been interpreted and applied differently in North America and Latin America.

"Functionalism" is defined as a way of studying how the media serve and sustain society, particularly the members of their audience, and is charged with being reductionist, positivist, and fundamentally supportive of the status quo (Martín Barbero, 1982). Functionalist research is typified by mainstream North American "effects" research, which accepts the structure and role of the media in society as natural. Functionalist investigations are seen as describing media processes in order to explain or predict the outcomes of media consumption. It is argued that such explanations and predictions support further ideological domination and market exploitation of media audiences (Beltrán, 1976; Esteinou, 1984).

Structuralism, however, challenges the legitimacy of media structure and purpose. Structuralist inquiry seeks to reveal national and international configurations of media ownership and control, as well as the economic, social, and political motivations underlying these configurations. Latin American critical scholars engaged in structural analysis are also concerned with latent media messages that generate "false consciousness" and deform or erode indigenous cultural identities; the material forms of mass media production, including transnational advertising, which foster the economic and cultural dependency of Latin American nations; and the hegemonic implications of the North-South transfer of new information technologies (Beltrán and Fox de Cardona, 1980; Mattelart, 1983; Mattelart, Biedman, and Funes, 1980; Piccini, 1982; Portales, 1981; Rada, 1981; Roncagliolo, 1982; Rota, 1982; Schmucler, 1982a).

Structuralism is fundamentally opposed to the notion of value-free, objective inquiry. Both Marxist and non-Marxist structuralist orientations are founded on an explicit commitment to radical changes in society, or what Beltrán (1975) has called a "communicology of liberation," which insists that researchers are embedded in the process of social destiny. From the structuralist perspective, researchers are responsible for the outcomes of their endeavors and cannot claim immunity in the name of "objectivity." Thus, researchers are accountable for the degree to which their values enable them to link theory with practice. This concept of "praxis," the actualization of theory in conduct, is a cornerstone of structuralism as articulated by critical communication researchers in Latin America (Marques de Melo, 1984; Paiva, 1983).

At the risk of oversimplifying, it might be said that this praxis involves two broad strategies that overlap in certain instances. The first type of strategy is aimed at influencing national communication policies that have regional and international repercussions, although efforts by Latin American critical communication scholars to affect the policy arena have met with limited or mixed results. Capriles (1982, p. 35) suggests that barriers to policy change are not necessarily the fault of critical researchers; nor are they solely due to recalcitrant public officials or military leaders:

In countries depending on the capitalistic sphere, the general imposition of merchandise form cannot but affect a research which becomes, as a production of knowledge, the meeting point for a financial, a labor and a merchandise market . . . [C]ommitted research thus appears or tends to appear as an exception, and such an exception tends in turn to be modified, forgotten, or wrongfully used.

Other problems faced by critical researchers in the Latin American communication policy domain include the lack of access to certain government and industry data; the preference of policy-makers for quantitative evidence on which to base decisions; the historical dependence on imported media software and hardware; and the lack of economic resources to create adequate indigenous replacements (Capriles, 1982; Gargurevich, 1981; Rada, 1981; Salinas and Paldan, 1979; Valdes, 1982).

The second type of strategy derived from the concept of praxis emphasizes alternative communication, democratic communication, and popular or participatory communication. These terms have sometimes been used interchangeably by critical Latin American scholars, and the thread that links them is the desire to foster substantially different structures and processes of communication that make possible egalitarian, interactive, and emancipatory discourse. Although these ideas are part of the same holistic vision, it is possible to detect slightly divergent nuances among them.

"Alternative communication" is probably the broadest term, encompassing local, regional, national, and international activities. Reyes Matta (1983) and Simpson Grinberg (1981) provide examples of efforts to promote community forums, media education and training, alternative print and broadcast media run by farm workers and labor union members, and the community use of computer and videocassette technologies. At the national and international levels, there are numerous efforts to create alternative forms of media and new technology production, as well as alternative news services and information distribution outlets (Action Committee for the Creation of ALASEI, 1982; Isaza, 1984; Mattos, 1982; Rada, 1982; Schneider, 1983; Schmucler, 1982b; Schulein and Robina, 1983). Hence, the goals of alternative communication endeavors include the creation of a New International Information Order (NIIO) as well as democratic and popular communication systems.

To comprehend the idea of democratic communication espoused by Latin American critical scholars, one must recognize how they distinguish "participatory democracy" from liberal Western "representative democracy," and how they connect participatory democracy with a unique outlook on development. Cardoso (1981, pp. 302–3) stresses that the Western capitalist ideology of development is increasingly being rejected not only by vast numbers of oppressed people in Third World countries, but also by those who live in "pockets of misery" in the industrialized nations. Even a growing number of the North American and Latin American elite are becoming disillusioned with their "developed" worlds of insecurity, stress, pollution, and isolation from any sense of community. Cardoso argues that traditional goals of development have created "a civilization of poverty for the majority and fear for all," and he suggests:

The alternative to it, beyond the value of equality, lies in its complement, which requires freedom, of the need to participate. It lies in democracy, but not a democracy deferred to the quasi-mystical body of a party, or identified with a liberalism relating representativeness to the division of powers and removing all effective political stake to the summit of large state organizations, to parliament, the executive, and the judiciary. Participatory democracy, which is an inherent part of another development model, starts by being more demanding and more inclusive. It turns to the new arenas in which the decisions of contemporary societies are made: the educational system, the world of labor, the organizations which control mass communication.

Consistently, critical communication scholars in Latin America have asserted that liberation, not liberalism, is the foundation for their desired form of democracy (Arrieta, 1980; Mattelart and Schmucler, 1982; Salinas and Paldan, 1979). They contend that such liberation cannot be achieved through democratic freedoms of enterprise and the marketplace, which in fact supply the "ideological substance that permits the freedom of action required for the powerful to increase their power" (Argumedo, 1982, p. 268; my translation). Thus, the key element in the notion of humanistic development is the participation of all sectors of society in decision-making processes—processes of self-actualization and self-determination that can be facilitated only by democratic communication systems, according to critical researchers.

Paiva (1983) emphasizes that the many definitions of alternative or popular communication should not delude one into thinking that they are merely "experiments" designed to oppose or replace current media systems. Rather, he suggests that popular communication activities are the result and expression of the social praxis of the lower classes, assisted in some instances by compatriot intellectuals and professionals. Contreras (1984, p. 185) says that the challenge of the many forms of popular communication is that they require researchers to redefine their parameters of orientation and ways of approximating reality. He suggests that critical communication scholars must engage in "participatory investigation," which means that being organically integrated into popular movements is a key element in the practice of research:

Certainly, this is not a new challenge. The methodological crisis in communication investigation transcends the problem of popular communication. But the specific opportunity that is offered is the ability to anchor methodological preoccupations in concrete referents . . . which will be described as part of a historic popular project. (My translation)

His argument, then, is that participatory investigation should not be confined to a particular area, but that education, reflection, and participation should be components of all types of inquiry.

What Contreras refers to is not just a method of observing, like the "participant observation" advocated by some North American communication scholars. His prescription is more aligned with Freire's (1973) assertion that investigation should be an involvement, not an invasion. Freire argues that those involved in liberation efforts must be witnesses to the fact that the struggle of the oppressed is a common task and work with people to learn about the realities of their world. Such witnessing, he suggests, mandates consistency between words and actions, boldness in confronting existence, and the courage to love, based on faith in the people.

Despite the relative consensus about these and other aspirations among Latin American critical mass communication scholars, internal debates and differences of opinion do exist. Conflicts among critical researchers and those adhering to more traditional positivist or functionalist views are also evident. For example, Martín Barbero (1982, p. 101) complains that although Latin

American critical communication research has been defined by a break with functionalism, this rupture has been more "affective" than "effective"; some critical scholars have disavowed functionalist theory, but continue to use functionalist methods, which means that they have discarded only the jargon and not the substance. Contreras (1984) argues that many critical communication scholars are still looking for short cuts and are ambivalent about the epistemological problems and methodological inadequacies of the critical approach. Mattelart (1983, p. 61) concludes that semiological research, once a powerful response to functionalist sociology, has lost "both its dynamism and its sociopolitical anchorage." These scholars and others provide evidence that many university settings in Latin America are still dominated by positivist approaches and research models (Peirano and Kudo, 1982; Munizaga and Rivera, 1983).

Discussing a slightly different issue, Gonzaga Motta and Silva (1982) note the importance of popular resistance to dominant ideologies and claim that mechanical Marxist axioms that look only at such ideologies are ignoring the lived interpretations of media consumers in Latin America. Salinas and Paldan (1979, p. 93) also stress the need for more study of the ways in which subordinated social groups use national culture to unify and struggle against oppression:

Above all, cultures and subcultures are the expression of men's and women's lived experience of the conditions of existence. Accordingly, the constant invasion of meanings that do not express this reality will often generate some limits to its assimilation. It is important, therefore, to study the conditions affecting the reception of the messages, as well as to examine the possible distance between the models of interpretation provided by the media and the real level of assimilation by the "audience" to them.

In more general terms, several scholars call for a more profound explication of existing knowledge and a more systematic synthesis of future research evidence. Yet by their own analyses of critical communication literature in Latin America, these same scholars attest to the richness and variety of work already completed (Marques de Melo, 1984; Martín Barbero, 1982).

Latin American Contributions to Critical Scholarship

Latin American critical scholars have made significant contributions to the field of mass communication inquiry in their respective regions, and they have promoted an authentic discourse on the most important communication issues facing their continent. In addition, Latin American scholars have offered valuable insights for consideration by critical mass communication researchers from other geographic areas, particularly the United States.

Clearly, there are important differences in the current economic, social, and political circumstances facing researchers in Latin America and North America. Yet it would be erroneous to assume that critical mass communication scholars in North America have no lessons to learn about confronting the kinds of inequities that have been experienced so acutely in Latin America. Mounting evidence suggests that the United States is undergoing a shift toward greater socioeconomic disparity, loss of basic civil rights, and ever-increasing concentration of power among conservative government and business elites (Galbraith, 1984). The direct influence of these trends is being felt in university settings as institutions ranging from the Defense Department to high-technology industries attempt to seduce researchers into their service (Carey, 1984; Gitlin, 1981; Kopkind, 1983; Lewontin, Rose, and Kamin, 1984).

Thus, one of the most timely and relevant aspects of Latin American critical approaches is the prominence given to linking theory with practice. This focus on praxis has philosophical, methodological, and pragmatic implications worthy of closer scrutiny by North American communication researchers and practitioners. Such scrutiny might begin to correct imbalances in the distribution of knowledge among South and North American scholars. Equipped with more informed perspectives, U.S. scholars can engage in meaningful dialogue with Latin American colleagues and collaborate on projects aimed at the international policy arenas most suited to collective endeavors.

Not all activities that may ultimately be mutually rewarding necessitate overt cooperation. The solutions to many dilemmas confronted by Latin American and U.S. scholars are often derived most appropriately from indigenous viewpoints and strategies. For example, alternative and democratic communication may be facilitated through somewhat different tactics in Latin America and the United States, and take distinct forms. Specific research agendas and types of data collection and analysis may vary as well.

In sum, critical communication scholarship in the Americas constitutes a vigorous challenge to positivist science and repressive society. The outcome of this challenge will depend, in large measure, on the degree of consistency between the values critical scholars articulate and the way they conduct their lives. Numerous critical researchers from Latin America have provided admirable examples of what Freire meant by "the courage to love," and they have sustained such courage through faith in the people they serve. This element of praxis in mass communication inquiry may turn out to be the most durable lesson from Latin America.

References

Action Committee for the Creation of ALASEI (1982). *Implementation Project for the Latin American Special Information Services Agency*. Panama City: SELA.

Argumendo, A. (1982). "Comunicación y Democracia: Una Perspectiva Tercer-

Mundista." In *Comunicación y Democracia en América Latina*, pp. 265–81. Lima: DESCO.

Arrieta, M. (1980). *Obstaculos para un Nuevo Orden Informativo Internacional.* Mexico City: Editorial Nueva Imagen.

Atwood, R. (1980). "Communication Research in Latin America: Cultural and Conceptual Dilemmas." Paper presented to the meeting of the International Communication Association, Acapulco, Mexico, May.

Atwood, R., and S. Mattos (1982). "Mass Media Reform and Social Change: The Peruvian Experience." *Journal of Communication,* 32, 2, pp. 33–45.

Beltrán, L. R. (1975). "Research Ideologies in Conflict." *Journal of Communication,* 25, 2, pp. 187–92.

Beltrán, L. R. (1976). "Alien Premises, Objects, and Methods in Latin American Communication Research." *Communication Research,* 3, 2, pp. 107–34.

Beltrán, L. R., and E. Fox de Cardona (1980). *Comunicación Dominada: Estados Unidos en los Medios de América Latina.* Mexico City: Instituto Latinoamericano de Estudios Transnacionales/Nueva Imagen.

Blumler, J. G. (1983). "Communication and Democracy: The Crisis Beyond and the Ferment Within." *Journal of Communication,* 33, 3, pp. 166–73.

Capra, F. (1982). *The Turning Point: Science, Society, and the Rising Culture.* New York: Simon and Schuster.

Capriles, O. (1982). "From National Communication Policies to the New International Information Order: Some Lessons for Research." In *New Structures of International Communication?: The Role of Research,* pp. 10–59. Leicester, England: IAMCR.

Cardoso, F. H. (1981). "Towards Another Development." In H. Muñoz (ed.) *From Dependency to Development,* pp. 295–313. Boulder, Colorado: Westview Press.

Carey, J. (1982). "The Mass Media and Critical Theory: An American View." In M. Burgoon (ed.) *Communication Yearbook 6,* pp. 18–33. Beverly Hills, Calif.: Sage Publications.

Carey, J. (1984). "High Tech and High Ed." *Illinois Issues,* March, pp. 22–28.

Carter, R. E. (1983). "Inter-American Collaboration in Sociology: Historical Tendencies and Current Changes." Paper presented to the meeting of the Latin American Studies Association, Mexico City, September.

Contreras, E. (1984). "Estrategias de Comunicación." In *Comunicación Popular Educativa,* pp. 147–56. Quito: CIESPAL.

Correl, M. C. (1982). *La Ciencia de la Comunicación en México: Origen, Desarrollo, y Situación Actual.* Mexico: Taller de Investigación en Comunicación Masiva.

Curran, J., M. Gurevitch, and J. Woollacott (1983). "The Study of the Media: Theoretical Approaches." In M. Gurevitch, T. Bennet, J. Curran, and J. Woollacott (eds.) *Culture, Society, and the Media,* pp. 11–29. New York: Methuen.

Dervin, B. (1980). "Communication Gaps and Inequities: Moving Toward a Reconceptualization." In B. Dervin and M. Voigt (eds.) *Progress in Communication Sciences,* vol. 2, pp. 73–112. Norwood, N.J.: Ablex.

Díaz Bordenave, J. (1976). "Communication of Agricultural Innovations in Latin America: The Need for New Models." *Communication Research,* 3, 2, pp. 43–62.

Esteinou Madrid, J. (1984). "CIESPAL y la Ciencia de la Comunicación." *Chasqui,* July–Sept., pp. 20–27.

Fals Borda, O. (1980). "The Negation of Sociology and Its Promise: Perspectives of Social Science in Latin America Today." *Latin American Research Review*, 15, pp. 161–66.

Fals Borda, O. (1985). *The Challenge of Social Change*. Beverly Hills, Calif.: Sage Publications.

Fish, M. (1984). "A Study of Mass Communication Research and Scholarship." Ph.D. dissertation, University of Texas, Austin.

Freire, P. (1973). *Pedagogy of the Oppressed*. New York: Seabury Press.

Fuenzalida, E. F. (1983). "The Reception of Scientific Sociology in Chile." *Latin American Research Review*, 18, pp. 95–112.

Galbraith, J. K. (1984). *The Affluent Society*. 4th ed. Boston: Houghton-Mifflin.

Gargurevich, J. (1981). "Perú: La Alternativa Dentro de la Alternativa." In M. Simpson Grinberg (ed.) *Comunicación Alternativa y Cambio Social*, vol. 1: *América Latina*, pp. 191–214. Mexico: Universidad Nacional Autónoma de México.

Gitlin, T. (1978). "Media Sociology: The Dominant Paradigm." *Theory and Society*, 6, 2, pp. 205–53.

Gitlin, T. (1981). "New Video Technology: Pluralism or Banality." *Democracy*, 1, 4, pp. 60–76.

Golding, P. (1974). "Media Role in National Development: Critique of a Theoretical Orthodoxy." *Journal of Communication*, 24, 3, pp. 39–54.

Gonzaga Motta, L., and U. da Silva. (1982). "Críticas a las Políticas de Comunicación." *Comunicación y Cultura*, 7, pp. 11–28.

Gouldner, A. (1970). *The Coming Crisis of Western Sociology*. New York: Basic Books.

Guback, T. (1969). *The International Film Industry*. Bloomington: University of Indiana Press.

Haight, T. (1983). "The Critical Researcher's Dilemma." *Journal of Communication*, 33, 3, pp. 226–36.

Halloran, J. (1981). "The Context of Mass Communication Research." In E. McAnany, J. Schnitman, and N. Janus (eds.) *Communication and Social Structure: Critical Studies in Mass Media Research*, pp. 21–57. New York: Praeger.

Hamelink, C. J. (1983). "Emancipation or Domestication: Toward a Utopian Science of Communication." *Journal of Communication*, 33, 3, pp. 74–79.

Hedebro, G. (1982). *Communication and Social Change in Developing Nations*. Ames: Iowa State University Press.

Horowitz, I. L. (1967). *The Rise and Fall of Project Camelot*. Cambridge: M.I.T. Press.

Hur, K. (1982). "International Mass Communication Research: A Critical Review of Theory and Methods." In M. Burgoon (ed.) *Communication Yearbook 6*, pp. 531–54. Beverly Hills, Calif.: Sage Publications.

Isaza, G. (1984). "La Documentación de Comunicación en Latinoamérica." *Chasqui*, July–Sept.

Kaplan, A. (1964). *The Conduct of Inquiry*. New York: Crowell.

Katzen, M. (1975). *Mass Communication: Teaching and Studies at Universities*. Paris: UNESCO.

Kopkind, A. (1983). "A Diller, a Dollar, an N.S.C. Scholar." *Nation*, June 25.

Lang, K., and G. E. Lang (1983). "The 'New' Rhetoric of Mass Communication Research: A Longer View." *Journal of Communication*, 33, 3, pp. 128–40.

Lewontin, R. C., S. Rose, and L. J. Kamin (1984). *Not in Our Genes: Biology, Ideology, and Human Nature*. New York: Pantheon Books.

Lindsay, R. (1980). "Third World Communication Development: Prospects for Cooperation." Paper presented to the meeting of the International Association for Mass Communication Research, Caracas, August.

Marques de Melo, J. (1975). "Evolution of the Communication Discipline in Brazil." *Gazette*, 21, 1, pp. 35–39.

Marques de Melo, J. (1984). "La Investigatión Latinoamericana en Comunicación." *Chasqui*, July–Sept., pp. 4–11.

Marsal, J. F. (1970). "Sobre la Investigación Social Institucional en las Actuales Circunstancias de América Latina." In R. Cortes (ed.) *Ciencias Sociales: Ideología y Realidad Nacional*. Buenos Aires: Editorial Tiempo Contemporáneo.

Martín Barbero, J. (1982). "Retos a la Investigación de Comunicación en América Latina." *Comunicación y Cultura*, 9, pp. 99–113.

Mattelart, A. (1979). "Communication Ideology and Class Practice." In A. Mattelart and S. Siegelaub (eds.) *Communication and Class Struggle*. New York: International General.

Mattelart, A. (1983). "Technology, Culture, and Communication: Research and Policy Priorities in France." *Journal of Communication*, 33, 3, pp. 59–73.

Mattelart, A., P. Biedma, and S. Funes (1980). *Comunicación Masiva y Revolución Socialista*. Mexico: Editorial Diógenes.

Mattelart, A., and H. Schmucler (1982). "Construir la Democracia." *Comunicación y Cultura*, 7, pp. 7–10.

Mattos, S. (1982). "Domestic and Foreign Advertising in Television and Mass Media Growth: A Case Study of Brazil." Ph.D. dissertation, University of Texas, Austin.

McAnany, E. (1980). *Communications in the Rural Third World*. New York: Praeger.

McAnany, E., J. Schnitman, and N. Janus (eds.) (1981). *Communication and Social Structure: Critical Studies in Mass Media Research*. New York: Praeger.

McQuail, D. (1984). *Mass Communication Theory*. Beverly Hills, Calif.: Sage Publications.

Melendez, E. L. (1970). "Ideología, Ciencia y Práctica Profesional." In R. Cortés (ed.) *Ciencias Sociales: Ideología y Realidad Nacional*. Buenos Aires: Editorial Tiempo Contemporáneo.

Melody, W. H., and R. E. Mansell (1983). "The Debate Over Critical vs. Administrative Research: Circularity or Challenge?" *Journal of Communication*, 33, 3, pp. 103–16.

Mosco, V. (1982). *Pushbutton Fantasies: Critical Perspectives on Videotext and Information Technology*. Norwood, N.J.: Ablex.

Mosco, V. (1983). "Critical Research and the Role of Labor." *Journal of Communication*, 33, 3, pp. 237–48.

Munizaga, G., and A. Rivera. (1983). *La Investigación en Comunicación Social en Chile*. Lima: DESCO.

Myrdal, G. (1969). *Objectivity in Social Research*. New York: Pantheon Books.

Nordenstreng, K., and T. Varis (1974). *Television Traffic: A One-Way Street?* Paris: UNESCO Press, Reports and Papers on Mass Communications, no. 70.

Paiva, A. (1983). "La Comunicación Alternativa: Sus Campos de Influencia, Sus Limitaciones y Sus Perspectivas de Desarrollo." In F. Reyes Matta (ed.) *Comunicación Alternativa y Búsquedas Democráticas*, pp. 29–56. Mexico City: Instituto Latinoamericano de Estudios Transnacionales.

Peirano, L., and T. Kudo. (1982). *La Investigación en Comunicación Social en el Perú.* Lima: DESCO.

Piccini, M. (1982). "Medios y Estrategias del Discurso Político." *Connotaciones*, 3, pp. 67–90.

Pool, I. S. (1982). "The New Structure of International Communication: The Role of Research." In *New Structures of International Communication?: The Role of Research*, pp. 60–75. Leicester, England: IAMCR.

Portales, D. (1981). *Poder Económico y Libertad de Expresión.* Mexico City: Instituto Latinoamericano de Estudios Transnacionales/Nueva Imagen.

Rada, J. (1981). "The Microelectronics Revolution: Implications for the Third World." *Development Dialogue*, 2, pp. 41–67.

Rada, J. (1982). "A Third World Perspective." In G. Friedrichs and A. Schaff (eds.) *Microelectronics and Society: For Better or Worse*, pp. 213–42. New York: Pergamon Press.

Real, M. (1980). "Media Theory: Contributions to an Understanding of American Mass Communications." *American Quarterly*, 32, 3, pp. 238–58.

Reyes Matta, F. (1983). *Comunicación Alternativa y Búsquedas Democráticas.* Mexico City: Instituto Latinoamericano de Estudios Transnacionales.

Rogers, E. (1976). "Communication and Development: The Passing of the Dominant Paradigm." *Communication Research*, 3, 2, pp. 121–48

Roling, N. G., J. Ascroft, and F. W. Chege (1976). "The Diffusion of Innovations and the Issue of Equity in Rural Development." *Communication Research*, 3, pp. 63–78.

Roncagliolo, R. (1982). "Comunicación y Cultura Transnacionales." In *Comunicación Transnacional: Conflicto Político y Cultural*, pp. 17–31. Lima: DESCO.

Rose, H., and S. Rose (1976). *The Radicalisation of Science.* London: Macmillan.

Rota, J. (1980). "The Study of Mass Media in Latin America: Conflicting U.S. and Latin American Perspectives and Some of Their Detrimental Effects on Human Rights." Paper presented to the World Media Conference, New York, October.

Rota, J. (1982). "Conflicting U.S. and Latin American Perspectives for the Study of Communication." Paper presented to the International Communication Association, Boston, May.

Salinas, R., and L. Paldan (1979). "Culture in the Process of Dependent Development: Theoretical Perspectives." In K. Nordenstreng and H. Schiller (eds.) *National Sovereignty and International Communication: A Reader*, pp. 82–98. Norwood, N.J.: Ablex.

Sarti, I. (1981). "Communication and Cultural Dependency: A Misconception." In E. McAnany, J. Schnitman, and N. Janus (eds.) *Communication and Social Structure: Critical Studies in Mass Media Research*, pp. 317–32. New York: Praeger.

Schiller, D. (1982). *Telematics and Government.* Norwood, N.J.: Ablex.

Schiller, H. (1979). "Transnational Media and National Development." In K. Nordenstreng and H. Schiller (eds.) *National Sovereignty and International Communication*, pp. 21–32. Norwood, N.J.: Ablex.

Schmucler, H. (1982a). "Communication Research in Latin America During the Computer Era." In *New Structures of International Communication?: The Role of Research*, pp. 137–50. Leicester, England: IAMCR.

Schmucler, H. (1982b). "La Sociedad Informatizada y las Perspectivas de la Democracia." In *Comunicación y Democracia en América Latina*, pp. 311–27. Lima: DESCO.

Schneider, A. (1983). "From Basgasse to the Electronic Page: Telecommunications in Cuba." Paper presented to the meeting of the Association for Education in Journalism and Mass Communication, Corvallis, Oregon, August.

Schulein, S., and S. Robina (1983). "Prensa Alternativa y Nuevas Fuentes de Información: La Experiencia ALTERCOM." In F. Reyes Matta (ed.) *Comunicación Alternativa y Búsquedas Democráticas*, pp. 155–69. Mexico: Instituto Latinoamericano de Estudios Transnacionales.

Simpson Grinberg, M. (1981). *Comunicación Alternativa y Cambio Social*, vol. 1: *América Latina*. Mexico City: Universidad Nacional Autónoma de México.

Slack, J., and M. Allor (1983). "The Political and Epistemological Constituents of Critical Communication Research." *Journal of Communication*, 33, 3, pp. 208–18.

Smythe, D. (1979). "Realism in the Arts and Sciences: A Systemic Overview of Capitalism and Socialism." In K. Nordenstreng and H. Schiller (eds.) *National Sovereignty and International Communication: A Reader*, pp. 99–111. Norwood, N.J.: Ablex.

Smythe, D., and T. Van Dinh (1983). "On Critical and Administrative Research: A New Critical Analysis." *Journal of Communication*, 33, 3, pp. 117–27.

Stevenson, R. L. (1983). "A Critical Look at Critical Analysis." *Journal of Communication*, 33, 3, pp. 262–69.

Thayer, L. (1983). "On Doing 'Research' and 'Explaining' Things." *Journal of Communication*, 33, 3, pp. 80–91.

Tuchman, G. (1979). "Women's Depictions by the Mass Media." *Signs*, 4, pp. 528–42.

Tuchman, G. (1983). "Consciousness Industries and the Production of Culture." *Journal of Communication*, 33, 3, pp. 330–41.

Tulchin, J. S. (1983). "Emerging Patterns of Research in the Study of Latin America." *Latin American Research Review*, 18, pp. 85–94.

Valdes, M. I. (1982). "Third World and the Conflicting Ideologies of the Information Age." Paper presented to the meeting of the International Association for Mass Communication Research, Paris, September.

White, R. (1984). "Democratisation of Communication: The Need for New Research Strategies." Paper presented to the meeting of the International Communication Association, San Francisco, May.

2 *Emile G. McAnany*

Seminal Ideas in Latin American Critical Communication Research: An Agenda for the North

The dominant communication research tradition in the United States has only recently and somewhat grudgingly broadened its perspective to include a critical tradition of long standing in other countries. Three events heralded this change: the special issue entitled "Ferment in the Field" of the *Journal of Communication* (Summer 1983); the introduction of the journal *Critical Studies in Mass Communication* in 1984; and the 1985 annual conference of the International Communication Association, organized around the theme of "Paradigm Dialogue." Although this does not mean that most researchers working in U.S. universities have adopted critical methods or approaches in their work (Fish, 1984), perhaps it does mean that issues of critical research are achieving respectability among some in the field.

In an effort to expand the communication research agenda, U.S. critical scholars like Herbert Schiller, Thomas Guback, and Dallas Smythe have for some years addressed issues with international dimensions, especially those that relate to the Third World. But the U.S. dialogue about the Third World has been asymmetrical in that authors from those areas are not heard in their own voices. This is due in part, of course, to a kind of paradigmatic insularity and in part, undoubtedly, to language and cultural barriers. In addition, vestiges of an intellectual colonialism generate a more subtle but impenetrable barrier to the real "free flow" of ideas across national boundaries.

Most of Latin America won political independence in the nineteenth cen-

28

tury, but it remains at best an economically dependent entity and, except for a few limited areas of creative expression, an almost unheard voice in most U.S. universities and academic disciplines. Communication is no exception. Aside from a few works by Armand Mattelart (a Belgian sociologist now working in Paris), Paolo Freire (who writes primarily on education), and Luis Ramiro Beltrán (who was trained in the United States and writes in English as well as Spanish), most U.S. communication researchers, even those working in the critical tradition, are unaware of the significant literature that has accumulated over the past quarter of a century in Latin America.

Several structural conditions of scholarly production in Latin America need to be noted at the outset. The intellectual colonialism referred to above meant not only that the first generation or two of Latin American communication researchers were trained in or influenced by U.S. functionalism, but also that certain material conditions affected and still affect the production of a discourse in communication. Schools of communication have grown exponentially over the past twenty-five years, from 44 in 1960 to 81 in 1970 to 163 in 1980 and 174 in 1984 (FELAFACS, 1982; Nixon, 1982). Still, there has been little material incentive to publish, despite conventional rhetoric about research as a university function. Most professors were and are employed part time and underpaid in comparison with U.S. and European colleagues (FELAFACS, 1982), and research is not part of the reward structure of most institutions, which have a professional rather than a research orientation. Much if not most research is generated either by students doing a required thesis for a degree or by members of independent research institutions.

Another reason much Latin American research remains unknown outside the continent is the limited and unstable life of journals devoted to communication. Again the root problems are not only a lack of rewards for publication and the limited financial base of most journals, but also the absence of a tradition of communication research.

The 1970s began to change much of this, as Latin America struggled to free itself of the imitative phase and to enter into a more critical phase of its intellectual discourse. As Oscar Jaramillo and Cristina Schwarz point out elsewhere in this volume, the beginnings of an indigenous tradition go back to the 1960s, when Antonio Pasquali in Venezuela, Armand Mattelart in Chile, and Eliseo Veron in Argentina—all significant pioneers—began their work. One might add Freire in Brazil. This tradition in research and publication achieved a much broader base in the 1970s, so that today, when financial restrictions are perhaps even greater than in the 1960s, the momentum for research and publication carries on and is moving toward a more authentic and a better-grounded approach (Marques de Melo, 1984a).

Even so, the reader may well ask what the critical tradition in Latin America has to offer researchers from metropolitan countries like the United States,

Canada, and most European nations. The answer must partly rest on the content of this volume. The task of this introductory chapter will be to examine seven themes that are common to much of the critical literature from Latin America and to relate these to the concerns of colleagues in other regions, especially the United States and Western Europe. These themes, which have emerged in critical research in both Spanish and Portuguese over the last two decades, are: the transnationalization of communication; cultural imperialism and dependency; Marxist and neo-Marxist social and cultural analysis; the role of communication technology in Latin American societies; national policies for communication and culture; alternative communication practices; and the need for an indigenous communication science.

The Transnationalization of Communication

Latin American discussions of the transnationalization of communication structures and products often strike U.S. researchers as either an exaggeration or a repetition of the obvious. The *Instituto Latinoamericano de Estudios Transnacionales* (ILET), founded in Mexico City in 1976,[1] has taken this phenomenon, in both communication and economics, as its primary focus, and it continues to produce a great part of the research on this topic. Mattelart in Chile, Beltrán in Colombia, Simpson Grinberg in Mexico, Reyes Matta in Chile, and Marques de Melo in Brazil are only a few of the better-known scholars who have published research concerning the problems attendant on the presence of transnational (usually U.S.) corporations in Latin American communications.

The concern may seem to be one that U.S. researchers cannot share, since the impact of transnational corporations lies outside their territory. Latin American researchers, however, see the problem as intimately related to the United States and believe that it ought to be a part of the critical research agenda there. Latin Americans can grasp the phenomenon only from the point at which transnational corporations affect their own societies, and it is important, they argue, to grasp it at its point of origin as well. What, for example, explains the burst of growth of transnational structures in Latin America during the 1960s and early 1970s? How has the United States become so dominant in technology, finance, marketing, advertising, and the distribution of cultural products in comparison with other metropolitan countries? The bottom line, in a sense, is the question whether a better understanding of transnational communication can produce a solution to the problem of dominance in Latin American societies.

1. Its main center moved to Santiago, Chile, in 1981, but it has offices in Mexico and Argentina.

The full spectrum of Latin American concerns about the transnationalization of communication cannot be reflected here. Research projects have ranged from well-documented studies of the U.S. presence in Latin American advertising (Fejes, 1980; Mattos, 1982, 1984; Roncagliolo and Janus, 1981) to analyses of the flow of television programs (Beltrán and Fox, 1979; Lee, 1980; Schement and Rogers, 1984; Varis, 1974) and the influence of international wire services on Latin American press content (Reyes Matta, 1979) and a general assessment of transnational media corporations (Beltrán and Fox, 1980; Varis and Guback, 1982) in Latin American societies. The ILET publications of the last decade illustrate, perhaps best of all, a detailed, empirical effort to document both the presence and the impact of communication transnationals throughout the area.

The tone of the analysis, as much as the depth of data gathering and the methodology, has been disturbing to U.S. readers who come into contact with Mattelart's works (1970, 1972, 1977, 1978, 1979), including his famous collaboration with Ariel Dorfman on *How to Read Donald Duck* (1975), or the writing of Luis Romero Beltrán. Some see it as a passing phase, like the unpopularity of Americans in parts of Europe during the Vietnam War or the "Ugly American" phenomenon of a decade previously. What these readers fail to recognize is that the transnationalization of cultural products has a long history, reaching back to the 1920s in film (Guback, 1969) and advertising (Janus, 1980) and to the 1930s and 1940s in radio (Fejes, in press). Moreover, the phenomenon is not a short-term problem as some seem to argue (see *Communication Research,* April 1984) on the grounds that Latin American products are becoming more important in certain media contexts. There has been an increasing tendency toward concentration in U.S. media (Compaine, 1982), and this has had effects in transnational settings (see Audley, 1983, for an example not in the Third World, but in Canada) that make it more difficult to change the structures.

From this intense study of transnational communication in Latin America and elsewhere (see Audley, 1983; Lee, 1980; Nordenstreng and Varis, 1974; and Varis, 1974, 1984), several issues emerge that are of particular relevance to U.S. researchers. Research on any one of the following topics would be especially useful: U.S. media concentration and its impact on transnational corporations in Latin America (Shore, 1983, has made an excellent beginning in his study of the structure of the music industry in the United States and internationally); the power structure of U.S. media industries, a long-neglected topic (Morrow, 1984); the way in which U.S. foreign affairs news influences U.S. foreign policy in Latin America (see Larson, 1984; Larson, McAnany, and Storey, 1986; McAnany, 1983); and U.S. international policies in the area of communication, a particularly appropriate topic in the second term of the Reagan administration, when the federal government seems intent on tying communication/information policies more tightly to foreign policy considerations ("Tune Up for Term Two," 1984).

Imperialism and Dependency

Cultural imperialism has been a familiar theme in Latin American critical research for the last fifteen years. It is often misunderstood by U.S. readers as an offshoot of the political and economic domination that the U.S. maintains in Latin America. In recent years Latin American scholars (e.g., Sarti, 1981) have themselves criticized the confusion between a simple-minded imperialism thesis, which focuses all problems on outside forces, and a more comprehensive and complex dependency thesis, which sees the primary problem as national class structure, aided and abetted by international economic dependency. The all-powerful effects model, which borrowed heavily from Gramsci's theory of hegemony, has also come in for recent criticism. Without falling into the opposite error of promoting a pluralistic theory of the media, several Latin American scholars point out that any theory of domination must leave theoretical space for social change to occur despite the presence of dominant media (see, for example, the essays by Roncagliolo, Lins da Silva, Janus, and Simpson Grinberg in this volume for such qualifying statements, and Marques de Melo, 1984; Salinas and Paldan, 1979; Sarti, 1981).

Three streams of literature have contributed to the cultural imperialism/ dependency thesis. First, as has been pointed out, the political-economic perspective on imperialism stems from classical Marxist authors writing early in the century. The language of this tradition was applied by Latin American writers to a cultural analysis, even though classical Marxism had not made such an application. Mattelart's early writings from Chile (1977) applied much of the rhetoric of Lenin's theory of imperialism, if not the theory itself, to the cultural aspect of foreign and especially U.S. domination in Latin America. Salinas and Paldan (1979) clarify some of the arguments in their analysis of the cultural aspect of foreign domination and its interaction with local class structures.

The second major stream in the imperialism/dependency literature is largely atheoretical. It consists of empirical, descriptive accounts of foreign domination in the communication and cultural fields. This research arose from the UNESCO debates of the 1970s over the New International Information Order and from the research on transnational corporations sponsored by ILET and other Latin American institutions at that time. Works by Beltrán and Fox (1979, 1980) and Schmucler (1983) are good examples of this approach. The first major empirical work in this tradition was the survey of the international flow of television programming (not limited to Latin America) by Nordenstreng and Varis (1974). This was followed by a number of more general works, including Lee (1980), Read (1976), Smith (1980), and Tunstall (1977). Latin American researchers' contribution was a closer examination of their own media systems in terms of ownership, distribution, content, and cultural impact (see, for example, Beltrán, 1976a, and Beltrán and Fox, 1979, for two surveys of the literature). The conclusions were not theoretical but rather pragmatic. They suggested that Latin American media, although not largely owned by foreign interests, were heavily influenced by the presence of foreign materials, foreign advertisements, and foreign cultural models and called for better control through national communication policies.

The third tradition contributing to the imperialism/dependency discussion derives from European neo-Marxist cultural analysis with emphasis on semiotics, structuralism, and cultural studies. Gramsci is often cited as influential in these approaches. Latin Americans like Eliseo Veron (1967, 1972) have contributed to this tradition, which proposes internal rather than external explanations of dominant ideology and has shifted its attention from foreign powers to local power structures. Salinas and Paldan (1979) and Sarti (1981) both criticize the one-dimensional analysis of some Latin American writers, though they are careful not to dismiss international influences on local structures.

The imperialism thesis sometimes implies cultural homogenization (Lee, 1980), and U.S. researchers have become increasingly aware of the issue over the past few years. The common response is on a methodological level (Lee, 1980; Rosengren, 1983; Stevenson, 1983, 1984), where the debate is supposedly safe from value questions, but problems involving cultural production and distribution are political and economic as well as cultural. Researchers in Canada, a traditional ally as well as a developed society, cannot easily be accused of Marxist rhetoric, as are so many Latin American critics. Audley (1983) has compiled a lengthy empirical account of the economic and structural problems created by Canadian cultural dependency on the United States. Such descriptions will perhaps help U.S. researchers who take critical analyses of U.S. domination personally to see beyond what they consider the rhetoric to a real set of policy (and political) issues. The relation between market forces and U.S. policy is an issue that U.S. researchers need to look at, while Latin American researchers need to examine their own country's policies regarding the flow of cultural products into their societies.

Marxist and Neo-Marxist Cultural Analysis

There has been a tendency among U.S. researchers to lump critical research with Marxism (for example, Schramm, 1983, seems to do this), but a number of distinctions are beginning to emerge that help to identify different tendencies both within and outside Marxist theory. (A number of articles in the *Jour-*

nal of Communication special issue in summer 1983 introduced these distinctions to U.S. researchers). Latin American communication research, as Jaramillo and Schwarz point out elsewhere in this volume, like social science research in general, has drawn heavily on both Marxist theory and Marxist vocabulary, and yet, as these authors assert, it would be a mistake to identify such research as Marxist in any monolithic sense.

Some have called the role of modern communication the blind spot of classical Marxist theory. Even in today's wave of neo-Marxist analyses, there is no single approach, much less a party line (Grossberg, 1984). Javier Esteinou Madrid is perhaps the clearest exponent of a detailed application of European neo-Marxist cultural theory to the Latin American situation (1979, 1980, 1984, and his essay in the present volume). Veron (1967, 1972) was an early proponent of a semiotic approach that applies a Marxist perspective on class structure and power to an analysis of Argentinian media codes. García Canclini's detailed cultural analysis (1977, 1979) calls upon similar concepts. It would be difficult to determine the degree to which the latter two writers should be described as Marxist, or how one should describe cultural analyses that are similar but perhaps use a different vocabulary.

The most clear-cut articulation of the influence of Marxist theory on practice in communications is made by Simpson Grinberg (see his essay in this volume), who asserts that Marxist vanguard theory embodies an authoritarian tradition, going back to Lenin, that is antidemocratic in its consequences. Simpson Grinberg argues for a democratic and decentralized approach in Latin American communication policy and practice and, at the same time, against the centralizing power of both vanguard theory and transnational practice.

Finally, Mattelart's studies (1974, 1979) are often identified as the classic Marxist writing about Latin America and U.S. cultural imperialism (see also his effort, with Siegleglaub (1979, 1983), to synthesize Marxist research in communication). But he has himself been accused by Marxists of a theoretically unacceptable eclecticism, and in his recent work with the Mitterand government in France he has shown considerable flexibility in national policies regarding communication technology (Mattelart and Piemme, 1982). His interview with Muller and Herz (1983) gives the reader the impression that political and social circumstances in Chile in the 1960s had more influence on his writing than strict neoclassical Marxist theory.

Current U.S. critical research is already beginning to draw heavily from the British neo-Marxist analyses of Raymond Williams, Stuart Hall, and many others who have appeared or have been referred to in such journals as *Media, Culture and Society* and *Critical Studies in Mass Communications*. A better understanding of Latin American scholars who have drawn upon similar sources would provide a Third World interpretation of this theory. The Latin

American experience has been uniquely under the influence of U.S. political and economic relationships. U.S. scholars should be aware that many mass media products of the United States will have cultural as well as economic impacts beyond its borders. Latin American Marxists have been more keenly aware of this transnational cultural phenomenon than have their European colleagues. Their insights may help sensitize U.S. scholars to these issues.

Communication Technology in Latin American Society

There are contradictions in the Latin American critical research approach to the role of technology. These seem to stem from uncertainty about whether new technologies can be transferred and used in socially beneficial ways for Latin American societies. Much of this ambivalence is reflected in the UNESCO MacBride Commission report, *Many Voices, One World* (1980), where the new information and communication technologies are promoted as leading to significant economic growth and yet are also seen as part of the dominant structures of transnational enterprise. It is not clear whether and to what extent technologies developed in metropolitan countries can do anything but reinforce existing social structures in Latin America (see Esteinou's essay in this volume). If they inevitably reinforce the status quo, the logical response might be a rejection of such technologies as a possible avenue of growth for Latin societies. Most critical researchers take a more positive if guarded position.

At least three attitudes toward technology may be distinguished. The first seems to be the most negative in that it spends much of its energy in attacking the simplistic protechnology forces that see satellites and microprocessors as a boon to Latin American societies. People like Mattelart and Schmucler (1983) have shown that technology needs to be viewed historically in terms of its origin and its likely applications in Latin American society. Their analysis shows that the new technology has tended to reinforce given social structures and political forces in Latin America. Nevertheless, they do not rule out all transfer but merely warn of the need to pay attention to the social context in which the transfer is made.

The second, more pragmatic position stresses the urgency of technological development for Latin American societies, lest they fall farther behind in an area of great importance for their economic growth. Rada (1981) exemplifies this position when he urges Latin American countries to adopt national policies that will promote growth in technological (especially microelectronic) areas even if some of this technology must be transferred in. Orellana and Rodriguez, in an ILET-sponsored study (1984), show that national strategies for development in new technologies vary widely. Brazil, for example, has a highly developed national policy aimed at promoting growth and self-reliance in new technologies, whereas Chile operates on a classical laissez-faire, free-market basis. The point that these and other authors make is that international economic structures make it difficult, but not impossible, for Latin American countries to transfer in the necessary infrastructure to build their own information and communication structures.

The third position characteristically distinguishes between large and small technologies in deciding whether their social impact will be positive. The idea is that smaller technologies will be more amenable to control by local communities, whereas large technologies, and especially the newer ones in information and telecommunication, have a centralizing tendency that will almost certainly reinforce the dominant power structures (see the Simpson Grinberg and Reyes Matta essays in this volume). Mattelart (1979) seems to make the same argument in his later writings (e.g., Mattelart and Schmucler, 1983). The argument involves certain assumptions about the role of power in any social order and the question whether non-power-holders should or could hold a dominant position in society. Control of smaller technologies would allow subordinate groups to gain a relative independence within a society that still maintains dominant power structures.

The Latin American discussion of new technologies is reminiscent of the work of certain critical researchers in the United States who have tried to counterbalance the protechnology bias so evident in the literature in this country. With some exceptions, works reflecting the first two positions have less relevance for the United States than works reflecting the third. Despite widespread paranoia about the Japanese technological edge, the United States is not likely soon to be overwhelmed by imported technologies, nor is it uncertain about maintaining its own hegemony. But the question of how different groups within U.S. society may best approach their role in an information society (or, as the French would have it, an informatized society) is still largely unexplored.

National Policies for Communication and Culture

In Latin America, as in other parts of the globe, there has been increased interest in policy studies in communication for the past decade. UNESCO's MacBride Report (1980) on international communication problems and the New International Information Order (NIIO) put a heavy emphasis on the need of each country to develop policies to promote national development goals as well as to regulate various foreign and transnational influences. As far back as the early 1960s, some Latin American and a number of U.S. communication researchers were promoting the role of the mass media in development (the *dessarollista* position often criticized in the Latin American critical literature of the 1970s) and implicitly or explicitly making policy recommendations.

In the 1970s concerns about national policies became explicit but were often couched in terms of the agenda of the NIIO (Beltrán, 1976b). A number of Latin American countries made more conscious efforts to coordinate communication policy with national objectives (as defined by prevailing governments). Mexico and Brazil (Mahan, 1984, and Mattos, 1981, respectively) moved in the direction of promoting the more efficient operation of a private enterprise model. Chile under Allende (1970–73) took some steps toward promoting socialist goals (Morel, 1973; Salinas, 1981) but essentially left intact the strong opposition press, which supported the military coup of Pinochet. Subsequent government policies under Pinochet were drastically repressive (Munizaga, 1981). In Peru under Velasco and his successor (1968–78), the military reformist government promoted the most radical restructuring of the media, including expropriation of the press and the reassignment of newspapers to different social sectors (see the exhaustive bibliography by Peirano and Kudo, 1982, and the studies summarized in English by Atwood and Mattos, 1982). Finally, Venezuela attempted to incorporate policy changes in line with NIIO values into its four-year plan under the Herrera administration (1979–83), although conflict with private sector forces reduced their effectiveness (Lizcano, 1984).

Beyond the mass media concerns of Latin American governments and communication scholars, there are a series of issues involving new communication technologies, including satellites, microelectronics, and telecommunications (Mattelart and Schmucler, 1983). As has been mentioned, Brazil has developed the most articulate and independent policies in the area (Orellana and Rodriguez, 1984), and other countries of the region need to follow its example (Rada, 1981).

One of the particular problems of critical scholars in Latin America is their relationship with repressive military governments. With the withdrawal of the military governments in Argentina, Uruguay, and Brazil, this oppositional stand may give way to a search for alternative policies. For example, the ILET group has spent more time since the early 1980s on the development of workable alternatives for democratizing mass communication in Latin America and less in critical analysis of the dominant media.

A number of policy questions raised by Latin American researchers resonate with the concerns of their U.S. colleagues. The development of policies regarding satellite parking space, transborder data flow, and future international satellite broadcasting to other countries is being watched closely by critical scholars in the United States. Relatively few critical scholars in the United States and Canada have a voice in government policy, but a focus on policy issues needs to be part of the critical research agenda (Melody and Mansell, 1983). International issues like the ones mentioned above point to areas where U.S. and Latin American researchers can and should collaborate. Such collaboration would provide a better understanding on each side of how the policy process works and how policies that provide the best options for both sides may be achieved.

Alternative Communication

The theme of alternative communication has been sounded frequently in Latin America in the 1980s (Reyes Matta 1981a, 1981b; Simpson Grinberg, 1981). In many ways this is a logical outcome of the extensive work done on transnationalization and cultural imperialism and dependency in the 1970s. By the end of the 1970s, many researchers had recognized two things: (1) that many of their mass media were dominated by foreign interests and local sub-classes with no interest in changing the status quo; and (2) that having documented this situation in a number of studies, simply denouncing the domination or calling for change was relatively unproductive. In order to promote change, research had to be directed toward action and applied to situations where the weight of existing structures did not prevent progress toward more open and democratic communication (Reyes Matta, 1981b).

Latin American researchers have been trying to find out how people in different settings have opposed or resisted the dominant power structure and the dominant (usually transnational) communication structure. As one of the spokespeople for this movement, Fernando Reyes Matta, points out in this volume:

> The primary reference point of alternative communication is the transnational model in the global expansionary phase. We must recognize that this model debilitates the full, integrated development and the political, economic, and cultural independence of the people of the Third World and the industrialized world. Consequently, the analytic challenge here is to integrate diverse phenomena that are all partial replies, in different societies, to still other phenomena that have a common origin.

Alternative communication may arise in opposition to forces other than the transnational presence in Latin American media; the movement also opposes all forms of censorship (see Simpson Grinberg's essay in this volume). Thus, for example, these researchers have taken an interest in the "new song movement" in Chile (Davagnino, 1980; Mattelart, 1970; Rivera, 1980).

A number of special themes have emerged from this search for alternative forms of communication, but two are especially important to critical research beyond Latin America. The first is the effort to democratize communication and especially to make the mass media and the new technologies serve the interest of the majority. The MacBride Report (UNESCO, 1980) emphasized this theme, although it made no recommendations on how this could be accomplished. Roncagliolo and Janus (1981) point out that the emphasis on electoral politics so often portrayed in U.S. foreign policy as the only way toward democracy overlooks the structures of social power and economic interest that make U.S.-backed "demonstration" elections meaningless. They argue that democratic communication must in some sense grant the power of expression to all, not simply the freedom to consume the products advertised in the mass media. Reyes Matta (in this volume) goes farther to argue that there are no absolutes in the struggle for more democratic and participative communication. Therefore, it will not do simply to denounce the large media that are controlled by dominant political and economic interests and to turn to the small media that may be more responsive to local control, since this strategy threatens to marginalize the alternative media and leave power in the hands of dominant groups. Rather, he argues that research should help to identify all forms of opposition at every level and to view the gains in relation to the goal of achieving greater participation for all (Díaz Bordenave, 1982). Such a theme is as relevant for the powerless segments of U.S. society as it is for Latin American societies, yet relatively little of this kind of research is evident in our critical literature (Downing, 1984).

The second significant theme that was generated under the rubric of alternative communication is termed "popular communication" or, to give it a more precise English equivalent, "grassroots communication" (Martín Barbero, 1983, 1984; Ossandón, 1981; White, 1980). The concept has both practical and theoretical antecedents. The rural and urban poor who make up the great mass of Latin American society have typically been marginalized within their countries. Although many of the urban poor have been exposed to the dominant media, they are not the target audiences for the products that advertising-based media are trying to reach. The rural poor are protected from the domination of the media by their physical isolation. These groups often have a culture of communication that speaks to their own needs and interests and expresses their resistance to the structures that oppress them.

On a theoretical level, there has been a reaction to the all-powerful media model emphasized by the scholars of cultural imperialism, and researchers are beginning to develop a more dialectical view of how people respond to domination. A clear statement of this new trend within a Marxist framework (Salinas and Paldan, 1979) suggests that a study of opposition movements among different sectors of Latin American society would indicate that many grassroots groups have not been totally dominated by the media. Researchers are discovering more promising theoretical as well as practical applications of this idea. As more careful study of the cultural history of the nondominant groups expands, a total hegemony model seems less plausible. Middle-class scholars are beginning to look to this grassroots experience as a guide to both theory and policy strategies for opposing the dominant power structures.

U.S. critical scholars have spent much of their time studying and denouncing a dominant structure that seems almost impervious to change. A return to the grassroots and to the culture of opposition might provide a more useful tack for those whose research is motivated in part by the goal of social change. There are, of course, notable historical differences between U.S. and Latin American societies. The majority populations in Latin America are often considered minorities in the U.S., and there is less likelihood that critical researchers there will turn to these minorities for theoretical and practical alternatives. Still, U.S. critical research needs a counterbalance to the repetitive themes of hegemony and a path toward more positive alternatives.

An Indigenous Communication Science

Latin American scholars have produced recurrent self-examinations centering on their dependence upon foreign sources for their ideas and research models. The ideal has been to create a new social science (Fals Borda, 1973), a new economic approach (Cardoso, 1979), or a new communication science (Beltrán, 1976b) that would be appropriate to the Latin American context and its historic necessities. Critical communication researchers have demonstrated the heavy influence of U.S. theories and models in the 1960s and the inappropriateness of such research for the region's basic development needs (Díaz Bordenave, 1976).

Mainstream scholars criticize any deviation from accepted social science models as "nonscientific," whether it is produced by U.S. or Latin American critical scholars (Rosengren, 1983; Stevenson, 1983, 1984). Latin American critical research may appear to those trained in the traditional social science models of the United States as "unscientific" (a vague, general criticism leveled at any deviation from the canons of a quantitative, experimental model); "nonempirical" (depending not on externally validated evidence but on preconceived values that seek confirmation by example rather than disconfirmation by hypothesis testing); "Marxist" (another vague and almost undefinable criticism, frequently made without supporting detail); "ideological" (based on rigid preconceived models not open to disconfirmation by objective evidence); "journalistic" (lacking a logical and coherent methodology); or "committed to change by means of violence" as opposed to knowledge creation (a critique advanced by researchers who denounce any goal beyond knowledge, and especially goals related to social change). Real (1984) presents a more complete discussion of these accusations.

Many of these criticisms can be dismissed as inaccurate or irrelevant to most works in the Latin American critical tradition. They miss much of the point of what critical communication research in Latin America has tried to do over the past two decades. If one looks beyond the narrower confines of the U.S. social science tradition between World War II and the mid-1970s (Bell, 1982) to other traditions in the United States itself that have undertaken the study of communication from non–social science perspectives (Carey, 1979;

Rowland, 1983), it is clear that criticism of one tradition by another does not invalidate the premises of the former. Moreover, it is not the case that Latin American critical research has entirely rejected the methodological tools of a quantitative approach to communication (on the contrary, a good deal of quantitative research is carried on by the ILET and other centers of critical thought), even if there is widespread skepticism about the epistemological premises of a strictly positivist science. Understood correctly, Latin American researchers' denunciation of U.S. traditional models was as much a critique of the irrelevance of U.S. research topics as a rejection of the premises of the model (Halloran, 1981). A researcher's personal commitment to study that is relevant to social change is a conscious recognition of the social function of knowledge building, a function that many U.S. researchers ignore. Latin American communication researchers, whether critical or not, are acutely conscious of their role in society and the relationship of that role to changing a status quo that in most countries is obviously unjust.

Latin Americans know their own needs and are attempting to build a coherent and scientific communication model for the purpose of knowledge building as well as policy change. Given the long history of social frustration and political repression in Latin America, most communication researchers are not naive about the possibilities of social change. Yet they refuse to disengage the attempt to build a more relevant and valid social science for their own environments and historical realities from the effort to create change in their societies.

Although critical scholars in this country cannot help directly in building a Latin American communication science, their own needs for a more socially relevant research are much in evidence. Articles in the special "Ferment in the Field" issue of the *Journal of Communication* (1983) expressed the need to adapt communication research to a new agenda. There were few calls to abandon the norms of social science. Rather, there were calls to include other aspects of communication problems in critical studies—the political and economic dimensions of new technologies, the negative social impact on some groups of those technologies, and the epistemological principles that underlie the scientific study of social communication. An expansion of the meaning of the "scientific" study of communication in the United States promises a growth in the field beyond the well-defined limits of science as it has been understood. Such a growth would parallel similar developments in Latin America.

Conclusion

The dialogue concerning critical communication in Latin America has a history of some twenty years or more, and yet in many ways it is just beginning. A *tradition* of scholarship and research is only now taking root. One manifestation of this is the appearance in the past few years of a number of national bibliographies in the communication area from different Latin American countries. For Peru (Peirano and Kudo, 1982) and Chile (Munizaga and Rivera, 1983), we have excellent overviews of the past twenty years of research; for Brazil (Marques de Melo, 1984a) we find a complete summary for the past century (1883–1983). Other bibliographies are promised soon for Mexico, Colombia, and Venezuela. A specialized bibliography on rural development was produced in Colombia several years ago (Beltrán, Isaza, and Ramirez, 1978). In addition, there are now a number of regularly published journals in both Spanish and Portuguese, not to mention a good record of book publication in Mexico, Brazil, Venezuela, Argentina, and Colombia. With this kind of infrastructure, it is becoming possible for the numerous Latin American communication schools to use indigenous works in their teaching instead of old and often irrelevant U.S. textbooks translated into Spanish or Portuguese. Once genuine incorporation of local materials has taken place in the teaching institutions of Latin America, there is real potential for the formation of a Latin American communication science.

All of this is an exciting prospect for Latin American communication scholars, and it promises to enrich U.S. critical communication scholars as well. The outlines of a world economic system have been in place for some time, thanks to pioneering work by Braudel (1979–1984) and Wallerstein (1974, 1979), and few economists would today argue that international concerns are not central to their field. In communication studies, U.S. scholars have been slow to recognize the operation of a parallel world communication system and even slower to see its implications for communication research and theory. A better understanding of European scholarship has been gradually emerging in U.S. communication research publications and has begun to influence our theories, but a similar awareness of Latin American scholarship has so far been confined to a minority of specialists. A wider definition of communication research and a more diverse view of theory will emerge from the exposure of the U.S. research community to Latin American contributions. Problems that are international in scope may not only be researched together, but may be solved in a way that helps promote both research and socially positive change in both parts of the hemisphere.

References

Atwood, Rita, and S. Mattos (1982). "Mass Media Reform and Social Change: The Peruvian Experience." *Journal of Communication*, 32, 2, pp. 33–45.

Audley, P. (1983). *Canada's Cultural Industries*. Toronto: Lorimer.

Bell, D. (1982). *Social Sciences Since the Second World War*. Rutgers, N.J.: Transaction Books.

Beltrán, L. R. (1976a). "TV Etchings in the Minds of Latin Americans: Conservatism, Materialism, and Conformism." Paper presented at the tenth General Assembly of the International Association of Mass Communication Research, Leicester, England, August 30–September 4.

Beltrán, L. R. (1976b). "Alien Premises, Objects, and Methods in Latin American Communication Research." *Communication Research*, 3, 2, pp. 107–34.

Beltrán, L. R., and E. Fox (1979). "Latin America and the United States: Flaws in the Free Flow of Information." In K. Nordenstreng and H. Schiller (eds.) *National Sovereignty and International Communication*. Norwood, N.J.: Ablex.

Beltrán, L. R., and E. Fox de Cardona (1980). *Comunicación Dominada: Estados Unidos en los Medios de América Latina*. Mexico City: Instituto Latinoamericano de Estudios Transnacionales/Nueva Imagen.

Beltrán, L. R., G. Isaza, and F. Ramirez (1978). *Bibliografía Sobre Investigaciones en Comunicación para el Desarrollo Rural en América Latina*. Bogota: International Development Research Center.

Braudel, F. (1979–84). *Civilization and Capitalism: Fifteenth to the Eighteenth Centuries*. 3 vols. New York: Harper and Row.

Canclini, G. N. (1977). "Cine Documental, Histórica, de Ficción, de Entretenimento: Caminos de un Cine Popular." *Arte, Sociedad, Ideología* (Mexico City), 1.

Canclini, G. N. (1979). "Teoría da Superestructura e Sociologia das Vanguardas Artísticas." *Encontros com a Civilização Brasileira*, 18, pp. 71–98.

Cardoso, F. (1979). "The Originality of the Copy: The Economic Commission for Latin America and the Idea of Development." In A. Hill (ed.) *Toward a New Strategy for Development*. New York: Pergamon Press.

Carey, J. (1979). "Mass Communication Research and Cultural Studies." In J. Curran, M. Gurevitch, J. Woollacott (eds.) *Mass Communication and Society*. Beverly Hills, Calif.: Sage Publications.

Compaine, B. (1982). *Who Owns the Media? Concentration of Ownership in the Mass Communication Industry*. 2d ed. New York: Harmony Books.

Davagnino, M. (1980). "La Experiencia de Nuestro Canto." In *La Comunicación Alternativa en Chile*, pp. 1–10. Mimeographed. Santiago: VECTOR, Serie Documentos de Talleres, 1.

Díaz Bordenave, J. (1976). "Communication of Agricultural Innovations in Latin America: The Need for New Models." *Communication Research*, 3, 2, pp. 135–54.

Díaz Bordenave, J. (1982). "Democratización de la Comunicación: Teoría y práctica." *Chasqui*, 1, Oct.–Dec., pp. 13–21.

Dorfman, A., and A. Mattelart (1975). *How to Read Donald Duck*. New York: International General.

Downing, J. (1984). *Radical Media: The Political Experience of Alternative Communication*. Boston: South End Press.

Esteinou Madrid, J. (1979). *El Estudio Materialista de la Comunicación de Masas*. Mexico City: Taller de Investigación en Comunicación Masiva, Universidad Autónoma Metropolitana-Xochimilco, no. 1.

Esteinou Madrid, J. (1980). *Aparatos de Comunicación de Masas, Estado y Puntas Hegemonía*. Mexico City: Taller de Investigación en Comunicación Masiva, Universidad Autónoma Metropolitana-Xochimilco, no. 6.

Esteinou Madrid, J. (1984). "Los Medios de Comunicación y Capacitación de la Fuerza de Trabajo." *Ciencia y Desarrollo*, 59, Nov.–Dec., pp. 89–99.

Fals Borda, O. (1973). *Ciencia Propia y Colonialismo Intellectual*. Mexico City: Editorial Nuestro Tiempo.

Fejes, F. (1980). "The Growth of Multinational Advertising Agencies in Latin America." *Journal of Communication*, 30, 4, pp. 36–49.

Fejes, F. (in press). *Imperialism, Media and the Good Neighbor*. Norwood, N.J.: Ablex.

FELAFACS (Federación Latinoamericana de Asociaciones de Facultades de Comunicación Social) (1982). *La Formación Universitaria de Comunicadores Sociales en América Latina*. Lima: FELAFACS.

Fish, M. (1984). "A Study of Mass Communication Research and Scholarship." Ph.D. dissertation, University of Texas, Austin.

Grossberg, L. (1984). "Strategies of Marxist Cultural Interpretation." *Critical Studies in Mass Communication*, 1, 4, pp. 392–421.

Guback, T. (1969). *The International Film Industry*. Bloomington: University of Indiana Press.

Guback, T. (1982). "Theatrical Film." In B. Compaine (ed.), *Who Owns the Media?* 2d ed. New York: Harmony Books.

Halloran, J. (1981). "The Context of Mass Communication Research." In E. McAnany, J. Schnitman, and N. Janus (eds.), *Communication and Social Structure: Critical Studies in Mass Media Research*. New York: Praeger.

Janus, N. (1980). "The Making of the Global Consumer: Transnational Advertising and the Mass Media in Latin America." Ph.D. dissertation, Stanford University.

Journal of Communication (1983). Special issue: "Ferment in the Field," 33, 3.

Larson, J. (1984). *Television's Window on the World: International Affairs Coverage on the U.S. Networks*. Norwood, N.J.: Ablex.

Larson, J., E. McAnany, and D. Storey (1986). "News of Latin America on Network TV, 1972–1981: A Northern Perspective on the Southern Hemisphere." *Critical Studies in Mass Communication*, 3, 2, pp. 169–83.

Lee, C. C. (1980). *Media Imperialism Reconsidered: The Homogenizing of Television Culture*. Beverly Hills, Calif.: Sage Publications.

Lizcano, M. (1984). "Communication Policies in Venezuela." M.A. thesis, University of Texas, Austin.

Mahan, E. (1984). "Government-Industry Cooperation and Conflict in Mexico and the U.S.: A Comparative Analysis of Commercial Broadcast Regulation." *Studies in Latin American Popular Culture*, 3.

Marques de Melo, J. (1984a). "La Investigación Latinoamericana en Comunicación." *Chasqui*, July–Sept., pp. 4–11.

Marques de Melo, J. (1984b). *Inventario de Pesquisa en Comunicação no Brasil*. São Paulo: INTERCOM/Sociedade Brasileira de Estudios Interdisciplinares da Comunição.

Martín Barbero, J. (1983). "Comunicación Popular y los Modelos Transnacionales." *Chasqui*, Oct.–Dec., pp. 4–11.

Martín Barbero, J. (1984). "Cultura Popular y Comunicación de Masas." *Materiales para la Comunicación Popular* (Instituto para América Latina, Lima), no. 3.

Mattelart, A. (1970). "Estructura del Poder Informativo y Dependencia." In *Los Medios de Comunicación de Masas*. Santiago: Centro de Estudios de la Realidad Nacional, Cuadernos no. 3.

Mattelart, A. (1972). *Agresión en el Espacio: Cultura y Napalm en la Era de los Satélites*. Mexico City: Siglo XXI.

Mattelart, A. (1977). "Prensa y Lucha Ideológica en los Cordones Industriales de Santiago: Testimonios." In A. Mattelart and M. Mattelart (eds.) *Frentes Culturales y Movilización de Masas*. Barcelona: Editorial Anagrama.

Mattelart, A. (1978). *La Comunicación Masiva en el Proceso de Liberación*. Mexico City: Siglo XXI.

Mattelart, A. (1979). *Multinational Corporations and the Control of Culture: The Ideological Apparatuses of Imperialism*. New York: Harvester.

Mattelart, A., and J.-M. Piemme (1982). "Cultural Industries: The Origin of an Idea." In *Cultural Industries: A Challenge for the Future of Cultures*. Paris: UNESCO Press.

Mattelart, A., and H. Schmucler (1983). *América Latina en la Encrucijada Telemática*. Mexico City: Instituto Latinoamericano de Estudios Transnacionales/Folios Ediciones.

Mattelart, A., and S. Siegleglaub (1979, 1983). *Communication and Class Struggle*. 2 vols. New York: International General.

Mattos, S. (1981). *The Development of Communication Policies Under the Peruvian Military Government (1968–1980)*. San Antonio, Tex.: V. Klingensmith.

Mattos, S. (1982). *The Impact of the 1964 Revolution on Brazilian Television*. San Antonio, Tex.: V. Klingensmith.

Mattos, S. (1984). "Advertising and Government Influences: The Case of Brazilian Television." *Communication Research*, 11, 2, pp. 203–20.

McAnany, E. (1983). "Television and Crisis: Ten Years of Network Coverage of Central America, 1972–1981." *Media Culture and Society*, 5, 2.

Melody, W., and R. Mansell (1983). "The Debate Over Critical vs. Administrative Research: Circularity or Challenge." *Journal of Communication*, 33, 3.

Morel, C. (1973). "Políticas de Medios de Comunicación en Chile, 1970–1972." Mimeographed. Santiago: Escuela de Artes de la Comunicación, Universidad Católica.

Morrow, F. (1984). "The U.S. Power Structure and the Mass Media." Ph.D. dissertation, University of Texas, Austin.

Muller, C., and D. Herz (1983). "Entrevista: Armand Mattelart." *Comunição e Politica*, 1, 1, pp. 85–99.

Munizaga, G., and A. Rivera (1983). *La Investigación en Comunicación Social en Chile*. Lima: Centro de Estudios y Promoción del Desarrollo.

Nixon, R. (1982). "Historia de las Escuelas de Periodismo." *Chasqui*, Jan.–March, pp. 13–19.

Nordenstreng, K., and T. Varis (1974). *Television Traffic: A One-Way Street?* Paris: UNESCO Press, Reports and Papers on Mass Communications, no. 70.

Orellana, R., and G. Rodriguez (1984). *Políticas de Información en América Latina: Chile, Argentina, Brasil*. Santiago: Instituto Latinoamericano de Estudios Transnacionales.

Ossandón, F. (1981). "Comunicación Popular y Rearticulación del Movimiento Popular en Chile Hoy." Paper presented to the Seminar on Comunicación y Movimiento Popular, CELADEC, Lima, September.

Peirano, L., and T. Kudo (1982). *La Investigación en Comunicación Social en el Perú.* Lima: Centro de Estudios y Promoción del Desarrollo.

Rada, J. (1981). "The Microelectronics Revolution: Implications for the Third World." *Development Dialogue,* 2, pp. 41–67.

Read, W. (1976). *America's Mass Media Merchants.* Baltimore: Johns Hopkins University Press.

Real, M. (1984). "The Debate on Critical Theory and the Study of Communications." *Journal of Communication,* 34, 4.

Reyes Matta, F. (1979). "The Latin American Concept of News." *Journal of Communication,* 29, 2, pp. 164–171.

Reyes Matta, F. (1981a). "La Comunicación Transnacional y la Respuesta Alternativa." In M. Simpson Grinberg (ed.) *Comunicación Alternativa y Cambio Social,* vol. 1: *América Latina.* Mexico City: Universidad Nacional Autónoma de México.

Reyes Matta, F. (1981b). "A Model for Democratic Communication." *Development Dialogue,* 2, pp. 79–97.

Rivera, A. (1980). *El Público del Canto Popular.* Santiago: CENECA, Serie Canto Popular, no. 10.

Roncagliolo, R., and N. Janus (1981). "Advertising and the Democratization of Communications." *Development Dialogue,* 2, pp. 31–40.

Rosengren, K. (1983). "Communication Research: One Paradigm or Four?" *Journal of Communication,* 33, 3.

Rowland, W. (1983). *The Politics of TV Violence: Policy Uses of Communication Research.* Beverly Hills, Calif.: Sage Publications.

Salinas, R. (1981). "Políticas Nacionales de Comunicación, Chile." In *Políticas Nacionales de Comunicación.* Quito: Editorial Epoca.

Salinas, R., and L. Paldan (1979). "Culture in the Process of Dependent Development: Theoretical Perspectives." In K. Nordenstreng and H. Schiller (eds.) *National Sovereignty and International Communication: A Reader.* Norwood, N.J.: Ablex.

Sarti, I. (1981). "Communication and Cultural Dependency: A Misconception." In E. McAnany, J. Schnitman, and N. Janus (eds.) *Communication and Social Structure: Critical Studies in Mass Media Research,* pp. 317–32. New York: Praeger.

Schement, J., and E. Rogers (1984). "Media Flows in Latin America." *Communication Research,* 11, 2.

Schramm, W. (1983). "The Unique Perspective of Communication: A Retrospective View." *Journal of Communication,* 33, 3.

Shore, L. (1983). "The Crossroads of Business and Music: The Music Industry in the U.S. and Internationally." Ph.D. dissertation, Stanford University.

Simpson Grinberg, M. (ed.) (1981). *Comunicación Alternativa y Cambio Social,* vol. 1: *América Latina.* Mexico City: Universidad Nacional Autónoma de México.

Smith, A. (1980). *The Geopolitics of Information: How Western Culture Dominates the World.* New York: Oxford.

Stevenson, R. (1983). "A Critical Look at Critical Analysis." *Journal of Communication,* 33, 3.

Stevenson, R. (1984). "Pseudo Debate." *Journal of Communication,* 34, 1.
"Tune Up for Term Two" (1984). *Chronicle of International Communication,* pp. 6–7.
Tunstall, J. (1977). *The Media Are American: Anglo-American Media in the World.* New York: Columbia University Press.
UNESCO (1980). *Many Voices, One World.* New York: UNIPUB.
Varis, T. (1974). "Global Traffic in Television." *Journal of Communication,* 24, 1.
Varis, T. (1984). "The International Flow of Television Programs." *Journal of Communication,* 34, 1.
Varis, T., and T. Guback (1982). *Transnational Communication and Cultural Industries.* Paris: UNESCO Press, Reports and Papers on Mass Communication, no. 92.
Veron, E. (1967). "Ideología y Comunicación de Masas: La Semantización de la Violencia Política." In Veron et al. (eds.) *Lenguaje y Comunicación Social.* Buenos Aires: Editorial Nueva Visión.
Veron, E. (1972). *Conducta Estructura y Comunicación.* Buenos Aires: Editorial Nueva Visión.
Wallerstein, E. (1974). *The Modern World System.* New York: Academic Press.
Wallerstein, E. (1979). *The Capitalist World Economy.* Cambridge: Cambridge University Press.
White, R. (1980). "Comunicación Popular: Language of Liberation." *Media Development,* 27, 3, pp. 3–9.

3 Cristina Schwarz and Oscar Jaramillo

Hispanic American Critical Communication Research in Its Historical Context

Critical communication research in Hispanic America[1] is not new, but it is almost unknown to U.S. scholars. Our purpose in this paper is to present a systematized view of the work developed by scholars and research groups in this region since the early 1960s.

Some attempts to analyze this tradition in a systematic way have already been made by scholars in Hispanic America,[2] but there is still a need for a

1. For methodological reasons our paper takes into account only those countries in continental and insular America that directly received Spanish cultural influences. Nations with an English, French, or Dutch tradition are excluded from the analysis. So is Portuguese-speaking Brazil—although its influence on the rest of Latin America is decisive and Freire, in particular, has had a profound influence on communication scholarship (see Freire 1974, 1975a, 1975b, 1976)—because the Brazilian process deserves a special study; likewise, Cuban communication research merits specific treatment given its unique historical circumstances.

2. Beltrán (1976a) systematizes the underlying assumptions and methods of U.S. communication research as they have impinged on Latin America's own experience with communication scholarship. Díaz Bordenave and Carvalho (1978) trace the developmentalist efforts behind Latin American communication planning strategies. Beltrán, Isaza, and Ramirez (1978) provide an annotated bibliography of research in the region on communication and rural development. Martín Barbero (1978, 1980) not only analyzes the positivist/functionalist premises of U.S. communication research, but explains why Latin America has turned to semiotics for a better understanding of the role of communication in the area. Simpson Grinberg (1981) attempts to systematize the phenomenon of alternative communication. Piccini (1982) explains the potential value of Marx-

48

more comprehensive and in-depth view of the field. By systematizing Hispanic American critical communication research, we intend to show the real progress that has been made in indigenous theory building. In fact, we argue that Hispanic America offers a consistent and coherent discourse on communication phenomena. Our goal is to explain the dialectical forces forming the body of theoretical reasoning in Hispanic America, evaluate its conceptualization, its methodology, and its rhetoric, and then weigh its contribution to the field of communication. Ultimately, we focus on the alternative modes of communication that have emerged from Hispanic America's own grassroots groups and opened new roads for scholarly research.

Historical Context

Ideas do not appear in men's minds spontaneously; nor do they exist, as Plato asserted, in a marvelous world "beyond heaven." They are forged and transformed daily by the encounter of human beings with the concrete reality of life. They result from the "active unity between human beings and the world, between matter and spirit, between product and its producer" (Kosik, 1983, p. 240)—in a phrase, from the praxis that makes history.[3] Thus, we have to locate the Hispanic American critical approach to communication processes within its historical context if we intend to understand its scope and significance.

Critical communication research in Hispanic America began in the 1960s and in the 1980s is striking out on new paths. This twenty-year period has been marked by such significant changes in global economic, political, religious, and cultural structures that it is difficult to compare today's human habitat with the one existing in the 1950s, not to speak of the first half of the twentieth century. Such changes have had important consequences for Hispanic American history and, of course, for the ideas that arose from it.

From Development to Liberation

The 1960s were crucial to these changes in perspective in Hispanic American countries. The victory of the revolutionary *guerrillas* in Cuba (January 1959) and the failure of the U.S.-backed attempt at counterrevolution at the Bay of Pigs (1961) gave Fidel Castro and his government a powerful influence on the psychology of the peoples of Hispanic America. Even North American writ-

---

ism and structuralism for an analysis of communication in the region. Echeverría (1984) and Fox (1984) debate about the weaknesses and strengths of Latin American communication research. Finally, Marques de Melo (1984) presents a panoramic view of the last twenty-five years of communication research in Latin America.

3. All translations from Spanish-language works cited are ours.

ers, analyzing this historical period, conclude that "not all of the Cuban experience has been negative and some *fidelista* policies seem likely to have considerable appeal to the new Latin American leaders" (Gonzalez and Einaudi, 1974, p. 55).

As a direct consequence of the Cuban Revolution, John F. Kennedy initiated the "Alliance for Progress" to "accomplish the Revolution of the Americas and build a hemisphere in which all people can live in an atmosphere of dignity and freedom" (Agudelo-Villa, 1966, p. 53). But the fabulous economic aid promised by Kennedy was never delivered, and the proposed reforms to create national planning systems and modify rural, fiscal, and administrative structures were never achieved. The "Alliance" died after two years of intense publicity and a few more of slow decay (Agudelo-Villa, 1966).

Meanwhile, in Hispanic American countries the "dependency model" evolved from the work of the Economic Commission on Latin America (ECLA) to achieve a widespread predominance. The commission understood underdevelopment as a consequence of the international division of labor. This vision of underdevelopment as induced backwardness (García, 1969) does not place all the responsibility for poor conditions in underdeveloped countries on external factors, but finds an "internal expression" of dependency "through the social practices of local groups and classes which try to enforce foreign interests, not precisely because they are foreign, but because they may coincide with values and interests that these groups pretend are their own" (Cardoso and Faletto, 1979, p. xvi).

As a logical consequence of this kind of analysis, *liberation* was identified as the solution for the problems of Hispanic American countries: " 'Liberation,' in fact, expresses the inescapable moment of radical change, which is foreign to the ordinary uses of the term 'development' " (Gutierrez, 1973, p. 27). "Liberation" assumed various meanings, but the concept dominated economic literature just as it dominated political activity during the 1960s and 1970s.

The Participation of the Church and the Military

The Roman Catholic Church is a basic element in this period as in any other in Hispanic American history. The papacy of John XXIII (1958–63) saw the church begin a process of *aggiornamento*—bringing itself up to date. Hispanic American populations are more than 90 percent Catholic, and some countries officially embrace Catholic practices. The *aggiornamento* brought a new understanding of the church's role in the historical process of Latin America. The case of Camilo Torres, the Colombian priest who died grasping a machine gun as a leftist *guerrillero,* was not an isolated example, even if it was the most powerful in its originality (Broderick, 1975).

Under these circumstances the "theology of liberation" was born. Its main proponent, Gustavo Gutierrez (1973), a Peruvian priest, saw it as a product of a "profound historical movement" and its framework as "the Biblical message which presents the work of Christ as a liberation" (p. 35). In 1968, with the Second Vatican Council already closed, Pope Paul VI opened the Second Plenary Conference of Latin American Bishops (CELAM II), which was to issue documents based on a socioeconomic analysis of the "dependency model" (see document on "Peace," CELAM, 1969) and on the theology of liberation.

The military, another important element in Hispanic American society, was also touched by the liberation ethos, as can be seen in the so-called Revolución de la Fuerza Armada in Peru in 1968, a very different phenomenon from the *coups d'etat* so common in some Latin American countries (Einaudi and Stepan, 1974).

The free election in Chile in 1970 of the Unidad Popular government, made up of socialists, communists, and other leftist parties and groups, marked the beginning of another important stage in Hispanic American history. Here was the first attempt to exchange the capitalist system for a socialist-Marxist alternative through democratic means (Gonzalez and Einaudi, 1974). The ideological and factional struggle of those years in Chile left a mark on Hispanic America, as did the tragic end of Salvador Allende's government (September 1973) and the bloody repression following his death.

Another landmark of the period was the triumphal comeback of "Peronism" in Argentina in 1973, after eighteen years of military dominance. Three years later, however, it would be replaced by a new military dictatorship, which, like Chile's, brutally punished any criticism of the system.

Recent Events

Events of the last few years illustrate the same processes of change and repression. The Central American socioeconomic and political situation has again compelled the region to turn its eyes to revolutionary movements: the fight against the Somoza family in Nicaragua, against the oligarchy and the military in El Salvador, Honduras, and Guatemala, and against the increasing presence of the United States in the area.

To these Central American processes and the confrontation between U.S. interests and those of Hispanic America we must add Washington's backing of Great Britain in the Malvinas crisis. The invasion of Grenada in 1983—so romantically presented by the media to the U.S. public—further underlined for Hispanic Americans their dependence on outside forces.

A final word concerning the current debt crisis is necessary in this brief presentation of the Hispanic American habitat. Indebtedness is not something new in the region. In the present monetary crisis, Hispanic Americans are once more pawns in a game in which the prices of basic exports and interest rates for loans are driven up or down by forces beyond their control.

The Intellectual Environment

The academic environment in Hispanic America has been widely influenced by Marxist historical and economic concepts since the 1930s and 1940s, and these have become increasingly prominent since the 1960s. Marxist theories on value and capital accumulation or on imperialism and the capitalist crisis, for instance, are implicit in the works of researchers who are not necessarily Marxists. Marxist concepts are as common in Hispanic American universities and research centers as Einstein's theories on physics or Freud's on psychiatry.

Furthermore, researchers explicitly employ principles of Marxist economic or historical analysis as acceptable tools for inquiry. The Hispanic American academy normally does not equate Marxism (a philosophical theory and a model for the analysis of reality) with communism (a political movement, which, in the form of a party, has legally existed in almost all Hispanic countries for much of the last thirty years).

Precisely because of the differences in historical conditions described here, concepts such as "democracy" and "freedom" do not always have the same meaning when pronounced or written in Hispanic American countries as they have when used by politicians or writers in the United States. The same is true of "freedom of information," and a review of the controversy surrounding the New International Information Order (Reyes Matta, 1977a, 1977b; UNESCO, 1980) highlights these differences.

The Pioneers of Critical Research

The beginning of the 1960s saw the emergence of diverse approaches to communication processes, all of which were opposed to the dominant functionalist tendency of U.S. research. What was the source of this change of perspective in Hispanic American countries? Was this, for all its diversity, an organized and coordinated movement? To answer these questions we will set forth the work of four major Hispanic American critical thinkers who have laid the foundations for an original, indigenous approach to communication phenomena in the region. To avoid the danger of reducing to a few names what was almost a wild blossoming of thought and debate, we will, as our discussion develops, refer to the work of other representative authors.

Communication Versus Information: Pasquali

The first critical research work in communication published in Hispanic America to achieve relatively wide resonance was written by Antonio Pasquali, then teaching ethics at Venezuela's Universidad Central. Pasquali, a philosopher with an existentialist expressive style,[4] whose writings reveal the influence of Martin Heidegger and Jean-Paul Sartre, first presented his own communication theory in 1963 in *Comunicación y Cultura de Masas* (2d ed., Pasquali, 1977).

Pasquali's theory is based on his distinction between the *communication relation* and the *information relation*. For him, the former is reciprocal—"any transmitter can be a receiver, any receiver can be a transmitter" (p. 49). In the information relation messages are sent "without any possibility of non-mechanical return" (p. 53). Genuine communication can only be achieved by rational beings, whereas information transmission can be performed by any machine equipped for this kind of activity. All the channels or media that mankind has at present for interrelating could be used either for communication or for information, but a progressive shift has taken place from bilateral communication to unilateral information.

Pasquali typifies a "mass society" as one where "information relations" prevail and where, as a consequence, society becomes massified: "Information *allocution* is fired without an explicit target because it will always find one" (p. 79). The "mediocrity" of content and form of mass media messages is due to their need to be universally interpreted. Real communication processes do not massify but create a community or a public characterized by "the presence of a free, rational discussion" (p. 85); they place a high value on individuals and are associated with the existence of an elite that is responsible to the public and not engaged in subduing it, as is the case in information processes. According to Pasquali, "mass communication" is a contradiction in terms. If it is a true communication, the receiver is not a mass; and if it is an information process, it is superfluous and redundant to describe it as "mass."

"Mass culture" is "the remnant of all omnibus messages (for all and for whomever) circulated by the information transmitters and deposited in the receiving pole, which is constituted by a mass society" (p. 86). A society where communication relations prevail does not have "mass culture"; it simply has "culture" in one of many stages of development" (ibid.).

Pasquali's analysis of the influence of the mass media on Venezuelan audiences (Pasquali, 1967) led him to promote the application of communication policies at national and international levels, a process that we will consider further below. He was active in several symposia promoted by UNESCO in the 1970s to study this issue (Capriles, 1981). In his own country Pasquali promoted national communication policies and attained a partial victory when his government sponsored the Preparatory Commission of the National Council for Culture, created to design a national policy for radio and tele-

4. Like the first U.S. communication scholars, most Hispanic American pioneers had academic backgrounds not directly related to the study of communication media or processes.

vision (RATELVE, 1976), whose content and style had Pasquali's imprint. In recent years Pasquali has worked as deputy director of UNESCO at the organization's headquarters in Paris.

Structure and Ideology: Veron

The same year that Pasquali's main work was published, at the opposite end of South America the Argentinian sociologist Eliseo Veron compiled and published several of his earlier papers and lectures in a book entitled *Conducta, Estructura y Comunicación* (1963; 2d ed. 1972). The concepts introduced in this book were more thoroughly defined in 1967, when Veron organized a symposium entitled "Communication Theory and Linguistic Models in the Social Sciences." The proceedings of that meeting, held in the Torcuato Di Tella Institute in Buenos Aires, were edited by Veron and associates (Veron et al., 1967).

Veron's conceptual roots were in structuralism and Marxism. First as a disciple of the structuralists Claude Lévi-Strauss and Roland Barthes, and later as a professor at the Sorbonne, Veron attempted to restate the concept of "ideology," which had been used by many authors but was recoined and made popular by Marxists. Veron sought to place mass communication within the sociological controversy on ideology. He expected in this way to find a more solid basis for a communication science as well as a reexamination of the methods for the study of ideology (Veron, 1967a, 1967b).

Veron's aim was to reach the structural source of operation for ideological processes—a structure that cannot emerge from typical research methods like general surveys or public opinion polling. Such methods only "reflect the way that surveyed people consciously perceive diverse aspects of society" (Veron, 1967b, p. 138). Veron wanted to examine the internal workings of the process: that is, the ultimate source of these opinions. How are individual ideas organized inside society? What is the world view (or *Weltanschauung,* to use the German word so loved by European philosophers and sociologists) underlying the atomized expression of opinion?

This organizing principle or this structure is precisely what does not appear, what is not manifest, what is not attainable either by individual consciousness or by content analysis techniques. The structure lies at another level, one that is "latent," "secondary," "connotative." (Martín Barbero, 1978, p. 31)

Veron, as a structuralist, uses the method designed and applied by Greimas (1984) to classify connotative units and discover signifier modalities within social life: in other words, semiology. Veron describes it plainly as "communication science," a field that allows the study of sign systems per se—that is, a field that concentrates on the syntax of these systems ("study of the relations of signs among themselves") and their semantics ("study of the relations of signs with their meaning"), without much reference to pragmatics ("the con-crete processes of these systems' uses among their users") (Veron, 1967a, p. 17).

Veron uncovers the effects of a *Weltanschauung* in a given society and then uses Marxist tools of analysis to explain the genesis of its particular ideology as a product of a society marked by class struggles (Veron, 1967b, pp. 189–90). Marxist analysis is concerned with the concrete conditions under which internal images are produced in people and signs are generated in the media and elsewhere. These conditions do not influence people at a conscious level, but they are related directly to the objective characteristics of a social system associated with people's so-called class consciousness. Ideology, then, is a pervasive environment within which all the members of a given society act and think. It is a consequence of that society's economic infrastructure. Ideas expressed by individuals, and even their expressive forms, are a function of those individuals' material existence.

It is important to note that according to Veron's thesis (1967b), "the appar-ent or expressed function of messages cannot be confused with their ideologi-cal operation" (p. 142). For instance, in Western societies it is normally held that the mass media have an information function, but when an ideological reading is done, it is easy to discover that their real function is to shape the consciousness and the lives of people. The task of communication researchers is, according to Veron, to unveil the real function of messages and to elucidate the processes of selection and exclusion of content that occur in every com-munication event.

"Return the Word to the People": Mattelart
As Veron was developing his ideological reading in Buenos Aires and Pasquali was publishing his theory of communication in Caracas, a Belgian lawyer and demographer was beginning to work on population problems and policies in Chile. Armand Mattelart arrived in Chile in 1963 after legal studies at Lou-vain University and subsequent graduate studies in sociology and demography at the Sorbonne. He went to Chile under a contract with the Catholic Univer-sity in Santiago, as researcher in the Centro de Estudios de la Realidad Na-cional (CEREN). His personal aim was to be a partner in the process of change that Latin American countries were experiencing at that time.[5] In Chile Eduardo Frei's Christian Democratic government was involuntarily opening the way for the Unidad Popular of Salvador Allende in 1970.

Demographic policies in Chile, as in almost all Latin American countries at that time, were dominated by functionalist North American sociology and

5. This and other biographical material was taken from an interview with Mattelart by Muller and Herz (1983).

the goal of promoting birth control in underdeveloped countries, for which communication research was a useful tool. Although Matellart's approach to demography was quite different, this was his introduction to communication processes and research. With his wife, Michelle (who had previously studied literature and sociology), he published his first work in the field, *La Mujer Chilena en una Nueva Sociedad: Un Estudio Exploratorio Acerca de la Situación e Imagen de la Mujer en Chile* (Mattelart and Mattelart, 1968).

Mattelart candidly confesses that he had no theoretical framework when he began his work in communication. He and his research partners tried to synthesize elements taken from structuralism, Marxism, linguistics, and other systems. His work attracted students, unions, political parties, and finally the Unidad Popular government until its overthrow in 1973.

Mattelart's work in Chile fell into two stages. Before the Unidad Popular government, his scholarly task centered on the denunciation of existing communication practices. Under that government Mattelart worked for the government publishing agency and later for radio and television. His work continued to be critical, but his main task was to design and try to construct new communication forms.

Mattelart rejects the traditional role assigned to social researchers ("to take communication as a mere object for observation") and postulates a political involvement: "Transforming reality is equal to abolishing differences between life and science, between life and art, between life and culture, in order to liberate men and women" (Mattelart, Biedma, and Funes, 1980, pp. 13–14).

In his new approach to communication, he deals with the concept of "fetishization" used by Marx. The concept refers to the process in which the qualities of inert objects are attributed to human beings, and the qualities of human beings are attributed to things: workers are considered "production factors" and capital is said to "work." For Mattelart, communication media were new fetishes: in capitalist society the media have a special kind of existence and have been transformed into actors on the world stage, treated as if they were natural forces. The same can be said of the concept of "public opinion," which allows publishers and politicians "to transmit a private opinion as a public one" (Mattelart, 1980, p. 23).

Given this reality, the task of communication research is to "de-fetishize" those processes and media (Muller and Herz, 1983). It will then be possible to "return the word to the people," an expression that Mattelart (1980) took from the Chinese leader Mao Zedong. In Mattelart's view, this expression meant "to take away the dynamics of information from the prevailing class; in a more global sense, it means to take away culture from that class" (p. 81). The first steps have to be taken inside the media owned by the parties and movements that back egalitarian or popular causes. Only later will it be possible to expropriate the media that are now controlled by the bourgeoisie.

The objective Mattelart proposed for media professionals in the early 1970s was "to link news with popular initiatives," to place grassroots people in the middle of news commentaries (Mattelart, 1980, p. 77). This was the time for diverse journalistic activities designed to bring alternative information or "counterinformation" to the *cordones industriales* (industrial belts) of Santiago and other Chilean cities (Mattelart, 1974).

The end of the Unidad Popular government came sooner than expected, and this was due in significant measure to the influence of the mass media, which were mostly in the hands of right-wing groups opposed to Allende (Biedma, 1980; Mattelart, 1974). Mattelart had to leave Chile, the country that had become his second home, and where his prolific work on communication had begun. Since 1973 he has worked mainly in France. He has not broken his connection with the Latin American scene, although he has added communication problems in Africa to his interests.

Communication Policies: Beltrán

The Bolivian-born scholar Luis Ramiro Beltrán, a journalist and a journalist's son, was the only one of the four pioneers discussed here to receive intensive academic and professional preparation in the communication field. He received M.A. and Ph.D. degrees from Michigan State University for theses whose very titles denounce the positivist orientation that prevailed in the United States: "Communication and Modernization: Significance, Roles and Strategies" (M.A. thesis, 1972); "Communication in Latin America: Persuasion for Status Quo or for National Development" (Ph.D. thesis, 1972). A Beltrán paper of 1970, "News Flow between Latin America and the U.S.: An Assessment of International Communication," raised the problems that would become central in his subsequent academic activity (see Rincon, 1979).

Beltrán returned to Hispanic America and took root in Colombia. There he began working in the field of rural communication, which was central to research in the region at the time (Beltrán, 1974b). His re-encounter with the reality of Latin America soon led him to react against those "alien premises, objects and methods" (1976a) prevailing in Latin American communication research as a result of U.S. influence. Because he knew those phenomena from the inside, Beltrán's criticism of North American functionalist theories and practices is perhaps the most serious and precise work published by a Hispanic American in this field. The "modernization" and "diffusion of innovations" models, the main targets of his critical analysis, led Beltrán to the conclusion that Latin America needs new methods for communication research, "hosted by a sociology of nonadjustment and a psychology of nonconformity" (Beltrán, 1976a, p. 129). This new "communicology of liberation" must be deeply rooted in Latin American realities (ibid.).

A good number of Beltrán's subsequent works have denounced the mechanisms by which the United States exercises a "cultural imperialism" over Latin America (Beltrán and Fox de Cardona, 1980). But his most important scholarly activity has been the promotion of national communication policies (Beltrán, 1974a, 1976b). In these efforts he has sometimes been joined by the North American researcher Elizabeth Fox, who was based for some time in Colombia, then in Argentina, and recently in Paris.

In his work on communication policies, Beltrán met with other Hispanic American researchers and got the backing of UNESCO. In 1970 UNESCO began helping member countries to design and implement national communication policies in accordance with the individual countries' development goals. In a series of conferences on this issue, UNESCO benefited from the advice of local experts like Beltrán. The climax of such activities for the Caribbean and Latin America took place in San Jose, Costa Rica, in July 1976. The preparation and final results of this conference were largely due to Beltrán's and Pasquali's work. The governments of the area came to an agreement on the need for an information balance between developed and underdeveloped countries, on the "right to communicate," and on the institutionalization of a Latin American news agency (Reyes Matta, 1977b). In 1984 Beltrán was appointed by UNESCO as the regional adviser on communications for Latin America and the Caribbean, based in Quito.

The Role of Research Centers

In concentrating on a few pioneers in critical communication research, we do not wish to minimize the importance of research institutions and other scholars who have contributed to this tradition. Research centers and institutes exerted a strong influence on the development of critical communication research in Hispanic America.

Schools of communication, by contrast, have had only a limited role in the appearance and growth of the new trends in research. Although there are more than a hundred such schools in Hispanic America, only two of them offer graduate studies (Nixon, 1982). Thus, few academics work full time in research, and the libraries in these schools are usually inadequate for communication research (FELAFACS, 1983). Furthermore, in some countries the schools have failed to find their own identity, under pressure to supply the job market through weak programs in journalism, advertising, or public relations.

This situation explains why scholarship found its main arena in such diverse centers as Centro de Estudios de la Realidad Nacional (CEREN) in Santiago, Chile (until 1973); Instituto Torcuato Di Tella in Buenos Aires; Instituto de Investigaciones de Comunicación (IININCO) and Centro Pellin in Caracas; Instituto Latinoamericano de Estudios Transnacionales (ILET) in Mexico City and recently also in Santiago; Taller de Investigación para la Comunicación Masiva (TICOM) in Mexico City; Centro Internacional de Investigaciones para el Desarrollo (CIID) in Bogota; Centro de Estudios y Promoción del Desarrollo (DESCO) in Lima; and Centro Internacional de Estudios Superiores de Comunicación para America Latina (CIESPAL) in Quito.

CIESPAL: A Special Case

As promoter of the new tendencies in communication research and teaching, CIESPAL had tremendous influence throughout Latin America. CIESPAL was founded in 1959 as the International Center for Superior Studies in Journalism for Latin America, with support from UNESCO, the Ecuadorian government, and the Universidad Central at Quito. It was one of four such centers promoted by UNESCO around the world with the goal of stimulating research and the teaching of journalism.

In 1974, however, several factors converged to create a new orientation for CIESPAL. A new general director was named, the Ecuadorian journalist Marco Ordoñez; the center's name was modified, substituting the word "Communication" for "Journalism" (without changing the acronym); and CIESPAL began to receive economic backing from the Friedrich Ebert Foundation (an institution financed by the Social Democratic Party of West Germany), which in addition to financial assistance gives the center continuing academic support in the person of the German sociologist Peter Schenkel (Nixon, 1982). These developments were immediately reflected in the conceptual framework produced by the invited instructors and lecturers, mostly Latin Americans working from a critical perspective, in the center's published materials, and in the new guidelines set by CIESPAL for the region's schools of communication (see Ordoñez, 1974). In fact, CIESPAL has produced a "resonance effect" for the new tendencies.[6]

A Critical Tradition

Hispanic America's critical tradition did not arise merely as a reaction to capitalist ideology or to the alien premises and methods of traditional social science (Beltrán, 1976a). The dialectical forces behind it are far more complex. The critical approach to communication in Hispanic America preceded U.S. concerns, as expressed in the mainstream publications. Pasquali's 1963 work, for example, was a landmark long before Schiller's first major book (1970) was published in the United States. Veron's and Mattelart's thought-provoking monographs were already circulating extensively in the area by the late 1960s and early 1970s. And Beltrán's major critique appeared at the same time as Rogers' (1976) analysis of a change of paradigms in the communication field. Freire, although a pedagogue and not a communication scholar, brought a linguistic and Marxist analysis to the study of communication two decades ago.

It is rarely recognized that these pioneering scholars and a host of other

6. For more information on CIESPAL, see *Chasqui,* July–Sept. 1984.

authors in the region are contemporaries of the European critical scholars, especially those at the Birmingham Centre for Cultural Studies (see Hall, 1981), whose propositions have had such a powerful influence on U.S. researchers. This lack of recognition can be seen in the special issue of the *Journal of Communication* titled "Ferment in the Field" (1983), which poses a U.S.-European debate on critical communication. Though the debate was defined as "international," no Latin American scholar was included except Mattelart, who is now actually based in Europe. That no scholar from Latin America or any other underdeveloped region participated is ironic, since it was mainly in the Third World that the "ferment" under discussion originated (see, for example, UNESCO's meetings on the debate over the New International Information Order: Jaramillo, 1978; Salinas and Paldan, 1979).

The Rhetoric of Critical Research: Five Meanings

"Critical" has a host of meanings in Hispanic America that we will not even try to define in this chapter. We can, however, identify a set of characteristics that, although they do not all appear in any one author or for any one topic, make up the rhetoric of critical communication.

First, the need to understand the capitalist hegemonic system in the region has forced scholars to address the issues of imperialism, economic dependency, and economic and cultural transnationalization. The arguments focus on alien communication technologies, media systems, and cultural products, which not only upset national sovereignties but act as ideological forces reproducing the existing unequal social relations. The logic behind this analysis is to find through alternative communication policies and practices the possibility for a more democratic, participatory, and liberating society.

Second, the recognition of the above issues compels critical scholars to publicly denounce the unfairness of both national and international information and economic orders. These critiques have been part of a conscious strategy aimed at focusing attention on a situation that would otherwise be unquestioned, the status quo being accepted as naturally rather than structurally created.

Third, criticism in this tradition does not concern itself only with communication issues but deals with the totality of economic, social, political, and cultural relations in society (Esteinou Madrid, 1980). The complexity of Hispanic America's reality does not allow scholars to extract communication from its historical context. Thus, the critical tradition tends to treat communication in the light of social theory rather than from a behavioral perspective.

Fourth, critical scholars are interested not only in describing and explaining the region's social reality but in determining how such knowledge can be used for social change. The emphasis is on relating the theoretical and the practical (Freire, 1976; Mattelart, 1978; Mattelart, Biedma, and Funes, 1980; Mattelart and Mattelart, 1981). This orientation has led Hispanic American scholars to publish most of their work in newspapers or magazines accessible to the general public—ultimately the subject of social change—rather than in academic journals geared to an elite group.

Lastly, the critical tradition deals with the basic assumptions that guide research. Hence, the literature manifests a concern for redefining what research is and what researchers are and what they do. Terms such as "intellectual colonialism" (Fals Borda, 1973) or "decolonization of the social sciences" (Stavenhagen, 1971) reflect this perspective. The goal is to establish a language and a scientific practice that describe and explain Hispanic America's reality in a more precise manner (see Díaz Bordenave and Carvalho, 1978; Martín Barbero, 1984).

A Critical Discourse

Having established the background from which critical communication in the region emerged, we will now turn to the substantive arguments of this tradition in an attempt to explain the initial concerns of this discourse and its development to its present expression.

U.S. Influences: Developmentalism

It was in the late 1950s and early 1960s that Hispanic American communication scholarship was most influenced by the United States and by international agencies' concerns for economic development (Díaz Bordenave, 1976). This developmentalist boom[7] spurred Hispanic American scholars at that time to seek graduate studies in U.S. universities. Moreover, those courses that were deemed appropriate were then transferred to Hispanic America with the hope of training students to bring about "modernization" in the region (see Beltrán, 1976a).

The emphasis on developmentalism led scholars to focus on agricultural extension and population control. The work of U.S. scholars in Hispanic America, such as Rogers and Svenning (1969) and Rogers (1973), typified this effort. Beltrán, Isaza, and Ramirez (1978) collected 490 titles of studies done in the region on rural development and communication. One of the last notable efforts of this type was a 1974 gathering of U.S. and Latin American scholars to discuss communication strategies for rural development. The Cornell-CIAT International Symposium, held in Cali, Colombia (Crawford and Ward, 1974), introduced to a wide audience Beltrán's (1974b) and Díaz Bordenave's (1974) criticism of U.S. explanations of their native reality. Both of these scholars, it is interesting to note, had been trained in the United States.

The application of communication to the field of demography led to the

---

7. "Developmentalism" as we use the term is the economic model that follows W. W. Rostow's doctrine of development as a linear path along which all countries travel.

creation of the Latin American Association of Demographic Communicators (ALACODE), based in Bogota, Colombia. ALACODE organized seminars for Latin American journalists and published a monthly newspaper, *El Demografico,* whose objective was to offer diffusion material for communication professionals.[8]

Disenchantment with Foreign Models

The disenchantment with using communication as the "psychosocial engineer of behavior" (Díaz Bordenave, 1976, p. 144) became evident in the 1970s. The international development boom of the previous decade began to falter. The enormous inequalities created and sustained within Third World nations in respect to standards of living and quality of life were a testimony to the failure of the developmentalist optimism of foreign models.

Because Hispanic American scholars were dependent on alien theories, even in selecting problems and social groups to be studied, they were not able to build a conceptual model based on the particular experiences of the region. Positivism and functionalism in the study of communication phenomena could not provide the tools for a diachronic analysis or for the generation of concepts that would allow a more accurate analysis of the Hispanic American reality; scholars could focus neither on collectivities as the unit of analysis nor on social theory as their research framework. Thus, the incongruity between local reality and the developmentalist model, which was heavily based on functionalist social science and the assumptions behind it, increased in the 1970s to the point where a systematic expression of that incongruity began to emerge in Hispanic American critical communication scholarship (Martín Barbero, 1978). From the early 1970s on, the pioneering works of Pasquali, Veron, Mattelart, Beltrán, and others were to greatly influence the rest of Latin American scholarship.

The Presence of Foreign Technology: A Fact to Live With

An important aspect of Hispanic American critical communication research is the fact that the very instruments of communication are produced in alien environments and then imported into Third World countries (Mattelart and Schmucler, 1983; Rada, 1981; Roncagliolo, 1983). Such technology, whether as hardware (e.g., satellites, computers, broadcast or cable television) or as software (e.g., the organization, format, and content of messages and media institutions) is not neutral:

8. ALACODE was founded in 1973 with support from the Population Reference Bureau, an organization based in New York City. In 1974 ALACODE substituted the words "para el Desarrollo" ("for development") for "Demograficos" ("demographic") in its name, largely because of the stigma attached to the concept of "demography" in the region. ALACODE disappeared in 1980, broken up by internal strife.

We [have] reach[ed] a point where the development prospects of the South are not only conditioned by the ways and means of transferring technology but by the very logic and dynamism of scientific development in the advanced countries. (Rada, 1981, p. 43)

The argument that the solution to the problem is to enable Hispanic Americans to adapt or create new communication technologies more adequate to their specific conditions and needs ignores the extremely complex political and economic implications of such activities. One must acknowledge "the irreversible marginality produced by the scarcity and nonselective concentration of scientific and technological resources in Latin America" (Hodara, 1984, p. 80).

If one accepts the above-mentioned point on technology's nonneutrality and the inherent logic of technological transfer, one can understand why critical scholarship is so concerned about the social implications of this transfer. Critical scholars realize that it is fruitless to try to explain the adaptation of communication theories and mass media without understanding the constraints that the technology imposes (Echeverría, 1984). Thus, they focus on technology as "the privileged vehicle of transnationalization" (IPAL, 1983, p. 12). Yet technology alone does not alter mass consciousness; it is rather the basic social relations generated by the technology that do so (Prieto, 1981). Against the dominant top-down mode of the imported communication technologies, critical scholars have taken a counterposition—horizontal communication (Gargurevich, 1981).

Critical Responses to Communication Technologies

The analysis of the social implications of communication technologies focuses on, among other things, the imbalance of information flow; cultural industries and foreign cultural products; respect for national sovereignty; and national communication policies. The assumption behind the discussion of technology is that communication media, as they are structured at present, do not provide the social benefits that Hispanic Americans are seeking for all groups in society.

Mattelart's *Agresion Desde el Espacio: Cultura y Napalm en la Era de los Satelites* (1975) was one of the first treatments of the problem of communication technologies for underdeveloped countries. Reyes Matta (1977b), Roncagliolo (1983), and Portales (1984), to mention only a few, have thoroughly analyzed this topic from diverse perspectives. Their discussions inevitably link communication technology issues to the debate over the New International Information Order. Beltrán and Fox de Cardona (1980) cite more than thirty-five Latin American authors who have analyzed this theme since 1967.

The Revision of Some Misconceptions in Critical Research

The discussion of "technological aggression" suggests that there may have been reductionist errors in some of the critical research done in the early

1970s and even later. Echeverría (1984) strongly criticizes present and past Hispanic American scholarship for thinking "that cultural imperialism is a Pandora's box from which all explanations of problems are extracted" (p. 37). He adds that technologies certainly have the power to transform the masses, but Latin American scholars have exaggerated it.

Even Mattelart and Schmucler (1983), who have in the past insisted on the dangers presented by the new transnational technologies, now criticize many of the old analyses and theories as "ideologisms" and "economisms" (pp. 61–62). Salinas (quoted by Schenkel, 1984) refers to a new style of realism: "Being for or against these [technological] changes is simply useless. It does not change anything, nor does it help. The way, I think, lies . . . in trying to establish which kind of actions our countries could take to reduce damages and to maximize possible benefits" (p. 50).

Salinas and Paldan (1979), Sarti (1981), and others criticize the related error of discussing the dynamics of national elites in the same terms one uses to discuss the international arena. This mistake not only confuses levels of analysis but ignores the particular ideological and historical evolution of national elites in their domestic and international interactions.

Hispanic American scholars are aware that these misconceptions could prevent them from adopting more appropriate solutions to present conditions. To expose the failures of the present international information order and to demand structural change was, and continues to be, commendable and necessary. Yet scholars today recognize that the definition of the problem requires them to play an active role in transforming the internal reality of Hispanic American nations, taking into consideration also the value of an appropriate use of the new communication technologies (Gargurevich, 1982; Prieto, 1982, 1983, 1984).

The Concept of Transnationalization

The Instituto Latinoamericano de Estudios Transnacionales (ILET) has been working successfully to bridge the conceptual gap between outside forces and internal factors. Founded in the mid 1970s, ILET has defined its subject matter as "transnationalization" instead of "aggression" or "invasion." The concept of transnationalization arose as a reflection of concrete historical conditions (Portales et al., 1982), and it allows for a better understanding of the technological importation problem; moreover, it offers a language for grounding the analysis of cultural imperialism in empirical facts (see Mattelart and Schmucler, 1983; Portales, 1981; Reyes Matta, 1977a, 1977b, among others).

This line of analysis is not completely new. In fact, a number of interesting examples appeared in the early stages of the critical research tradition. A well-known example is the celebrated Dorfman and Mattelart book *How to Read Donald Duck* (1975), which explains the process of the transnationalization of culture through a foreign media product, the Disney comics. Fox de Cardona (1977) likewise analyzes U.S. investment in television in Latin America.

A joint U.S. and Latin American discussion on media flows in the region is presented in a recent volume of *Communication Research* (1984). The main focus is on the structural conditions for and the catalytic actions of the international flow of television products in Latin America (Schement et al., 1984). The consensus of the participants was that the fact that Brazil, Mexico, and other Latin American countries are now exporting cultural products weakens or refutes the argument that the region is culturally dependent and indicates that the flow of information is now more equitable. Yet there is strong empirical evidence to the contrary, and many Hispanic scholars would object strenuously to these conclusions.

The Struggle for National Communication Policies

The "technological aggression" issue deals mostly with cultural dependency, and the "transnationalization" analysis tries to bring empirical evidence to bear on otherwise abstract arguments. It is the movement for "national communication policies" that sets forth a series of alternatives for action in Hispanic America. Several experts on communication have stressed the importance of national communication policies (Beltrán, 1974b, 1976b; Canclini, 1983; Díaz Bordenave and Carvalho, 1978; Pasquali, 1976; Reyes Matta, 1977a; UNESCO, 1980).

The experience of a few countries may throw some light on how Hispanic America has faced the challenging task of developing such policies. Venezuela's RATELVE project designed a national policy for radio and television broadcasting (RATELVE, 1976) that was clearly marked by Pasquali's influence, as mentioned above. The project was never implemented fully, however, because of intensive lobbying by pressure groups (Lizcano, 1984).

The military process in Peru created a landmark in the analysis of communication phenomena because it sponsored the first Latin American attempt—outside Cuba—to elaborate a national communication policy that corresponded to UNESCO's suggestions for the region. That the Peruvian plans were never fully completed—in this case because of a change in government—does not eliminate the issues the project raised. One such issue is the control of the content of commercial advertising to bring it into line with national development plans (Mattos, 1981).

Orellana and Rodriguez (1984) have studied the responses of the governments of Argentina, Chile, and Brazil to the new communication/information technologies and found that only Brazil has a specific set of policies, which have been implemented since 1971. Besides Brazil, these authors suggest that "Mexico and Cuba are possibly the only Latin American countries that present a highly structured and regulated policy that includes the bureaucratic and legal tools for making their guidelines effective" (p. 16). The military government of Chile, they observe, explicitly rejects the possibility of developing a policy on the subject "in accordance with its own decision to leave policies to be automatically developed by market forces themselves" (p. 3).

A different kind of policy has crystallized in ALASEI (Latin American Agency for Special Information Services), a regional organization specifically designed to meet the area's need for news of real interest to it—an example of an effort to respond to the propositions of the New International Information Order (ALASEI, 1982).

Hispanic America is very much aware of the need to confront new communication technologies in an organized way. However, little research is geared toward policy making (Díaz Bordenave and Carvalho, 1978). Moreover, the absence of a clear conception of the kind of national development Hispanic American nations need undermines the ability of researchers to produce communication policies, and many national and international interests oppose such policies (Reyes Matta, 1977b).

Piccini (1982) warns that national communication policies in the region may be developed by hegemonic groups that have historically been authoritarian (see also Collier, 1979). This could limit the potential for democratization and structural change within nations, though it would perhaps help to protect national sovereignties from international influence. Thus, Canclini (1983) recommends grounding national policies in "the actual existential conditions of the grassroots sectors" (p. 24), and Mattelart (1978) and Mattelart, Biedma, and Funes (1980) argue for policies that are not only democratic but restore the people's voice.

The European Influence

Overlapping the above-mentioned themes in Hispanic America's discourse is the analysis of capitalism as a mode of production, of the interaction between capitalism and civil society, and of capitalism's bearing on communication and vice versa. Here descriptions and analyses deal with ideology, ideological apparatuses, and hegemony in a capitalist system as they reproduce unequal social relations and impede the possibility for social change (Echeverría and Castillo, 1973; Muraro, 1974). Analysts rely heavily on the theory of historical materialism because of its power to incorporate history and explain phenomena in the light of specific social forces (Mattelart, 1978; Mattelart, Biedma, and Funes, 1980; Piccini, 1982). The most comprehensive work on the subject at present is that of Esteinou Madrid (1980, 1981), the director of Taller de Investigacion para la Comunicación Masiva (TICOM) in the Universidad Autónoma Metropolitana-Xochimilco in Mexico City, which has produced a number of monographs and studies on the region.

It is in this analysis of capitalism that one can detect the European influence on Hispanic American thought. Marxist analysis appeals to scholars because it offers a language for describing and explaining the functions of communication in their economic context (Esteinou Madrid, 1980). Concepts such as "class" and "class consciousness" are useful for capturing the dialectics of thought and action, consciousness and practice (Echeverría and Castillo, 1973). Liss (1984) offers a succinct overview of Marxist thought in Latin America that traces Marxist variants in the works of the area's critical thinkers.

Other Hispanic American scholars, interested in the formation and social conditions of discourse, have borrowed from Europe's structuralist and semiotic traditions (Martín Barbero, 1978). The former tradition is appealing because it studies the events of social existence and their saturation with signification; the latter, because it offers a model for understanding the meaning-structures of those events (Paoli, 1977).

Ultimately, what all these conceptual tools offer is the possibility of explaining the "links that articulate mass media rhetoric and mythology with the market logic, and all of these with the global structure of production" (Martín Barbero, 1978, p. 26). Each in his own way, Pasquali, Mattelart, Beltrán, and particularly Veron are pioneers in the analysis of the latent meanings of media messages (Gargurevich, 1982; and see Beltrán, Isaza, and Ramirez, 1978, for references to other scholars engaged in similar work).

A Search for Communication Alternatives

Another theme in Hispanic American communication scholarship is the elaboration of an incipient theoretical approach and a long-standing empirical one. Scholars engaged in this work advocate a focus on alternative communication, variously referred to as "participatory," "popular," "democratic," and "horizontal" communication. As the definitions of these terms are still not clearly fixed, "subordinate" and "oppositional" communication and "counter-information" are also thrown into the same basket (see Simpson Grinberg, 1981).

"Alternative communication" has several meanings. As defined by some, it seems to have been born out of the *comunidades de base* (Martinez-Terrero, 1980; White, 1980). These community-based religious groups, influenced by the theology of liberation, stress action-oriented practice at the grassroots level, based on interpersonal and group communication. Others trace it to the involvement of grassroots groups in media practices in response to the dominant vertical modes of communication (Capriles, 1981; Cassigoli, 1981; Reyes Matta, 1983). Still another conception of alternative communication defines it not as communication events per se—events characterized by the constraints of the roles of sender and receiver—but as cultural manifestations grounded in the historical flow of popular culture and folklore (Canclini, 1983; Martín Barbero, 1984). Whatever the definition of alternative communication, it is above all a popular or grassroots practice.

Born out of the experiences and social practices of Hispanic America's diverse and heterogeneous popular sectors, alternative communication has compelled scholars to reflect on the dynamics of these new modes and the possibility of liberation through them (Freire, 1974, 1975a, 1975b, 1976; Mattelart, 1974, 1975, 1978, 1980; Martinez-Terrero, 1980; and Reyes Matta, 1983). Although they may have appeared at first to be subordinate alternatives to the dominant vertical model, it soon became obvious that they offered a framework for exploring different structures of media ownership, production, distribution, and consumption. Furthermore, they have made researchers focus for the first time on the active role of audiences as they receive, reject, create, recreate, and transform mass-mediated messages (Esteinou Madrid, 1980; Canclini, 1982, 1983). Researchers are thus driven to participate, in a nonmanipulative way, in the people's communication processes.

Alternative communication is not, however, always liberating. Ossandón (1983) argues that for liberation to occur the historical subject as such must first come into being. Simpson Grinberg (1981) stresses that communication technologies are not the alternative: they are only the instruments for an alternative. And Kaplún (1981) adds that unless subjects use mechanisms and send messages that are autonomous, participation in alternative modes cannot be effective. Moreover, alternative communication does not reject foreign technology but adapts it to a new logic elaborated from native reality (Martín Barbero, 1980; Portales, 1981).

Conclusion

We have attempted in this paper to examine the historical environment of Hispanic American critical communication research. This is the only way to grasp how Hispanic American scholarship arose, how it developed, and what the perspectives that have already emerged from it mean.

Our focus on the works of those we have defined as "the pioneers," although it has excluded a host of equally deserving authors, demonstrates how a group of researchers from diverse backgrounds arrived at a common definition of their subject matter and their methods of approaching it.

The critical tradition in the 1960s concentrated on denouncing a status quo that had proven unfair. In subsequent years, however, an impressive accumulation of knowledge about the region's communication phenomena has emerged. Hispanic American discourse is thorough in pinpointing its assumptions, raising pertinent questions, and conceptualizing problems. Such discourse is not to be disregarded for its supposed lack of scientific "hard evidence" or its persistent rhetoric of denunciation. The framework is a consistent and coherent set of theoretical propositions that, despite their shortcomings in positivist terms, have a validity and explanatory power for their Hispanic American contexts. Critical scholarship is not seeking quantifiable evidence to predict and control behavior in an atmosphere detached from its historical context. Nor does it aim to build theory separated from the material conditions that generated it. Perhaps what Hispanic American critical communication scholars seek is to know the history, clarify the processes, and understand the dialectical forces of a given moment so that the articulations for structural change could be put into motion.

In fact, it is people—not theories—who make change possible. Because of this, the present moment is passionately challenging for Hispanic American scholars: they have to find ways to interpret the communication processes that have been developed by grassroots sectors in spite of their own lack of resources and the oppressive transnational media systems. New theory must then be generated from this starting point.

What the Hispanic American critical tradition has done is to establish the prolegomena for a fresh approach to the field of communication, emerging from the dialectical experience of societies that have suffered the consequences of an unfair planetary socioeconomic order. This experience—if adequately understood by scholars—could be enlightening for the rest of the world as well.

References

Agudelo-Villa, H. (1966). *La Alianza Para el Progreso: Esperanzas y Frustración.* Bogota: Editorial Tercer Mundo.

ALASEI (Agencia Latinoamericana de Servicios Periodísticos Especiales) (1982). *Implementation Project for the Latin American Special Information Services Agency.* Panama: SELA.

Beltrán, L. R. (1974a). "Las políticas nacionales de Comunicación en América Latina: Los Primeros Pasos." Mimeographed. Paris: UNESCO.

Beltrán, L. R. (1974b). "Rural Development and Social Communication: Relationship and Strategies." In R. H. Crawford and E. B. Ward (eds.) *Communication Strategies for Rural Development: Proceedings of the Cornell-CIAT International Symposium.* New York: New York State College of Agriculture and Life Sciences.

Beltrán, L. R. (1976a). "Alien Premises, Objects, and Methods in Latin American Communication Research." *Communication Research,* 3, 2, pp. 107–34.

Beltrán, L. R. (1976b). "Políticas Nacionales de Comunicación en América Latina: Los Primeros Pasos." Mimeographed. Quito: CIESPAL.

Beltrán, L. R. (1976c). "TV Etchings in the Minds of Latin Americans: Conservatism, Materialism, and Conformism." Paper presented at the Tenth General Assembly of the International Association of Mass Communication Research, University of Leicester, England, August 30–September 4.

Beltrán, L. R., and E. Fox de Cardona (1980). *Comunicación Dominada: Estados Unidos en los Medios de América Latina.* Mexico City: Instituto Latinoamericano de Estudios Transnacionales/Nueva Imagen.

Beltrán, L. R., G. Isaza, and F. Ramirez (1978). *Bibliografía Sobre Investigaciones en Comunicación Para el Desarrollo Rural en América Latina*. Bogota: CIID.

Biedma, P. (1980). "Prensa Burguesa, Prensa Popular y Prensa Revolucionaria." In A. Mattelart, P. Biedma, and S. Funes, *Comunicación Masiva y Revolución Socialista*, pp. 205–89. Mexico City. Editorial Diógenes.

Broderick, W. J. (1975). *Camilo Torres: A Biography of the Priest-Guerrillero*. New York: Doubleday.

Canclini, N. G. (1982). *Las Culturas Populares en el Capitalismo*. Mexico City: Editorial Nueva Imagen.

Canclini, N. G. (1983). "Políticas Culturales en América Latina." *Chasqui*, July–Sept., pp. 18–26.

Capriles, O. (1981). "Venezuela: Política de Comunicación o Comunicación Alternativa?" In M. Simpson Grinberg (ed.) *Comunicación Alternativa y Cambio Social*, vol. 1: *América Latina*, pp. 149–66. Mexico City: Universidad Nacional Autónoma de México.

Cardoso, F. H. (1979). "The Originality of the Copy: the Economic Commission for Latin America and the Idea of Development." In A. Hill (ed.) *Toward a New Strategy for Development*, pp. 53–72. New York: Pergamon Press.

Cardoso, F. H., and E. Faletto (1979). *Dependency and Development in Latin America*. Berkeley: University of California Press.

Cassigoli, A. (1981). "Sobre la Contrainformación y los Asi Llamados Medios Alternativos." In M. Simpson Grinberg (ed.) *Comunicación Alternativa y Cambio Social*, vol. 1: *América Latina*, pp. 29–39. Mexico City: Universidad Nacional Autónoma de México.

CELAM (Consejo Episcopal Latinoamericano) (1969). *La Iglesia en la Actual Transformación de América Latina a la Luz del Concilio*. 2 vols. Santiago: Ediciones Paulinas.

Chasqui—Revista Latinoamericana de Comunicación (1984). Special issue: "25th Anniversary of CIESPAL," July–Sept.

Collier, D. (ed.) (1979). *The New Authoritarianism in Latin America*. Princeton: Princeton University Press.

Communication Research (1984). Special issue: "Television Flows in Latin America," 11, 2.

Crawford, R. H., and W. B. Ward (eds.) (1974). *Communication Strategies for Rural Development: Proceedings of the Cornell-CIAT International Symposium*. New York: New York State College of Agriculture and Life Sciences.

Díaz Bordenave, J. (1974). "Communication and Adoption of Agricultural Innovations in Latin America." In R. H. Crawford, and W. B. Ward (eds.) *Communication Strategies for Rural Development: Proceedings of the Cornell-CIAT International Symposium*, pp. 205–17. New York: New York State College of Agriculture and Life Sciences.

Díaz Bordenave, J. (1976). "Communication of Agricultural Innovations in Latin America: the Need for New Models." *Communication Research*, 3, 2, pp. 43–62.

Díaz Bordenave, J., and H. M. Carvalho (1978). *Planificación y Comunicación*. Quito: Ediciones CIESPAL.

Dorfman, A., and A. Mattelart (1975). *How to Read Donald Duck*. New York: International General.

Echeverría, L. (1984). "La Televisión: Utopías y Realidades." *Chasqui,* Jan.–March, pp. 35, 37–39.

Echeverría, R., and F. Castillo (1973). "Elementos Para la Teoría de la Ideología." In R. Echeverría (ed.) *Ideología y Medios de Comunicación,* pp. 9–44. Buenos Aires: Amorrortu.

Einaudi, L. R., and A. C. Stepan (1974). "Changing Military Perspectives in Peru and Brazil." In L. R. Einaudi (ed.) *Beyond Cuba: Latin America Takes Charge of Its Future,* pp. 97–105. New York: Crane, Russak.

Esteinou Madrid, J. (1980). "El Estudio Totalizador de la Comunicación de Masas." *Cuadernos de Comunicación,* pp. 50–57.

Esteinou Madrid, J. (1981). "La Utopía de la Comunicación Alternativa en el Aparato de la Cultura de Masas." In M. Simpson Grinberg (ed.) *Comunicación Alternativa y Cambio Social,* vol. 1: *América Latina,* pp. 41–60. Mexico City: Universidad Nacional Autónoma de México.

Esteinou Madrid, J. (1982). "Medios de Comunicación y Acumulación de Capital." *Comunicación e Informática,* 2, 3, pp. 16–27.

Fals Borda, O. (1973). *Ciencia Propia y Colonialismo Intelectual.* Mexico City: Editorial Nuestro Tiempo.

FELAFACS (Federación Latinoamericana de Facultades de Comunicación Social) (1983). *La Formación Universitaria de Comunicadores Sociales en América Latina.* Report presented to UNESCO. Mexico City: Editorial ITESC.

Fox, E. (1983). "Communication and Civil Society," *Comunicação e Politica,* 1, March–May, pp. 35–41.

Fox, E. (1984). "La Televisión: Utopías y Realidades." *Chasqui,* Jan.–March, pp. 34, 36–37.

Fox de Cardona, E. (1977). "American Television in Latin America." In G. Gerbner (ed.) *Mass Media Policies in Changing Cultures,* pp. 57–62. New York: John Wiley and Sons.

Freire, P. (1974). *Conscientización.* Bogota: Asociación de Publicaciones Educativas.

Freire, P. (1975a). *Extensión o Comunicación? La Conscientización del Medio Rural.* Mexico City: Siglo XXI.

Freire, P. (1975b). *La Educación como Práctica de la Libertad.* Mexico City: Siglo XXI.

Freire, P. (1976). *Pedagogía del Oprimido.* Mexico City: Siglo XXI.

Furtado, C. (1982). *Economic Development of Latin America.* 2d ed. Cambridge: Cambridge University Press.

García, A. (1969). *La Estructura del Atraso en Latinoamérica.* Buenos Aires: Editorial Pleamar.

García, A. (1975). *Dialéctica de la Democracia.* Buenos Aires: Ateneo.

Gargurevich, J. (1981). "Perú: La Alternativa Dentro de la Alternativa." In M. Simpson Grinberg (ed.) *Comunicación Alternativa y Cambio Social,* vol. 1: *América Latina,* pp. 191–214. Mexico City: Universidad Nacional Autónoma de México.

Gargurevich, J. (1982). "Comunicadores y Periodistas: Necesidades de América Latina." *Chasqui,* Jan.–March, pp. 20–29.

Gonzalez, E., and L. R. Einaudi (1974). "New Patterns of Leadership." In L. R. Einaudi (ed.) *Beyond Cuba: Latin America Takes Charge of Its Future,* pp. 45–57. New York: Crane, Russak.

Greimas, A. J. (1984). *Structural Semantics: An Attempt at a Method.* Lincoln: University of Nebraska Press.

Gutierrez, G. (1973). *A Theology of Liberation: History, Politics and Salvation.* New York: Orbis.

Hall, S. (ed.) (1981). *Culture, Media, Language.* London: Hutchinson.

Hodara, J. (1984). "La Medición del Avance Científico en América Latina." *Ciencia y Desarrollo,* May–June, pp. 80–88.

IPAL (Instituto Para América Latina) (1983). *Centre on Transnational Culture Program.* Lima: IPAL.

Jaramillo, O. (1978). "La Información Internacional." In G. Ortíz (ed.) *La Información en el Marco del Nuevo Orden Internacional,* pp. 19–33. Bogota: ALACODE-UNESCO.

Journal of Communication (1983). Special issue: "Ferment in the Field," 33, 3.

Kaplún, M. (1981). "Participación: Práxis, Propuesta y Problema: La Experiencia del Casete-Foro." In M. Simpson Grinberg, (ed.) *Comunicación Alternativa y Cambio Social,* vol. 1: *América Latina,* pp. 215–35. Mexico City: Universidad Nacional Autónoma de México.

Kosik, K. (1983). *La Dialéctica de lo Concreto.* 8th ed. Mexico City: Editorial Grijalbo.

Liss, S. (1984). *Marxist Thought in Latin America.* Berkeley: University of California Press.

Lizcano, M. (1984). "Communication Policy in Venezuela." Master's thesis, University of Texas, Austin.

Marqués de Melo, J. (1984). "La Investigación Latinoamericana en Comunicación." *Chasqui,* July–Sept., pp. 4–11.

Martín Barbero, J. (1978). *Comunicación Masiva: Discurso y Poder.* Quito: Ediciones CIESPAL.

Martín Barbero, J. (1980). "Retos a la Investigación de Comunicación en América Latina." *Comunicación y Cultura,* 9, pp. 100–111.

Martín Barbero, J. (1983). "Comunicación Popular y los Modelos Transnacionales." *Chasqui,* Oct.–Dec., pp. 4–11.

Martín Barbero, J. (1984). "Cultura Popular y Comunicación de Masas." *Materiales para la Comunicación Popular* (Instituto para América Latina, Lima), no. 3.

Martinez-Terrero, J. (1980). "Alternative Media in Latin America." *Media Development,* 27, 3, pp. 22–25.

Mattelart, A. (1974). "Prensa y Lucha Ideológica en los Cordones Industriales de Santiago." *Comunicación y Cultura,* 2, March, pp. 77–108.

Mattelart, A. (1975). *Agresión Desde el Espacio: Cultura y Napalm en la Era de los Satélites.* 4th ed. Mexico City: Siglo XXI.

Mattelart, A. (1978). *La Comunicación Masiva en el Proceso de Liberación.* Mexico City: Siglo XXI.

Mattelart, A. (1980). "Comunicación y Cultura de Masas." In A. Mattelart, P. Biedma, and S. Funes *Comunicación Masiva y Revolución Socialista.* 4th ed., Mexico City: Editorial Diógenes, pp. 12–205.

Mattelart, A., P. Biedma, and S. Funes (1980). *Comunicación Masiva y Revolución Socialista.* 4th ed. Mexico City: Editorial Diógenes.

Mattelart, A., and M. Mattelart (1968). *La Mujer Chilena en una Nueva Sociedad: Un Estudio Exploratorio Acerca de la Situación e Imagen de la Mujer en Chile.* Santiago: Editorial del Pacífico.

Mattelart, A., and M. Mattelart (1981). *Los Medios de Comunicación en los Tiempos de Crisis.* Mexico City: Siglo XXI.

Mattelart, A., and H. Schmucler (1983). *América Latina en la Encrucijada Telemática.* Mexico City: Instituto Latinoamericano de Estudios Transnacionales/Folios Ediciones.

Mattos, S. (1981). *The Development of Communication Policies Under the Peruvian Military Government (1968–1980).* San Antonio, Tex., V. Klingensmith.

Muller, C., and D. Herz (1983). "Entrevista: Armand Mattelart." *Comunicação e Politica,* 1, 1, pp. 85–99.

Muraro, H. (1974). *Neocapitalismo y Comunicación de Masa.* Buenos Aires: Editorial Universitaria.

Nixon, R. B. (1982). "Historia de las Escuelas de Periodismo." *Chasqui,* Jan.–March, pp. 13–19.

Ordoñez, M. (1974). *El Rol de la Comunicación en la Sociedad: Planteamientos Generales Para Establecer un Marco Conceptual Entre Sociedad, Comunicación y Formación.* Quito: Ediciones CIESPAL, Colleción Documentos, Serie Comunicación y Educación, no. 1.

Orellana, R., and G. Rodriguez (1984). *Políticas de Informática en América Latina: Chile, Argentina, Brasil.* Santiago: Instituto Latinoamericano de Estudios Transnacionales.

Ossandón, F. (1983). "Comunicación Popular y Rearticulación del Movimiento Popular en Chile Hoy." *Comunicacão e Politica,* 1, 1, pp. 71–83.

Paoli, A. (1977). *La Comunicación.* Mexico City: Edicol.

Pasquali, A. (1967). *El Aparato Singular: Análisis de un Día de TV en Caracas.* Caracas: Universidad Central de Venezuela.

Pasquali, A. (1976). *Comunicación y Cultura de Masas.* Caracas: Monte Avila Editores.

Piccini, M. (1982). "Medios y Estrategias del Discurso Político." *Connotaciones,* 3, pp. 67–90.

Portales, D. (1981). "Perspectivas de la Comunicación Alternativa en América Latina." In M. Simpson Grinberg (ed.) *Comunicación Alternativa y Cambio Social,* vol. 1: *América Latina,* pp. 61–74. Mexico City: Universidad Nacional Autónoma de México.

Portales, D. (1984). *Poder Económico y Libertad de Expresión.* Mexico City: Instituto Latinoamericano de Estudios Transnacionales/Nueva Imagen.

Portales, D., et al. (1982). *Comunicación Transnacional: Conflicto Político y Cultural.* Lima: DESCO.

Prieto, D. (1981). "Una Experiencia de Comunicación Intermedia en un Proceso Histórico de Democratización." In M. Simpson Grinberg (ed.) *Comunicación Alternativa y Cambio Social,* vol. 1: *América Latina,* pp. 253–66. Mexico City: Universidad Nacional Autónoma de México.

Prieto, D. (1982). "Teoría y Práctica de la Formación Profesional." *Chasqui,* Jan.–Mar., pp. 30–38.

Prieto, D. (1983). "La Formación Universitaria de Comunicadores Sociales." *Chasqui*, Oct.–Dec., pp. 89–90.

Prieto, D. (1984). "Comunicación y Cultura: De los Productos a los Procesos." *Chasqui*, Jan.–Mar., pp. 63–65.

Rada, J. (1981). "The Microelectronics Revolution: Implications for the Third World." *Development Dialogue*, 2, pp. 41–67.

RATELVE (1976). *(Proyecto) Diseño para una Nueva Política de Radiodifusión del Estado Venezolano.* Caracas: Ediciones Suma.

Reyes Matta, F. (ed.) (1977a). *La Información en el Nuevo Orden Internacional.* Mexico City: Instituto Latinoamericano de Estudios Transnacionales.

Reyes Matta, F. (ed.) (1977b). *La Noticia Internacional.* Informes ILET, no. 1. Mexico City: Instituto Latinoamericano de Estudios Transnacionales.

Reyes Matta, F. (ed.) (1983). *Comunicación Alternativa y Búsquedas Democráticas.* Santiago: Instituto Latinoamericano de Estudios Transnacionales.

Rincón, H. (1979). *La Comunicación Social en Colombia.* Bogota: Editorial Andes.

Rogers, E. (1973). *Communication Strategies for Family Planning.* New York: Free Press.

Rogers, E. (1976). "Communication and Development: The Passing of the Dominant Paradigm." *Communication Research,* 3, 2, pp. 213–40.

Rogers, E., and Svenning, L. (1969). *Modernization Among Peasants: The Impact of Communication.* East Lansing, Mich.: Holt, Rinehart and Winston.

Roncagliolo, R. (1983). "Comunicación y Democracia en el Debate Internacional." *Chasqui,* July–Sept., pp. 12–17.

Salinas, R., and L. Paldan (1979). "Culture in the Process of Dependent Development: Theoretical Perspectives." In K. Nordenstreng and H. I. Schiller (eds.) *National Sovereignty and International Communication,* pp. 82–98. Norwood, N.J.: Ablex.

Sarti, I. (1981). "Communication and Cultural Dependency: A Misconception." In E. G. McAnany, J. Schnitman, and N. Janus (eds.) *Communication and Social Structure: Critical Studies in Mass Media Research,* pp. 317–32. New York: Praeger.

Schement, J. R., D. Gonzalez, P. Lum, and R. Valencia (1984). "The International Flow of Television Programs." *Communication Research,* 11, 2, pp. 163–82.

Schenkel, P. (1984). "América Latina y la 'Comunicación'" (part 1). *Chasqui,* Jan.–March, pp. 48–56.

Schiller, H. I. (1970). *Mass Communication and the American Empire.* New York: A. M. Kelly.

Schmucler, H. (1981). *La Sociedad Informatizada y las Perspectivas de la Democracia.* Mexico City: Instituto Latinoamericano de Estudios Transnacionales.

Simpson Grinberg, M. (ed.) (1981). *Comunicación Alternativa y Cambio Social,* vol. 1: *América Latina.* Mexico City: Universidad Nacional Autónoma de México.

Stavenhagen, R. (1971). "Decolonializing Applied Social Sciences." *Human Organization,* 30, 4, pp. 333–57.

UNESCO (1980). *Many Voices, One World.* New York: UNIPUB.

Veron, E. (1967a). "Hacia una Ciencia de la Comunicación Social." In E. Veron et al., *Lenguaje y Comunicación Social,* pp. 9–27. Buenos Aires: Editorial Nueva Visión.

Veron, E. (1967b). "Ideología y Comunicación de Masas: La Semantización de la Violencia Política." In E. Veron et al., *Lenguaje y Comunicación Social*, pp. 133–91. Buenos Aires: Editorial Nueva Visión.

Veron, E. (1972). *Conducta, Estructura y Comunicación*. 2d ed. Buenos Aires: Editorial Nueva Visión.

Veron, E., et al. (1967). *Lenguaje y Comunicación Social*. Buenos Aires: Editorial Nueva Visión.

White, R. (1980). " 'Comunicación Popular': Language of Liberation." *Media Development*, 27, 3, pp. 3–9.

II. CRITICAL THEORY, TRANSNATIONAL COMMUNICATION, AND CULTURE

4 *Rafael Roncagliolo*

Transnational Communication and Culture

I am not in a position to fully define the place of cultural-ideological phenomena or the means of communication within the process of transnationalization. A task of such magnitude can only be the result of a systematic and interdisciplinary program of cumulative research efforts. I will use the framework established by the Instituto Latinoamericano de Estudios Transnacionales (ILET) to set out certain issues that must be resolved before we embark on such efforts. There are three crucial questions:

1. What is the place of culture in the transnationalization process and of communication within cultural processes?
2. What does the transnationalization of consumption consist of, if it signifies something more than the homogenization of demand at the international level?
3. Is there such a thing as a "transnational culture," or are there simply internationalized patterns of behavior?

I will limit myself to repeating and condensing here a body of propositions that have proved indispensable within the effort alluded to and that, to some extent, mark out the path for a long-term research effort. Certain consistent features of ILET's work have influenced premises of this essay. Among them are: the link between rigorous analysis and proposals for actions and policies at all levels (group, regional, national, international); analysis of communication against a background of political processes and particularly of social conflict, which offers researchers both a context and an explication; a concern for the democratization of communication, understood as the absence of interference by either the state or economic powers and as the effective development of the capacity of expression in all segments of society; and the desire to understand the transnationalization process through joint analysis, cross-referencing its economic, cultural, and political dimensions.

What Latin American researchers have achieved in the field of communications is by no means either limited or trivial. Latin America is the region in which concern with and exposure to the various forms of international domination in communications are most highly developed. For the same reason, it has led the intergovernmental debate on these matters in UNESCO and elsewhere.

Let us return to our original assumptions in order to attempt a critical, and indeed self-critical, overview of Latin American research (not only, nor even principally, by ILET) during the past decade. From this review there emerge at least four themes that have successively held center stage:

1. International news flow, in the treatment of which attacks have been made on the "mercantile concept of news" and the notion that "information is a social good" has been asserted.
2. "Transnational culture," understood (though not defined) as a totality of processes that compulsively urge us toward a universalization of culture and that are promoted by means of transnationalizing the media themselves.
3. The expansion of the new communication technology, particularly data processing and telecommunication.
4. Alternative communication, seen as a broad populist response to the aforementioned transnationalization of culture.

With regard to these four themes, researchers have had to struggle constantly against a "communicationist" bias, which would serve not only to impede the intellectual interchange with those analyzing other dimensions of transnationalization, but would also hamper the understanding of our own objects of study.

The following propositions summarize the research efforts in Latin America over the past decade.

Proposition 1: The enunciation of "news as a good," "information as a social good," and the value of "the free and balanced flow of news" served as an effective means of attacking news imbalances and distortions was not a sufficient basis for an explanation of communication phenomena, which absolutely requires an approach that goes beyond communication itself.

Empirical studies of the relationship between transnational corporations and communication first focused on the news agencies and the international flow of information. The crucial demands for change that were generated, particularly in Latin America, fuelled the emergence of extremely valuable considerations of a normative or ethical nature. These were juxtaposed, not always within a fully adequate theoretical framework, with certain intriguing findings by empirical researchers. Thus, Echeverría (1978) has shown that the claim that "information is a social good" doubtless possesses a normative and political value, but does not allow for a theoretical grasp of international communication. Something of the same sort occurs with the opposing claim that "news is merchandise." To be more precise, Echeverría states:

Information today is not merchandise to the extent that it is not information that is marketed and realized for a given value or price. What is actually exchanged is the informational medium that carries the news, whether this is the press, radio, or television. Meanwhile, where there also exists a commercial operation, it is in the forms utilized by the medium to ensure its financing by means of advertising, in the absence of state or other subsidies. Finally, the news service may also be considered as a good, but not the news itself. All of this, however, does not prevent recognition of the fact that information is built up and transmitted within a process based on mercantile logic.

The mercantile involvement in communication thus does not consist, even principally, of the mercantile nature of the news itself, but of a much broader range of factors, the most important of which is the transformation of the means of communication into advertising vehicles and the consequent treatment of the public as a market to be offered to advertisers. It is possible to recognize at least three aspects of this involvement: news as merchandise, the medium as merchandise, and the public as merchandise. Although none of these formulations fully describes the phenomenon, all three help to define the functions and contradictions of mass communication as well as their products (messages and advertising) and to reveal the predominance of the secondary market (the marketing of time to advertisers, and, thus, of publicity) over the primary market (the marketing of messages).

The nature and consequences of mercantile involvement in communications are matters that go well beyond our original framework. Thus, the problem no longer consists of the fact that some impersonal market mechanism causes the United States to offer less news about Latin America than Latin America provides about the United States, which is the complaint implicit in the call for a "free and *balanced* flow." This situation is not an arbitrary one but rather a logical consequence of the existence of transnational communication within international relations: everything is dependent on the real weight, economically and politically, of one country over another country, or other countries. That is, it is economic and social relationships, viewed globally, that generate and explain communication flows. The imbalances in the latter are a logical manifestation of transnational structures as a whole. In this regard, there has sometimes been a failure to deal with communication as a dependent variable to be explained in a systematic manner. And it is with this in mind that we should approach the idea of advertising as the "dominant cultural word" (Cathelat, 1976) in the study of transnational communication.

Proposition 2: The transnationalization of messages is not a mechanical consequence of a supposed transnationalization of the media as such, but is a complex process accompanying the transnationalization of the economy and of politics.

There is no need to review the figures that demonstrate the transnationalization of messages. What matters is that the penetration of news agencies, advertising agencies, television programs, films, or what have you has always followed the expansion of transnational corporations properly described as industrial. In spite of this, there is a crucial paradox that cannot be resolved simply on the basis of an analysis of the messages and the media: studies of the ownership of the media suggest that the media themselves remain relatively impermeable to transnationalization. Thus, new approaches to the issue are needed, which, on the one hand, can establish analytically the umbilical cord linking the structural involvement of the media with the content of their messages and their psychological and social effects, and, on the other, are capable of acceptably resolving the paradox outlined above.

The long-term history of the media has been characterized by a dual process of differentiation: a growing specialization and separation between the message-production function and the message-distribution function (Portales, 1981), and a significant shift in the sources of financing for the media.

Although the communication industry appeared originally as a producer-distributor of communications, the picture has altered substantially. The means of communication now tend to specialize in the distribution of messages, leaving the production of a substantial part of their content to others: advertising agencies, public relations offices, and so on. If we consider the large Latin American commercial dailies, we find that approximately 60 percent of their space is devoted not to journalism but to advertisements produced by transnational advertising agencies or advertising companies. A further 10 percent, approximately, comes from news agencies, while between 5 and 10 percent consists of virtually word-for-word reproductions of communiqués issued by various public relations offices. In such cases the daily itself performs a secondary task: the placement of the advertisements within the newspaper's basic format, the selection and provision of headlines for cables, and so on. In terms of exercising their journalistic function, the staff are left with a bare 20 to 30 percent of the total space in each daily.

This phenomenon is even more striking in the case of radio and television, as record- and tape-producers, the film industry, and the emergence of program-producing companies have merely confirmed a general historical trend. Part of this trend in the region has been the legal separation of the entities that distribute television messages (channels) and the producing entities. This separation provides a kind of shield against any attempt to deprivatize radio and television. A typical example is provided by what happened in Peru in 1969, when the state bought a majority holding in the channels. In the case of the most important of these, channel 5, the state ended up owning nothing more than the aerial and the transmitting installations. The bulk of the programming was tied up in a program-purchasing contract with a different legal entity, which, though it operated on the same premises, had assumed autonomous control over production (Gargurevich, 1977). As a consequence, the means of mass communication are to an ever-increasing extent the means of distributing messages rather than exclusive centers for their production.

This differentiation process demands that any analytical perspective extend from the media themselves to their structural context. And it is in this way that we can begin to explain the paradox of transnationalization. Indeed, it may be stated today, with some degree of conviction, that the transnational corporations never exercised direct control over the Latin American means of communication as a whole. They were nothing more than the owners—and then only partially—of a few radio stations, in their early days, and then of television stations and certain periodicals of crucial ideological importance: comics, women's magazines, and so on. In other words, they failed to penetrate the dailies.

Nevertheless, the relative absence of the transnational corporations from the lists of direct owners of the media does not signify any abandoning on their part of communications, but rather a strategic displacement of their efforts into control of the message producers. That is, to the extent that a differentiation in functions occurs between production and distribution, a movement is generated among the transnational corporations from the distribution subsector to the production subsector. This is why we find them in the film industry, in the record- and cassette-producing companies, and among the producers of radio and television programs, but not in the dailies, nor in radio, nor to any great extent among the owners of television stations.

It is by virtue of the specialization of functions within the communication system that the transnational power structure (Somavía, 1977) effectively intervenes in national communications, through messages ensuring both its ideological presence and its basic economic function of articulating production and consumption by means of advertising campaigns. These campaigns are intended to widen markets in order to adapt them to levels of production achievable on the basis of the economic logic of maximization of profits.

In complementary fashion, the transnational structure exercises control over the means of communication through its manipulation of financial flows. And it is here that the second differentiation process alluded to comes into play. Indeed, as a general rule the media are increasingly less dependent on the sale of their products than on the sale of space or time for advertising purposes. Daily newspapers, for example, offer a good of a very particular kind within the capitalist system, since they are sold to consumers at a price below the cost of production. This in itself suggests that the real product of the journalistic enterprise is not the physical newspaper that is sold, but the creation of "needs" and the expansion of a market for advertisers. The large private Latin American dailies depend on advertisements for approximately 70 percent of revenues and on sales for only 30 percent. In the cases of radio and television, dependence on advertising rises to 100 percent (except, of course, for the small number of stations that enjoy state subsidies). Thus it is that control over production and manipulation of financial flows create a pincer movement by means of which the transnational power structure limits the options open to the media without the necessity of actually owning them directly.

The fact that most of the large Latin American dailies belong to local capitalists does not mean that they are exempt from or impermeable to the transnationalization of our economies and our cultures, or that they cease to be instruments of informational colonialism. Trapped as they are by the production-financing pincer, they are influenced to an extraordinary degree by the power of the transnational structure, though this effect is always counteracted by impulses toward autonomy of a nationalistic, and sometimes popular, nature.

The transnationalization paradox can only be resolved, as I have indicated, when the mass media are viewed as an integral part—and not as the whole—of the communication and social structure. The major limitation of partial approaches to the communication issue resides in their inability to take account of the complex relationships between messages and their social effects and the structural and economic infiltration of the media (Roncagliolo, 1977a and 1977b).

Proposition 3: The expansion of new communication technology, far from implying some sort of Machiavellian move on the part of major corporations, is nothing more than a way of accelerating the transnationalization process.

An analysis of the penetration of new technologies requires avoidance of the two forms of Manicheism to which their owners themselves are vulnerable: a facile enthusiasm over the possibilities that are opened up, especially by the so-called data-processing revolution or the computerization of society, and the moralistic and humanistic condemnation of the depersonalizing effects of these technologies. We are dealing, in fact, with a technological transformation that, unlike its predecessors, is characterized by the utmost flexibility. Progress in the field of data processing can be put to direct use in all spheres of the economy and of human activities. At the same time, the potential for control over the citizenry, whether by a state apparatus or by foreign powers, is increased to an unprecedented level.

However, technology does not possess an autonomous history, nor can it be managed without reference to the economic and political forces that implement, develop, and expand it. One even hears about the "alternative uses of technology," a phrase that refers to the utilization of the most modern techniques to benefit the most downtrodden sectors of society. IBASE (the Brazilian Institute for Social and Economic Analysis), in Rio de Janeiro, suggests that such a prospect is not necessarily utopian.

In any case, we still do not have a complete analysis of the penetration effected by these technologies in Latin America, and such an analysis would be impossible without measuring their political and economic infiltration.

Proposition 4: The alternative aspect of alternative communication can only be defined by the relevance of these communication experiences to the national and popular pole, which is antithetical to the transnational one. The alternative is not definable in terms of communications themselves.

There is in Latin America a justifiable enthusiasm for what has been called "alternative" communication. ILET has played a key role in arousing interest in and support for these forms of communication, and it must be added that its role has been a pioneering one. At times the enthusiasm is accompanied by a comparable degree of ambiguity in defining the universe that comes within the scope of "alternative communication." Thus, the phenomenon is identified with the small-scale press, with craftsmen's publications, and with the opposition press. But to define alternative communication in terms of size, technical characteristics, or political stance as related to current circumstances inexorably leads to utter confusion of the issue. Even more seriously, it produces a profound theoretical and practical error, which starts with the image of the "nonalternative" means of communication as totally functional instruments of the given structure, and not as spaces and stages for social struggles. The practical and political consequence of this view is the belief that the task is to create and not to question, and that the nourishing of small and socially insignificant media operations is a better response than waging the fight on the great communication battlefields. Amid the widespread crisis in Latin American political institutions, such enthusiasm could easily give rise to the attitude Kaplún (1980) calls "communication as a party."

In the face of these dangers, a concern has been expressed for some time within ILET about the need for a theoretical definition of alternative communication. Rather than a communication genus, what we are perhaps involved with here is a dimension capable of penetrating means of communication of the most varied scope, as well as technical resources and current political formations.

There is an "alternative" option in every type of social conflict. The alternative is what alters (Reyes Matta, 1981)—that is, what is inscribed in the construction of counterhegemonic historical subjects (Munizaga, 1981). The alternative to alternative communication, therefore, can only be identified by an analysis of its emergence in civil society.

The four propositions enunciated above seek to point out some possible deficiencies in the research of Latin American experts in communication. These deficiencies have a counterpart in the frankly marginal place that economists and analysts of Latin American society in general have set aside for communication phenomena in their reflections. The following propositions, therefore, aim at restoring to communication its important place in the region's transnationalization process.

Proposition 5: The transnationalization process, far from being a strictly economic phenomenon involving the expansion of corporations, is defined in the political and cultural spheres—that is, in changes within political and civil society.

Economic research under way in ILET suggests the existence of a new phase in the history of capitalism, the transnational phase, characterized by a leap forward in the capital-concentration process, a process that, in this stage, comes to be realized above and beyond political boundaries. This implies, when the process reaches its apogee, a progressive independence on the part of the transnational corporations with regard to their countries of origin. The multilateral ordering of production without regard for national borders and the combination of the resources available in each country enhance the advantages for the activities of the transnational corporations as a whole.

The principal consequence of this transformation—and the one that permits us to speak of a new "transnational phase"—is political in nature: the break in the dike that national boundaries formerly constituted against capitalist concentration radically alters the nature and functions of states (whether at the center or on the periphery) by diminishing their erstwhile capacity to intervene in the economy and in their own historical development (Trajtenberg and Vigorito, 1981).

Transnationalization, therefore, is not a purely economic phenomenon but rather a process that erodes the basis of national states, weakens sovereignty, and requires, for this very reason, a transnational communication apparatus that enables transnational corporations to take action while maximizing consensus and minimizing conflict. That is, transnational expansion not only makes monopolistic corporations extranational protagonists in the world economy, but requires at the same time the existence of a "global super-market" and the "global village" of which McLuhan speaks.

Proposition 6: In the transnational phase, the means of communication tend to be converted into a dominant "ideological apparatus" and "agency of socialization," partially displacing the family, the church, and the educational apparatus.

It is widely recognized that since the very beginnings of capitalism the loosening of family relationships and the general secularization of society have weakened the ideological strength and socializing function of both family and church—hence the complaints one hears that the church-family combination has been superseded by the school-family one. Room must be made for a complex discussion of the relative weight of the school and mass communications. It has been shown that the quantitative and qualitative presence of the media in the network of social relationships has become greater than that of the school (Esteinou Madrid, 1980; Roncagliolo, 1977c; and Roncagliolo and Janus, 1980). Indeed, the scope and intensity of the media presence have endowed the media with an unprecedented socializing efficiency.

This assertion leads us to a recognition of the first factor in the definition of the "transnational cultural phase": the occurrence of a clear change in the structural hierarchy of ideological apparatuses and the agencies of socialization. The decline of the family within this hierarchy culminates, during the transnational cultural phase, with the consolidation of the media as agents of mass socialization and ideological control and mobilization. Obviously, this does not imply omnipotence on their part, but neither does it suggest ultrarationality or all-embracing wisdom on the part of the recipients. What we are dealing with is, simply, the achievement of a superior degree of efficiency compared with the other agents of socialization—hence the prominent place of communication in the analysis of the links between culture and transnationalization.

If to this is added the fact that, alongside their ideological function, the mass media also fulfill the increasingly important function of adapting demand to the production levels determined by the logic of maximization of profits (Portales, 1981), nothing would appear to be more unsatisfactory than to continue to regard mass communications as a "superstructure."

References

Cathelat, B. (1976). *Publicité et Société*. Paris: Payot.

Echeverría, R. (1978). "Capitalismo e Información: Consideraciones en Torno a un Debate." Manuscript. Mexico City: Instituto Latinoamericano de Estudios Transnacionales.

Esteinou Madrid, J. (1980). *Aparatos de Comunicación de Masas: Estado y Puntas de Hegemonía*. Mexico City: Taller de Investigación en Comunicación Masiva, Universidad Autónoma Metropolitana-Xochimilco, no. 6.

Gargurevich, J. (1977). *Introducción a la Historia de los Medios de Comunicación en el Perú*. Lima: Editorial Horizonte.

Kaplún, M. (1980). "La Comunicación Participativa Como Praxis y Como Problema." In *Comunicaçao e Sociedade*, 3, July.

Munizaga, G. (1981). "La Industria de las Comunicaciones y los Micro-Medios Alternativos: El Caso de Chile." Paper presented to the Seminar on Economics and Communications, sponsored by the Instituto Latinoamericano de Estudios Transnacionales. Santiago, December.

Portales, D. (1981). *Poder Económico y Libertad de Expresión*. Mexico City: Instituto Latinoamericano de Estudios Transnacionales/Nueva Imagen.

Reyes Matta, F. (1981). "La Comunicación Alternativa Como Respuesta Democrática." Paper presented to the CLACSO Working Group meeting on communications, Santa Marta, Colombia, March.

Roncagliolo, R. (1977a). *La Reforma de la Prensa Peruana*. DEC/D/16. Mexico City: Instituto Latinoamericano de Estudios Transnacionales.

Roncagliolo, R. (1977b). *Libre Flujo Internacional de Noticias y Libertad de Prensa*. DEC/D/30. Mexico City: Instituto Latinoamericano de Estudios Transnacionales.

Roncagliolo, R. (1977c). *Comunicación: Cambio Social y Necesidad de un Nuevo Marco Conceptual*. DEC/D/29. Mexico City: Instituto Latinoamericano de Estudios Transnacionales.

Roncagliolo, R., and N. Janus (1980). "Publicidad Transnacional, Medios de Comunicación y Educación en los Países en Desarrollo." *Perspectivas: Revista Trimestral de Educación* (Paris), 10.

Somavía, J. (1977). "La Estructura Transnacional de Poder y la Información Internacional." In *La Información en el Nuevo Orden Internacional*. Mexico City: Instituto Latinoamericano de Estudios Transnacionales.

Trajtenberg, R., and R. Vigorito (1981). "Economía y Política en la Fase Transnacional: Algunas Interrogantes." Mexico City: DEE/D/58e.

5 *Carlos Eduardo Lins da Silva*

Transnational Communication and Brazilian Culture

The economic phenomenon of transnationalization and its effects on the societies of the so-called Third World have been the object of innumerable deliberations and studies; transnationalization is now one of the most popular subjects in the social sciences. The specific matter of cultural transnationals and their effects on the cultural life of peripheral capitalist nations has gained the attention of various scientists, whose findings have contributed to a clearer understanding of the intricate course of contemporary international relations.[1]

However, few of these studies have avoided the shortcoming detected by Raymond Williams in almost all Marxist thinkers: an inability to give a material quality to the notion of culture, relegating it instead to the superstructure, the field of ideas, beliefs, arts, and customs that is determined by the basic history of a people (Williams, 1979).

This paper examines cultural phenomena within a framework influenced by Gramsci's theories and those of some Latin American authors who have made

The author wishes to express his thanks to the CNPq, which sponsored his participation in the June 1982 meeting in Austin, Texas, and to Intercom (the Brazilian Association for Interdisciplinary Studies on Communication), where many of the ideas here presented have been discussed in the last few years.

1. Some of the most important works in this field are Dorfman and Mattelart (1977), Mattelart (1976), Mattelart (n.d.), Schiller (1976a), and Schiller (1976b).

significant advances in this area. Outstanding examples of such advances are investigations by Néstor García Canclini and Javier Esteinou Madrid, currently under way in Mexico, and the work of research groups from the Instituto Latinoamericano de Estudios Transnacionales and the Brazilian Society for Interdisciplinary Study of Communication. We shall look at culture, above all, as the set of values and beliefs through which members of a social formation (in the Marxist sense of *Form*) explain their experience, express their artistic creativity, and motivate society as a whole to act. Special attention will be given to those values and beliefs transmitted through the communication media.[2]

The first part of this paper will attempt to make the aforementioned theoretical framework explicit. Then I will examine the complexity of transnational relations in the contemporary world, with special attention to the cultural issue in Latin America in general and Brazil in particular. A brief account of Brazilian culture follows, with emphasis on foreign influences. Finally, I will attempt to profile the several fields of culture transmitted by the communication media in Brazil.

My principal aim is to give a broad view of the problem of foreign influence in the formation, development, and present state of Brazilian culture, not to delve into theoretical matters or to examine the socioeconomic structure of Brazilian culture and its concrete manifestations in the production, circulation, and consumption of cultural goods. Such considerations are prior to the problem of the influence of transnational communication. My purpose is simply to introduce the subject and provide perspectives for more detailed studies.

The Material Quality of Culture

The apparent separation between symbolic production and economic life in societies before the emergence of the mass media (newspapers aimed at mass consumption and, later, film, radio, and television) is one of the reasons for the difficulty many theorists face in trying to relate one to the other. However, this separation was an illusion, since the producers of cultural goods have always lived in an intimate relation with the material life of society, even if they have not had direct ties with economic activity. Until the middle of this century, intellectual and artistic life was always dependent on the church, the state, or on patrons for sponsorship.

2. According to Darcy Ribeiro, culture is "the social heritage of a human community, represented by its total patrimony of standardized methods of adapting to nature to guarantee subsistence, the norms and institutions that regulate social relations, and the collected wisdom, values, and beliefs with which its members explain their experience, manifest their artistic creativity, and motivate the community for action" (1978, p. 127). Here I emphasize the third part of Ribeiro's definition.

Pierre Bourdieu describes the historical process through which cultural activity gains autonomy, concomitantly clarifying its ties with economic life, until it is self-sufficient and must assume the responsibility of creating its own means of support (Bourdieu, 1974). In the second phase of the industrial revolution in European countries, the consuming public became ever more extensive, favoring the independence and legitimation of the producers of symbolic goods. Consequently, a professional corps of producers and entrepreneurs of symbolic goods was formed, with admission and technical norms. Simultaneously, the demand for diffusion and legitimation of symbolic goods multiplied.

"Once a market for the work of art has been constituted, writers and artists can affirm the impossibility of reducing works of art to the stature of simple merchandise, and also affirm the singularity of the intellectual and artistic condition" (Bourdieu, 1974, p. 103). The production of symbolic goods in a capitalist formation cannot escape the logic of that formation. Some, however, are horrified and indignant when confronted with this reality and therefore insist on the nonmaterial character of artistic, cultural, and intellectual activity. Even today, many consider the submission of art to the logic of the market economy to be a perversion and look down on the symbolic products produced according to that logic.

This is an idealistic position. In a society in which the mode of production (capitalist) presupposes a hegemony of one class (the bourgeoisie), how can the cultural universe isolate itself from the process that guarantees the maintenance of that hegemony? Why should the production of symbolic goods escape the logic of capitalism, if the reproduction of the ideological component is essential for the reproduction of the mode of production itself?

However, simply understanding the ties between cultural and material life is not enough to put an end to the confusion in this area. Marx's image of the infrastructure and the superstructure is the basis for another type of error found in many analyses of cultural problems. Rather than idealistic deviations, we are now faced with mechanistic ones.[3] Reading Marx's texts only partially, many authors have misunderstood his concept of the relation between material life and ideology.[4] In reductionist accounts, cultural goods are seen simply as distorted reflections of economic life. Especially when treating the production of symbolic goods in communication media, these authors transform such goods into simple instruments used by the dominant classes to "manipulate" the dominated classes in order to maintain the status quo.

3. The best example of this tendency is found in Theodoro W. Adorno (1975) and the works of his disciples, including those who, in various Latin American countries, insist on defending positions that he himself has reconsidered (1978).

4. See Williams (1979), especially the chapters that deal with infrastructure, superstructure, and the concept of determination (pp. 77–92).

The best works in the field of culture, especially so-called mass culture, have been unable to reach a higher level of criticism than this and thus grasp only a part of the whole reality. It is evident that culture is ideology and that one of the roles of ideology is to furnish an interpretation of social conflicts that is distorted by class interests. It is also obvious that if the bourgeoisie is the hegemonic class in a capitalist social formation, the bourgeoisie will have hegemony over ideology. However, as Canclini (1979) points out, although the concepts of manipulation and domination are useful in describing the coercion that the dominant classes exert over the popular ones, they do not explain why the dominated classes accept that coercion. What the majority of critical authors lack is a dialectical vision that could help explain not only the ideological actions of the hegemonic class but also how members of the subordinate class elaborate their own cultural production and select, interpret, reinterpret, absorb, and use the cultural production of the hegemonic classes.

This same lack of dialectical vision appears also in works examining the relation between the production of symbolic goods and economic life. Most studies limit themselves to the effects of the second on the first, as if there were no action by culture on the economy. It is in fact rather difficult to separate the infrastructure from the superstructure; material goods have a strong symbolic charge, and symbolic goods are themselves material. However, if it is possible to separate them for analytic reasons, it is also possible to perceive that each acts continually on the other, and if the infrastructure is "determinant," it is so only in the sense that Williams (1979) uses the term: to describe how the economic characteristics of a given social formation limit the realm of action of cultural activities. For example, in a social formation in which economic conditions are such that the majority of the population is not served by electricity, cultural action through television is impossible. It is in this sense that the economy "determines" cultural activity, and not in the reductionist sense that treats culture as a distorted reflection of economic activity.

The "relative autonomy" of cultural activity demands that its peculiar socioeconomic structure be studied, since it will have an important influence on the content of symbolic goods. The content, the part that expresses ideology, is to a large extent the result of specific conditions of production. As Canclini says: "Statements like 'art is a commodity' or 'art is determined by the laws of the capitalist system' have little explanatory value until we precisely describe the forms that those laws adopt to produce works of art as unique means and relations of production" (1979, p. 80). For example, the balance of power between employee and employer in a cultural production medium can decisively influence the symbolic representation of a specific cultural good.

The conditions of production, circulation and consumption of cultural goods are mediators of the utmost importance between the global economic base of society and the representation of those cultural goods. Countless authors have wasted their talent and their readers' intelligence on exhaustive content analyses of communication media without helping to illuminate the cultural phenomenon as a whole, since they omit any and all reference to the intermediary areas that explain the passage from the material base to the ideological representation.

Thus, an analysis of cultural activity cannot be limited to an understanding of the product's representation, to what the cultural good "says." To cite Canclini once again, "art not only represents relations of production, but also puts them into practice. And the forms of representation are a consequence of the mode of production in which art is produced, and they vary with it. . . . Thought not only interprets reality, but also organizes all social practices according to that reality, thus contributing to the production of new social realities. . . . We must underscore the fact that the reproduction of the structure in the superstructure occurs not with mimic-like equivalence, but as a functional convergence, since the superstructural reproduction of materials, techniques, and social relations serves both the extension of interests in the ideological field and the specific objectives of the cultural forces (Canclini, 1979, pp. 81–94).

International Networks of Culture

The same reductionist and mechanistic flaws that appear in analyses of the relationship between material and cultural life are found in analyses of international cultural relations. As always, the mechanistic and reductionist vision sees only part of reality, ignoring the complexities that could impede the simplistic statements its practitioners are so fond of.

It is evident, of course, that capitalism is an international mode of production. And just as the ideology of the hegemonic class is the hegemonic ideology in the capitalist social formation, the bourgeois ideology of the central nation will naturally be hegemonic on the international level, as it is reproduced, valued, and disseminated in the peripheral nations by their national bourgeoisies. It is also evident that just as the reproduction of the hegemonic ideology is an essential condition for the reproduction of relations of production in a capitalist society, the reproduction of capital on a worldwide basis demands the reproduction of culture on a worldwide level. Various authors have shown the special importance of the communication media and their cultural productions in the international strategy of the central capitalist nation—the United States (Dorfman and Mattelart, 1977; Mattelart, 1976; Mattelart, n.d.; Schiller, 1976a; Schiller, 1976b).

But even though all this is evident, there is still no reason to fall into reductionist logic of the type that asserts that "the culture of the hegemonic nation is imposed on the peripheral ones, which limit themselves to reproducing it" or "the culture of the hegemonic nation promotes the manipulation of subordinate classes in the peripheral nations." Sarti offers a crushing criticism of one of the most prominent reductionist manifestations, the theory of cultural dependency: "Because it uses a mechanistic approach, which creates the mirage of a dichotomy in the social reality, 'cultural dependency' is unable to untangle the knot of colors and emotions we call 'Latin American culture.' From this woefully misguided perspective, the cultural process is explained in terms of a division of the world into dominated and dominating people and/or nations, powerful and oppressed, active and passive, creative creators and apathetic consumers, or even elite and plebs, urbanites and peasants. Only as a result of this sad mistake was it possible for the 'cultural dependency' literature to reduce the activity to the absorption of externally imposed values and *to aspire to* 'national autonomy' as a solution for this continent's conflicts" (Sarti, 1981, pp. 240–41; italics in original).

This vision of international relations results in an exacerbated, inconsequential nationalism of the type that has been seen on several recent occasions. Some authors, however, manage to see that things are not as simple as the defenders of the cultural dependency theory would have it. Beltrán and Fox de Cardona, for example, note the existence of "Latin American facilitators" in the process of cultural exchange between the central and the peripheral capitalist nations: "It becomes clear enough that—in all aspects of the problem (economics, politics, culture, and communications)—the transnational interests and operations of the United States receive decisive assistance from the coinciding interests and practices of powerful native Latin American elites. These elites benefit from the state of international domination, exercising, in turn, a no less crushing domination over the majority of the people in their own countries, a phenomenon documented in hundreds of studies" (1982, p. 38).

Thus, the fundamental concept of social classes, which remained obscure in the theory of dependency, is introduced into the debate on the transnational question. It is impossible to study the transnational communication phenomenon without considering the international ties of the diverse social classes. And these ties are extremely complex, especially at the point where the monopolistic phase of international capitalism reaches its peak with the appearance of transnational corporations. "The answer isn't simply to mechanically nationalize the media, its sources, and programs," as Reyes Matta has warned (1980, p. 17).

The complex network of international relations becomes much more complicated during the monopolistic accumulation phase. Just as there are no more nations that import industrialized products and export raw materials, in the cultural and communication field it appears that the phase in which Latin American nations simply bought television programs and films is being superseded. At least a few production centers have been created in peripheral countries, such as Brazil, which produces and exports television programs, films, and records to other Third World nations and even to the Spanish-speaking population in the United States.

De Souza's analysis helps explain this phenomenon (1980). According to this author, the process of the internationalization of capital should be understood as the internationalization of the productive process on a worldwide scale, which should result in new contradictions among nations, classes, and states. The internationalization of capital should not be seen as simply a more sophisticated form of the central nations' imperialism, since this interpretation leads one to believe that the state is the centerpiece in a movement to overcome bourgeois domination, a thesis that, under capitalism, is not sustained by the facts. Neither can the transnationalization process be seen as just another form of capital accumulation, internationalizing the internal markets of the dependent nations, since the central object of this reasoning is consumption and not production. Furthermore, the political consequence of this explanation, contrary to the previous one, is an overestimation of the role of civil society in obtaining social transformations: given the characteristics of capitalist formations, this explanation too is insufficient.

De Souza's explanation for the internationalization of capital seems most promising. It allows him to drop the ambiguous term "dependency," which survives in other theories on the subject. His approach recognizes that the capitalist productive system is today articulated on a worldwide basis, thus consumating one of the tendencies that Marx noted. Although research from this angle is in its early stages, it seems to have opened some very promising avenues (de Souza, 1980). It is necessary to elaborate the concept of a worldwide capitalist system that is articulated with, and consumates itself in, national social formations, not nullifying their national dimensions but introducing into them a new qualitative element that needs to be better studied, especially with regard to its effects both on the economic level and on the class structure and the state.

To better understand this phenomenon, it is also necessary to analyze the concrete historical forms by which the worldwide capitalist productive system articulates with national productive subsystems. It would then be possible to verify that these articulations may take the characteristic form that has been called "dependent" or "imperialist" but may also take a form that could be better called "associative." Both types of articulation can perfectly well coexist.

This type of analysis opens up avenues for much more worthwhile studies, since the differences between dominated and dominating classes within the worldwide capitalist system could be grasped more precisely. For example, it would be easier to separate the interests of the different factions of the bourgeoisie according to their positions in the different productive subsystems, and the same could be done in the case of the proletariat. That is, it would be easier to define the common interests of and the contradictions between factions of the bourgeoisie and the proletariat according to the way they fit into the various subsystems that are either directly tied to the worldwide production system, as occurs with multinational corporations, or indirectly connected with it, as with autonomous national enterprises. The role of the state, where all the class contradictions are condensed, would also be better defined with this type of analysis.

The theoretical framework suggested by de Souza is of the utmost importance in the case of culture. Transnational capital has become involved in the Brazilian means of symbolic production in several ways, ranging from the simple investment of money in national enterprises and the importation of equipment, techniques, and production concepts to the content transmitted by the media, with all its ideological implications. Nevertheless, a concomitant strengthening of autonomous national enterprises in the culture industry can be observed, as well as the transformation of the Rede Globo television network into a production center for television programs exported to other Latin American countries and Africa, thus consumating the internationalization of production observable for some time in other areas of the economy.

Complicating the Latin American case is the fact that several forms of capital accumulation coexist within the social formations in a typical process of unequal and combined development under capitalism. The result is the emergence of different types of cultural manifestations, each one corresponding to a different stage of capitalist development and all consistent with a hegemonic type of cultural manifestation corresponding to a hegemonic form of accumulation, which, in the Brazilian case, is monopolistic. "If the dynamics of unequal development and combined development of socioeconomic formations like those of Brazil are understood, it becomes easier to explain and understand, for example, the extreme interest shown by the state, in certain historical moments, in defending nonbourgeois, and even precapitalist, cultural expressions (like folklore), even using the media of the culture industry itself to do so (as occurred during the Geisel administration)" (Lins da Silva, 1980, pp. 173–74). The theory of unequal and combined development helps explain the coexistence, within a single social formation, of communication media typical of competitive capitalism side by side with others typical of monopolistic capitalism.

In any case, as Sarti warns:

It seems clear that the answers to [our] questions will come only from concrete analyses of specific historical contexts in which one preserves a global perspective on society while not only considering the divergence of interests between the two fundamental classes . . . but also maintaining the distinction between the different class sectors that occupy diverse positions in the productive process. Instead of generic analyses concerning the continent or entire nations, one needs concrete studies of specific class sectors that illustrate the interests of each sector. It is unrealistic, to say the least, to think that a message is received in the same way by all the individuals spread along the pyramid formed by the income-distribution graphs in our countries. The effect of what is said can only be evaluated when one knows to whom it is said: an elementary communication principle that cannot again be forgotten, as it was in the studies on "communication and cultural dependency." (1981, pp. 247–48)

This is what several Latin American scholars are doing at the moment: attempting to understand the real state of communication and culture in specific historical periods and in concrete manifestations, limiting the analysis to specific classes or fractions of classes, to provide a more realistic view of the problem of dependency and, in addition, to gather evidence for safer generalizations about the issue of cultural transnationalization itself.

For example, Canclini's study on the sociology of Argentine art in the 1960s, reaches conclusions of the utmost importance (1979). Canclini verified that in the sixties a firmer and more diversified economic development began to take shape in Argentina, involving changes in the economic use of industrial production, internal market growth, increased industrial imports, and increased capacity to create employment. It was a process similar to that which took place in other Latin American nations—a process of integration of national capital during the monopolistic period of capitalist exchange, which gave an impression of relatively autonomous internal development.

According to Canclini, Argentine society did modernize; industry grew, and the middle classes acquired new consumer habits. All these developments influenced culture and were influenced by it. Television expanded rapidly, and weekly information magazines appeared, helping to disseminate the new industrial products and, likewise, the political aspirations and ideology of the advanced bourgeoisie. This climate was also favorable to new artistic experiments as well as to the new aesthetic standards of the international avant-gardes. Later, with the failure of the apparent economic development, many of the cultural experiments also failed.

Canclini concludes as follows:

The Argentine case, like others, shows two functions of the artistic experience: on the one hand it served the industrial part of the bourgeoisie in its effort to extend its struggle against the agro-exporting part of that class into the symbolic area—that is, in the struggle between two models of capital accumulation. (The faction that pursues economic growth through the expansion of traditional agricultural resources defends a conservative cultural policy, and the faction that supports technological and industrial development promotes a cultural line based on the experimental modernization of procedures and materials.) On the other hand, the projects of these class factions serve cultural groups clashing in the struggle for artistic legitimation, in conflicts of aesthetic tendencies. . . . The unity and coherence between structure and superstructure derive, nonetheless, from the need of each class to legitimize and ensure economic power through the accumulation of symbolic capital. The faction that pushes industrial change must create cultural organizations and an ideological apparatus that correspond to and guarantee its modernization project. In order to legitimize itself, it develops a discourse of justification through like-minded scientists, artists, and writers. (1979, pp. 95–96)

Canclini's essay is an example of a study of concrete cultural manifestations, in a specific historical context, that contributes to the general understanding of the communication problem in Latin America. Since other countries on the continent have experienced similar situations, it is possible to understand other specific cases through this study.

The International Presence in Brazilian Culture

The cultural history of Brazil differs substantially from that of other colonized countries, even within Latin America itself. One of the main reasons is the absence of a powerful indigenous culture that might have presented an obstacle to the penetration of European culture: "All one needs do is think of the Arab world, China, India, or even Peru and Mexico, to immediately understand the difference in the Brazilian case. In Brazil, even during the time of formal subordination . . . the fundamental classes of our socioeconomic formation found their ideological and cultural expressions in Europe" (Coutinho, 1979, p. 23). And just as there was no resistance to the penetration of European culture, later, during the first centuries of colonization, there would be few elements of indigenous culture to mix with the culture of the colonizer: "Much more than in Spanish America, where native cultures, although inarticulate, endured in the form of residues . . . capable of entering as parts in new articulations, among us culture was imposed from the top as part of a scorched-earth policy. Culture became a privilege of the white man, who was interested in the indigenous ways only as a means of advancing acculturation—that is, destroying its possessor. . . . The native culture did not survive, even as an underground current, and its traces were transmitted only to the marginalized population of mamelukes, who could not be socially recognized" (Lima, 1978, p. 28).

Though more positive about the role of Brazil's indigenous culture, Ribeiro recognizes that European sociocultural institutions operated as "homogenizers" of the country's diverse cultural patterns, "organizing the rising society as a colonial dependency" and making it conform to Lusitanian cultural standards (1978, p. 141).

The spurious character of Brazilian culture is a result of . . . the exogenous and mercantile nature of the enterprise that gave it birth as a slave-based colonial formation, organized to provide the European market with certain products. Brazil was born under these conditions, and it grew as an external proletariat destined to fulfill the conditions of survival, comfort, and wealth of the European societies. Consequently, the Brazilian dominant class had from the beginning the responsibility of managing foreign interests, having to be more sensitive to the demands of these than to the conditions of the national population. This did not mean that it constituted a seignorial, elite stratum of an autonomous society; rather, it was an alienated local representation of another society whose culture it tried to mimic. (Ribeiro, 1978, p. 142)

In cultural terms, for most of their history the Brazilian hegemonic classes tried to be Portuguese, English, French, and, later, North American. As Ribeiro admits, foreign imitation (which was inevitable, given the country's conditions of economic formation) was not harmful in itself. It was probably even beneficial, since cultural transplants are often associated with progress. "The harm lay, and still lies, in the rejection of everything that was national and, especially, popular, on the grounds that it was impregnated with the subordinate status of the tropical lands, as well as the inferiority of colored people" (Ribeiro, 1978, pp. 143–44).

Even if this observation holds true for the hegemonic classes, especially when these were formed by the landed rural aristocracy, it cannot be generalized to the whole of Brazilian society. The penetration of European culture (which at the time of Brazil's discovery was becoming universal) occurred throughout Brazilian society, but its assimilation was not uniform: it varies according to class and according to the historical moment in which exposure occurred.

Once again, an effort is necessary to avoid falling into the mechanistic fallacy. Coutinho's description seems close to reality:

The history of Brazilian culture . . . can be schematically defined as the history of the assimilation—mechanical or critical, passive or transformative—of the universal culture (which is certainly a highly differentiated culture) by the several classes and social strata of Brazil. In sum: when Brazilian thought 'imports' a universal ideology, it is proof that a specific class or social stratum of our country found (or thought it found) in that ideology the expression of its own Brazilian class interests. For example, when the Brazilian working class took shape, it did not look for adequate theoretical expression in Bororo myths or in African religions. (1979, p. 23)

Thus, the foreign element in the formation and development of Brazilian culture does not necessarily mean that that culture is alienated in total and absolute terms. Diverse elements in the foreign cultural products that come to Brazil, as well as elements from within Brazilian society and from different periods in the country's history, impede homogeneous and uniform absorption, resulting in unique effects. In countless cases the uncritical assimilation of European (or U.S.) cultural products, created by social formations experiencing historical situations very different from those of Brazil, has resulted in what Robert Schwarz (1977) classifies as "out-of-place ideas." Yet imported ideas have been adapted to the national reality, and purely Brazilian cultural expressions have been (and still are) born within the subordinate classes in the form of original cultural products or critical reinterpretations of foreign cultural elements. We are not dealing with a uniform, homogeneous picture but, on the contrary, one composed of highly differentiated elements that forbid hasty generalizations.

The style of Portuguese colonization in Brazil (for several reasons very different from the Spanish colonization in the rest of Latin America) is responsible for some of the peculiar aspects of Brazilian culture. The delay in the arrival of the printing press is one example. Until the beginning of the nineteenth century, print shops were prohibited in Brazil. As Lima notes, this means that there was no Brazilian reading public that could encourage writers to modify European standards (1978, p. 29). This situation remained practically unaltered even after political independence in 1822 and throughout most of the monarchy. Thus, Brazilian culture was marked by an oral character that, according to Lima, is present even in written works, which use basically auditive styles, and, what is more important, basically European and elitist auditive styles. "Perhaps there was no other way, but the fact is that the characteristics of our intellectual system do not seem to be explained merely by the type of economic relations that characterized us. Perhaps a better hypothesis, capable of revealing the intermediate instances, might be found in the absence, on the part of the oppressed classes and underprivileged social segments, of means of furthering their aspirations and formulating their opposition to the official culture" (Lima, 1978, p. 32).

This situation would endure as long as the hegemonic classes continued to be formed of those who lived basically from the extraction and export of raw materials and thus had no need for a more vigorous internal market that would be capable of consuming cultural goods. The situation began to change about 1930, when new relations of production, new classes and fractions of classes taking over social hegemony, and new developments in international relations would make new and growing cultural demands.

The replacement of British preponderance at the economic level by North America began in the 1920s. In 1922 Brazil obtained its first loan from the United States, and North American influence increased throughout that decade, (which saw the installation of the first U.S. industries in Brazil), became stronger during the 1930s, when the growing industrial bourgeoisie gained control over the internal political hegemony (with interests very close to those of the United States), and consolidated itself during and after World War II, when the other central capitalist nations that could have disputed dominance over Latin America (England, France, Germany, and Japan) were penurious.

In the cultural area, corresponding developments were taking place. It was in the thirties that radio, film, and the music industry, all heavily influenced by U.S. capital, style, and content, imposed themselves as hegemonic cultural products. The North American presence in cinema was almost absolute. Yet the first modern plays by national authors were staged, and in the music industry some Brazilian cultural manifestations—and popular ones at that—managed to cross class frontiers and reach society as a whole as the samba and other popular rhythms were for the first time recorded and consumed by a large number of people. Even though transmitting facilities were owned by Brazilian entrepreneurs, radio was financially controlled by American advertising agencies and advertisers and subjected to heavy musical influence through the records played.

The predominance of the United States increased throughout the 1950s with the advent of television in Brazil, later transformed into the country's hegemonic means of cultural diffusion. Yet the number of Brazilians effectively participating in the cultural process remained small, even after the changes that occurred in the Brazilian economy between 1930 and 1964 and the emergence of communication media capable of reaching a large number of people. Except for radio, which can reach diverse strata, the arts and techniques of the communication media are beyond the field of interest of the landed classes, and certainly beyond the interests of workers, laborers, semiproletarians, and those who work on the land. The high bourgeoisie, on the other hand, has often displayed such an interest. One of the obstacles to Brazil's material development is the progressive incorporation into the market economy of vast areas in which the precapitalist economy still prevails. A parallel cultural problem is the progressive incorporation into its public life of social strata that remain distant from and indifferent to its manifestations (Sodré, 1979, p. 70).

It may be argued that the exclusion of vast sectors of the population from the market economy (as well as from the usufruct of the hegemonic culture) is essential to the maintenance of the Brazilian economy's current place in international capitalism. Despite the considerable growth of the middle class (including some sectors of skilled labor) after 1964, when the Brazilian economy adopted monopolism as a form of hegemonic capital accumulation in order to complete its participation in international monopolistic capitalism, these modifications failed to include all the classes that form Brazilian society. Even radio and television overlook a considerable minority of the population, especially in the rural areas of northern and northeastern Brazil.

Nevertheless, the growth of the middle classes and Brazil's entry into the order of international capitalism—a process initiated in the second half of the 1950s and consolidated after the 1964 military coup—vitalized the national cultural production by expanding the internal consumer market for symbolic goods as well as the external market catering to the consumer needs of other countries on the cultural circuit of international capitalism. Thus, the national film industry received a great impetus during this period, as did the music, publishing, and television industries, all of which placed Brazilian products on the international market.

However, an economic crisis checked the post-1964 options and provoked crises in the Brazilian cultural industry beginning in 1975. The middle classes, which form the main consumer sector of that industry, are among the hardest-hit victims of the trying times that have extended from 1975 to the present. Consequently, records, books, and films, which are considered non-essential items, have been consumed with less enthusiasm. Television, however, has reaffirmed itself as the diffusion vehicle of hegemonic culture, and national production has become stronger and more extensive, leading some adherents of cultural dependency theory to wonder whether it is on its way to extinction in Brazil's case. In fact, however, external influences on Brazilian television have not diminished but only changed in form. The national programming on Rede Globo reflects one of the needs of transnational capital, and it abides by transnational rules of style, format, and content. It has simply, for reasons of convenience, ceased to be produced in the United States and has begun to be made in Brazil, inciting new contradictions at the production as well as the consumer level, since internal productions have positive aspects.

The Present Situation

Two features of the present situation, though not exclusive to Brazil, appear in marked fashion there. First, the large-scale importation of production techniques for cultural goods, at a time when an autonomous consumer market for such products is just beginning to appear, is causing certain asynchronisms that have permanently marked the country's cultural and communication systems.

This is the case with journalism, for example. Marques de Melo states in his sociological examination of Brazilian journalism (1973), for a long time the majority of newspaper-publishing firms in Brazil were not structured like modern capitalist enterprises, nor were they able to maintain themselves exclusively through the product they produced. In fact, this is still true of a great part of the journalistic enterprises in Brazil, in keeping with the logic of unequal and combined capitalism. However, even though they are not structured according to the capitalist mold, in journalistic values and technology these enterprises have almost always kept up with their counterparts from capitalism's central countries. Nowadays, for example, in some northeastern states it is possible to find newspapers with ridiculously low circulation showing a deficit and maintained only because the group that owns them gains political advantages through their publication; yet they are produced with the most modern cold-type composing systems and they reproduce in content and form the values of the best North American dailies.

The introduction of advanced communication technology like television (and later videotapes and videocassettes), before there was a mass public for the printed media, gave Brazil's cultural and communication systems a peculiar character. It is evident that the introduction of audiovisual technology is related to the interests of transnational enterprises and the political objectives of capitalist nations. But it is also related to the interests of the country's own hegemonic classes. For example, the rapid expansion of television in Brazil, with the installation of a very modern microwave system capable of connecting the country from end to end, occurred after the 1964 military coup, when the new hegemonic arrangement of classes and fractions of classes opted for the monopolistic form of accumulation. And this rapid expansion of television, which became the country's hegemonic ideological apparatus, was not a mere "consequence" or "reflex" of that option for monopolistic capitalism; rather, it was an essential condition for putting that option into practice and consolidating it, in what was another demonstration of reciprocal influence between the infrastructure and superstructure.

The second noteworthy characteristic of Brazilian cultural life is the massive presence of the state, especially since 1964, when national cultural production began to expand exactly at the moment when the country's economy was being inserted into the circuit of transnational capital. As in the Argentinian situation described by Canclini (1979), the Brazilian option for monopolistic capitalism also resulted in effective modernization, enrichment of the middle class, the growth of the internal consumer market, the sharpening of contradictions, the creation of a class-conscious working class, a larger public for cultural products, and a sudden awareness on the part of the intelligentsia of the country's peripheral situation in cultural as well as political and economic terms. All these factors together would result in an acceleration of national cultural production.

When this happened, the fragility of the national bourgeoisie was once again revealed, since it was clear that such an acceleration would not be possible without the help of the state. Brazilian communications, unlike the communication systems of the central capitalist nations, suffer the direct interference of the state as advertiser or subsidizer. This happens in all spheres of cultural production: from film to theater, from television to newspapers, from magazines to folklore.

These two aspects are of the utmost importance for an understanding of both the cultural phenomena that have taken place in Brazil in the last twenty years and the influence of cultural transnationals during the same period. The acceleration of national cultural production at the exact moment when the economy was put on the transnational circuit reflects a necessity of that circuit in its more developed stage. At first the presence of foreign capital is overt. However, this situation changes rapidly when the interests of transnational capital are better served by national capital enterprises. Cultural production subcenters may be more attractive to the transnational system. For example, a Brazilian hero on Latin American (or African) television is much more useful than a North American one, since the United States is stigmatized as a colonial power and such a hero avoids the problems of the language barrier and disparate cultural traditions. Similarly, it can be more efficient and economical for transnational capital to obtain services from autonomous national enterprises. Therefore, Brazilian culture is full of contradictions. This is especially true of the communication media, and of television above all, which are the centers around which turn the production and consumption of the country's symbolic goods. These contradictions can be better perceived when each medium of communication is examined individually.

Television, as already noted, experienced extraordinary growth after the 1964 military takeover and served as one of the most important instruments (ideological and economic) for the consolidation of the option for monopolistic capitalism, which it represented. Whereas in 1970 only 24.1 percent of all households were equipped with television, in 1980 this figure had already reached 54.9 percent—73.1 percent in the cities. The first extraordinary contradiction (evidencing the decisive importance of television for the regime's politico-economic project) is the fact that according to official census figures, many more homes have television than refrigerators (42.2 percent of urban residences) or sewage services (37.8 percent). There is no significant difference between television and radio ownership figures for urban centers (there are radios in 79.2 percent of Brazilian urban households), though the gap increases in rural areas, where 68.0 percent of all homes have radios, against 14.7 percent with television (all figures from "O País de Televisão," 1982).

The foreign presence in Brazilian television should be analyzed from two points of view. In terms of content, it is much smaller today than it was in 1970. Even though it is difficult to come up with trustworthy statistics, since small television stations might rely more on foreign programming, it can be affirmed that today the absolute majority of programs broadcast by Brazilian television are national. The Rede Globo television network, which today dominates 75 percent of the country's total audience,[5] does not broadcast more than one hour of foreign programming during prime time (from 6:00 p.m. to 12:00 p.m.). The rest of its programming comprises *telenovelas* (similar to U.S. "soap operas," but usually of a much higher quality), news programs, series, humor programs, documentaries, and musicals produced in Brazil. The style and format of all these programs is heavily influenced by North

5. See "Força e Magia da Imagem Fugaz" (1980). There were two national television networks besides Globo in 1982; another was added in 1983.

American models, but they represent an undeniable nationalization of content and themes.

There is, however, a second aspect that must be taken into consideration: the sponsors of Brazilian television. Here no change has occurred. Of the fifteen biggest television advertisers in 1979, only four were Brazilian. In 1980 only five of the fifteen were Brazilian. The principal advertisers continue to be transnational enterprises with headquarters in the United States, Switzerland, England, Holland, and Liechtenstein, and the United States predominates ("Os 15 Maiores Anunciantes," 1981). Although the state, through its countless mixed companies and banks or through public organs themselves, is becoming an ever more important advertiser on Brazilian television (as it already was in newspapers, magazines, and radio), the state itself is under the hegemony of a group of classes and class factions with interests associated with transnational capital and thus does not differ substantially from the transnationals themselves as an advertiser.

Rede Globo programs have extensively penetrated other countries, principally in Latin America and Africa, but also in Europe and even in the United States. At present Rede Globo sells programs to seventy-one countries, chiefly childrens programs, *telenovelas,* musical programs, and series. This provided Rede Globo with almost $2 million in revenue in 1979. Furthermore, Rede Globo has received numerous international awards, including some North American ones, and evidently is seeking prestige in the international market ("Globo Multinacional," 1980). As noted above, we see here the beginning of the process of internationalization of production in the area of culture, paralleling the process that took place in certain areas of industrial production.

Television claimed 55.9 percent of the 1979 advertising budget shared among all the communication media. The extraordinary development of the Brazilian advertising sector, seventh in the world in financial terms, is attributed mainly to television. One of the most outstanding contradictions in Brazilian communications is the fact that despite the vitality of the advertising market, the number of consumers in the country is not comparable to consumer figures for other advertising leaders. The president of the Brazilian Advertisers' Association stated that "a large part of the products advertised [on television] are beyond the reach of the viewer's buying power, simply because it is estimated that the number of consumers is 35 percent smaller than that of viewers" ("Expressivos Numerous da Publicidade," 1980). This is one of the countless distortions of the economic model: in order to attend to the need for rapid capital reproduction and the superappropriation of labor for the creation of an economic surplus destined for foreign markets, the economic strategy requires an exaggerated consumption of superfluous goods in limited population strata, while it spreads misery over most of the country.

Another contradiction involves the state's presence in all communication media, which has a distinctive character in the case of television. The state plays three roles in the configuration of Brazilian television. In addition to its licensing power, the state is one of television's main advertisers, as well as its regulator. It grants licenses to operate television stations, mainly using political criteria and not market laws, as can be seen in a recent bidding in which superstructured groups were set aside in favor of the politically servile. But it also enters the market relations as a major advertiser, and, furthermore, it censors and pressures the television stations in cases of political or moral "abuses."

Finally, it must be observed that television has suffered the effects of the economic crisis that has marked Brazilian life since 1974, though to a lesser extent than other communication media. The main effect was on the advertising budget, which did not grow during 1980 and 1981 as it had in previous periods, especially during the first five years of the 1970s. This factor may dampen the nationalizing process in programming, since it is still much cheaper to buy canned programs from the United States (on the average, a Brazilian series costs 30 to 40 percent more than an imported American one). This tendency can be seen in Rede Globo's decision in 1982 to take Brazilian series off the air, even though this action could also be attributed to censorship pressure as a result of the liberality with which some of those series treated diverse moral issues.

Radio, present in close to 65 percent of homes all over the country, and accounting for 8.5 percent of the advertising budget, is also of great importance in Brazil. In coverage it is even more important than television; in cultural impact, however, it is way below television, and a great part of its content is influenced by television.

In terms of international influence, radio is in many respects similar to television. Although precise data are unavailable, the participation of foreign capital in advertising is greater, U.S. capital being particularly important. It is harder to determine foreign participation in decisions about content—there are close to 1,200 radio stations, and none monopolizes the audience, as Rede Globo does with the television audience. Even though the presence of American music is marked, it can be affirmed with reasonable certainty that more than 60 percent of radio's programming time is devoted to Brazilian cultural productions: music, newscasts, reporting, educational programs, interviews, sports, religious programs, and others. A factor that contributed decisively to the rebirth of radio as a communication medium in Brazil and has been important in advertising terms in recent years was the rise of FM radio stations. These cater to the expanded middle classes, which constitute one of the country's most important consumer markets.

Newspapers and magazines together claim one-third of the advertising budget, even though they reach less than 20 percent of the population. Countless contradictions, mainly in the case of newspapers, are evident. Some of these have already been mentioned, like the contrast between modern equipment and very small circulation. During the peak years of the 1970s, journalistic enterprises were proportionately much more lucrative than their large counterparts in the United States:

O Estado de São Paulo, with a daily circulation of 183,000 on weekdays and 288,000 on Sundays, in a country of 107 million inhabitants and an average per capita income—in 1973—of $433, showed a profit of $8.5 million in 1975; the *New York Times*, with an average daily circulation of 832,614 on weekdays and 1,480,141 on Sundays, in a country of 203 million inhabitants and a per capita income of better than $5,600, showed a profit of $18.744 million. Average profit of *O Estado* per newspaper sold: 0.12 cents; average profit of the *Times* per newspaper sold: 0.06 cents, exactly half. ("Nossos Jornais e Suas Empresas," 1976)

Large journalistic enterprises have, nonetheless, suffered a drop in their profit rates during the last five or six years: newspapers' participation in the advertising market dropped from 23.4 percent in 1970 to 21.8 percent in 1975, and to 20.0 percent in 1979, and the drop in the overall advertising market during the same period must also be considered. Moreover, large journalistic enterprises—those really structured along modern capitalist lines—are very few. In keeping with the logic of unequal and combined development of capitalism, a great part of Brazilian newspapers could be categorized as handicraft outfits; others have modern graphic equipment, but operate at a loss. Nonetheless, the profit margin of the large journalistic enterprises is impressive in a country that has 37 copies of a daily newspaper circulating for every 1,000 inhabitants.

International influence is even more evident in the case of newspapers and magazines than in that of television. The main advertisers continue to come from transnational capital, and the content of newspapers and magazines—or at least the international news—is basically produced abroad by the big news agencies. Although most space is occupied by national production, international news is rarely produced by Brazilian journalists, since only the large editorial groups are able to maintain correspondents abroad.

Furthermore, we have the case of Editora Abril, which controls 80 percent of the Brazilian magazine market and is owned by a person who is not Brazilian (which is contrary to the country's constitution), a former employee of the Time-Life group ("O Fraude da Informação," 1982). Editora Abril was responsible for the introduction of a *Time*-style weekly magazine; it publishes thousands of copies of Disney children's magazines weekly; it controls a great part of the market for men's magazines (which are almost a copy of *Playboy*), women's magazines (which are almost a copy of *Cosmopolitan*), and business magazines (which are almost a copy of the *Economist*). In most cases the content is almost totally imported and translated. The national production is much less significant than in the case of television, radio, or newspapers. Editora Abril has recently published a scientific magazine based totally on translations, just as it publishes countless volumes of translated encyclopedias in fascicle form. It is undoubtedly in this area of the Brazilian cultural industry that content denationalization is currently the strongest.

Brazil has one of the most powerful film industries in the world. In 1977 it was the world's third-largest producer of feature films, surpassed only by the United States and Italy (Barreto, 1981). This extraordinary progress was due to state intervention through the creation of a powerful enterprise, EMBRAFILMS, that began large-scale financing of film productions in the 1970s. Even though film is also suffering the consequences of the economic recession that began in the second half of the 1970s, it has penetrated ever farther into the consumer market, countering the once-complete hegemony of North America films in Brazilian movie theaters. The virtual state monopoly over production, however, influences the choice of topics, since censorship and self-censorship are very much alive.

Brazilian films are now as commercially successful in Brazilian movie theaters as the biggest American box-office hits. In 1981, for example, the movie *Eu Te Amo* (*I Love You*) brought more than 800,000 spectators to the movie theaters and netted more than $1.5 million in three weeks of exhibition. Although the audience for the most successful foreign films is still normally larger than that for the most successful Brazilian movies, the growing success of national films predicts a turnaround in the near future. The most popular film in Brazilian history was *Jaws,* with 12,822,000 spectators, compared with 10,864,000 for *Dona Flor e Seus Dois Maridos,* the biggest national success. However, the sixth-ranked national film surpassed the sixth-ranked international film, and this difference in favor of Brazilian cinema was maintained up to the tenth place (all figures from "O Rico Cinema Novo," 1981). Furthermore, national cinema is starting to penetrate the foreign market. Several national films have received major awards in international film festivals and are attaining success among both critics and the public, not only in Third World countries, but also in the United States and Europe.

The music industry is the sector where the presence of transnational capital is most obvious. Together, CBS, RCA, WEA, Odeon, RGE, Polygram (Philips), and Ariola (a German firm) control 66 percent of the recorded music market ("Os Riscos do Disco," 1981). Nevertheless, the number of national artists under contract with these companies has grown significantly in the last few years. The biggest sales hits are by Brazilian singers, composers, instrumentalists, and musical groups—that is, the television contradiction repeats itself in the record industry.

A similar tendency appears in other areas of the cultural industry. Brazilian records are being launched on foreign markets, especially in Latin America, but also in the central nations. Brazilian singers under contract with multinationals sell more than a million copies of each of their records in Latin American countries ("MPB—Um Artigo de Exportação?" 1980). Others record in Spanish, not just to market their records in South America, but also to reach the Spanish-speaking population of the United States.

The record industry, compared with the other cultural sectors, has suffered especially severely from the country's on-going economic crisis, after having been a particular beneficiary of the economic expansion of the first half of the 1970s. Classified as the fifth most important music industry in the world in 1978, it fell to ninth place in 1980. The internal market consumption fell 35 percent between 1979 and 1980 ("Os Riscos do Disco," 1981).

Although unimportant in economic terms, the presence of independent record producers in the music industry is a noteworthy phenomenon. This outlet was opened with great difficulty by musicians and composers who did not wish to submit themselves to the rules of transnational capital. Their cultural influence has not been meager, especially among the university public.

Books are another medium in which content is being nationalized. As in other sectors of the cultural industry, economic control has stayed basically in the hands of foreign firms or their subsidiaries. These enjoy help from the state, which is a great partner in this realm of cultural production. Brazil produces approximately 220 million books per year (less than two per inhabitant) and about 13,000 titles, of which about 60 percent are national, thus making it the largest book producer/consumer in Latin America ("O Brasileiro," 1980).

Brazilian theater is confronted with great difficulties especially in times of crisis like the present, but it continues to be an important component of the nation's culture, especially in the large urban centers. Although some foreign plays are staged, the majority are by national authors, and it is rare that a foreign company performs in Brazil. The state presence is decisive for the survival of this sector, although assistance is much less enthusiastic than it has been for television, radio, and film. Brazilian theatrical productions have also been successful in other Latin American nations and even in the United States.

Finally, even in cultural areas where national production was once nonexistent—cartoons, for example—the first Brazilian products are beginning to appear. Because of the excessive cost of this type of production, no Brazilian feature-length cartoon appeared until the mid 1970s. The first ones were produced with support from EMBRAFILME, and the fourth was finished at the end of that decade ("Para Breve," 1979).

Conclusion

Certain characteristics of the Brazilian cultural system emerge from this quick sketch of the national communication media:

1. The so-called mass communication media—particularly television—maintain hegemony over Brazilian cultural life today.
2. A tendency toward nationalization of the content of those media, compatible with the economic and social characteristics of the present historical conditions, can be noted, especially since the 1970s.
3. Despite the nationalization of content, economic control of the communication media remains basically in the hands of transnational capital.
4. Since the late 1970s one can clearly see the beginning of an internationalization process in cultural production, with Brazil emerging as an important producer for the Latin American region, especially in the areas of television and recorded music.
5. The state is an important element in the maintenance of the communication media, not only as a regulatory organ, but also as an economic partner and as a patron, with all the implications of control that stem from those positions.

These characteristics are all compatible with the theoretical framework introduced in the first part of this paper. However, more profound and specific studies along the previously recommended lines are necessary to fully understand their meaning. Given that internationalization of production is essential for the maintenance of the international capitalist system, it is only through the analysis of concrete cases that we can fully interpret the complex network of cultural production in a peripheral country in that system during the era of hegemony of international capital.

References

Adorno, T. W. (1975). "A Indústria Cultural." In Gabriel Cohn (ed.) *Comunicação e Indústria Cultural*, pp. 287–95. São Paulo: Editora Nacional.
Adorno, T. W. (1978). "Tiempo-Libre." In *Consignas*. Barcelona: Amarrortu.
"A Fraude da Informação" (1982). *Brazil Hoje*, 3, Feb.
Barreto, B. (1981). "Um Mecenas Quase Falido." *Veja*, Aug. 26.
Beltrán, L. R., and E. Fox de Cardona (1982). *Comunicação Dominada*. Rio: Paz e Terra.
Bourdieu, P. (1974). *A Economia das Trocas Simbólicas*. São Paulo: Perspectiva.
Canclini, N. G. (1979). "Teoria da Superestructura e Sociologia das Vanguardas Artísticas." *Encontros com a Civilização Brasileira*, 18, pp. 71–98.
Coutinho, C. N. (1979). "Cultura e Democracia no Brasil." *Encontros com a Civilização Brasileira*, 17.
De Souza, H. J. (1980). "America Latina: A Internacionalização do Capital e o Estado na Obra de Autores Contemporâneos." In Luis Maira et al., *America Latina: Novas Estratégias de Dominação*, pp. 57–85. Petrópolis: Vozes.
Dorfman, A., and A. Mattelart (1977). *Para Ler o Pato Donald*. Rio: Paz e Terra.
"Expressivos Numeros da Publicidade" (1980). *O Estado de São Paulo*, Sept. 14.

"Força e Magia da Imagem Fugaz" (1980). *Jornal do Brasil,* April 27.

"Globo Multinacional" (1980). *Isto É,* Oct. 29.

Lima, L. C. (1978). "Da Existência Precária: O Sistema Intelectual no Brasil." *Ensaios de Opinião,* 2–5.

Lins da Silva, C. E. (1980). "Indústria Cultural e Cultura Brasileira: Pela Utilização do Conceito de Hegemonia Cultural." *Encontros com a Civilização Brasileira,* 25.

Marques de Melo, J. (1973). *Sociologia da Imprensa Brasileira.* Petrópolis: Vozes.

Mattelart, A. (1976). *As Multinacionais da Cultura.* Rio: Civilização.

Mattelart, A. (n.d.). *Multinacionais e Sistemas de Comunicação.* São Paulo: Ciências Humanas.

"MPB—Um Artigo de Exportação?" (1980). *O Estado de São Paulo,* Oct. 12.

"Nossos Jornais e Suas Empresas" (1976). *Visão,* Aug. 9.

"O Brasileiro Iê Tudo, Enfim, Desde Que Tenha Dinheiro" (1980). *Isto É,* Aug. 13.

"O País da Televisão" (1982). *Isto É,* Jan. 20.

"O Rico Cinema Novo" (1981). *Veja,* April 28.

"Os 15 Maiores Anunciantes Privados da TV Brasileira" (1981). *Movimento,* May 4–10.

"Os Riscos do Disco" (1981). *Isto É,* Nov. 25.

"Para Breve, o quarto Desenho Animado Brasileiro" (1979). *O Estado de São Paulo,* April 29.

Reyes Matta, F. (1980). "The Concept of News in Latin America: Dominant Values and Perspectives of Change." In *News Values and Principles of Cross-Cultural Communication.* Paris: UNESCO.

Ribeiro, D. (1978). *Os Brasileiros: Teoria do Brasil.* Petrópolis: Vozes.

Sarti, I. (1981). "Comunicação e Dependência Cultural: Um Equívoco." In J. Werthein (ed.) *Meios de Comunicação: Realidade e Mito.* São Paulo: Nacional.

Schiller, H. (1976a). *Communication and Cultural Domination.* New York: International.

Schiller, H. (1976b). *O Império Norte-Americano das Comunicações.* Petrópolis: Vozes.

Schwarz, R. (1977). *Ao Vencedor as Batatas.* São Paulo: Duas Cidades.

Sodré, N. W. (1979). *Síntese da História da Cultura Brasileira.* Rio: Civilização Brasileira.

Williams, R. (1979). *Marxismo e Literatura.* Rio: Zahar.

6 *Javier Esteinou Madrid*

Means of Communication and Construction of Hegemony

The objective of this study is to formulate some general provisional hypotheses that will allow us to discuss the specific structural and superstructural functions of the dominant mass media. Such functions operate within both the social processes or apparatuses of hegemony that promote the reproduction of the capitalist system and the social relations that support it. It is not my purpose to demonstrate which system of cultural apparatuses is dominant in every particular formation (in the Marxist sense of *Form*)—this would require historical-empirical investigation within every society—but only to point out some of the principal hegemonic apparatuses of modern capitalism.

The following theoretical and historical reflections will, I hope, contribute to the determination of the role of the dominant mass media in a capitalist state. To this end I will attempt to specify the function of the mass media within the process of the reproduction of the capitalist bloc in so far as it is related to the cultural superstructure and its implementing organs.

The Capitalist State: Creating Its Own Cultural Supports

Structural antagonisms arise from the basic inequality of the capitalist form of production. The ruling class controls and mitigates these contradictions through the machinery of the state to create and conserve the equilibrium needed for the existence, reproduction, and transformation of capital. During the period when the dominant class maintains the cohesion and direction of society by cultural action, the ideological state apparatuses (ISAs) are the most important political means for maintaining the levels of the social formation. The ISAs are thus of fundamental importance to the cyclical reproduction of the system, permanent tools for the creation of the capitalist bloc. It is on this basis that the social formation achieves authoritarian and vertical stability through cultural action.

The modern capitalist state faces the need to apply its policies of cultural domination and at the same time its global plan of social subjugation. It must continually create and select the most appropriate superstructural institutions in order to inculcate the reasonableness of its domination. This involvement tends to manifest itself extensively and intensively in every cultural field and in every social group, and especially in those that constitute the base of support for capitalist society: the labor forces and working-class people in general.

This means that the ruling class, in order to survive, must continually revolutionize its forms of capital accumulation and its mechanisms of political control and continually modernize the material and cultural infrastructure of its historical legitimation. With this mechanism, the state protects its sources of surplus and confronts the structural antagonisms generated by its unequal economic system. We cannot forget that the main problem faced by every elite on its way to power, or already in power, is how to legitimate the basis of its domination day by day.

With this in mind, we find that every capitalist state carefully selects the means, instruments, and subjects of its ideological efforts to achieve the highest degree of ideological domination in all the fields of human awareness and behavior. This allows the state to impose its particular concept of society as the model of social reference and expectation—that is, to implement the ideology of its own class as the dominant one.

This practice is not stable but changes depending upon the different requirements of different phases of capital reproduction. In each phase the most advanced cultural system, or a combination of the most advanced means, is chosen by the ruling class to inaugurate its hegemony among the unlimited number of ideological positions that vie with one another at the level of the superstructure.

Privileged by their central role in capitalist development, the advanced means of communication are converted into the principal ideological apparatuses of the state to implement the program of cultural subjugation required for the stability of the social system. Through these cultural institutions, the dominant class produces and circulates its class-in-power ideology and inculcates it into the consciousness of the rest of society. Capital thus produces its principal ideological tendency throughout the consciousness industries that represent for the state the political control of ideology by means of consensus.

We must recognize the importance of specifying which of the state's ideological mechanisms is being used to dominate each social formation. To make this more manageable, we must locate the principal superstructural mechanism in every social formation that is shaping the consciousness of the working class to the value accumulation demands of each situation.

The Dominant Mass Media as Principal Means of Hegemony

The modern capitalist state has a wide repertory of ideological mechanisms for its own legitimation and for cultural socialization—educational systems, cultural organizations, churches, labor unions, mass media, professional associations, laws, and so on. The most effective ideological mechanisms today are the mass media: television, radio, and other new communication technologies. In both central and peripheral areas of capitalism, the communication media are used culturally to integrate the demands of capital in its different cycles of development with other forms of social consciousness.

In today's capitalist societies, and especially the dependent ones of Latin America, the mass media have become the most efficient instruments of consensus building. This can be attributed to two causes. First, scientific advances in the electronic and space industries have allowed a substantial reduction in the time and material conditions required for the development of social communications. Second, the increased efficiency of these technologies is being used by modern states and transnational groups to refine and promote efforts that result in an unequal development for others.

The new structural position of the mass media results in a new division of social tasks. The cultural functions of the mass media are many, and they change according to historical circumstances. Through their ideological practices, they influence politics, economics, morality, and other social behaviors as well as fulfilling functions in such areas as finance, birth control, and economic organization. However, the main structural importance of mass media lies in their triple role in the reproduction of capitalism. Through symbolic and cultural practices, the mass media carry out three functions critically required by the global structure of the capitalist state:

1. Speeding up the circulation of material goods
2. Inculcating ideologies
3. Contributing to the reproduction of the labor force

Speeding Up the Circulation of Material Goods
The first structural function of the mass media is to accelerate the circulation of capital. As the primary transmitters of the advertising discourse, they help

to spark the mass consumption phase required by the circulation of capital in its current state of amplified reproduction in order to reproduce itself as productive capital. This in turn solidifies the value process, which generates value from the surplus extracted from the labor force in the capitalist reproduction process.

Advertising uses the mass media to reduce the time that elapses between the moment of production and the moment of consumption. Capitalist society thus achieves the necessities of production, distribution, and particularly consumption through the superstructural forms of consciousness and behavioral influence. This makes possible the effective integration of the cultural economy and the superstructure, which harmonizes the functioning of the capitalist system. From this perspective we find that the mass media do not operate as simple entertainment institutions or information channels, as their owners would like them to appear. Rather, they are mechanisms in the production and reproduction of society through their involvement in the circulation of goods.

Thus, the mass media cannot be considered as complementary institutions in the reproduction system. Their task is not performed by any other mechanism of hegemony. It is unique to the dominant mass media and especially in conditions of socioeconomic crisis within the cultural system.

Inculcating Ideologies

A second organic function of the mass media within the social structure is to make the dominant class ideology the only one. Capitalism enters a new phase of development from the moment when the mass media, while maintaining their "relative autonomy" and their character as an "open" field for class struggle, produce, transmit, and collectively teach the various dominant ideologies and their ideological subgroups (required for different classes and class fractions, both foreign and national). Thus they solidify the many projects of capital accumulation through their respective mechanisms and their fetishization of reality.

The media, as noted above, serve to integrate the material sphere of society and the superstructural spheres dealing with political socialization and individual behavior, thus helping to achieve the social harmony required for the conservation of capitalism. This function is not exclusive to mass media but involves the group of ideological mechanisms of the capitalist state that support the cultural superstructure. What is special about the media is their massive audience, immediacy, and advanced technology. The following properties of the mass media have converted them into the principal form of hegemony in the civil societies of the modern capitalist states:

1. The wide scope of ideological action
2. The capacity for continuous and rapid legitimation

3. The capacity for social mobilization and consensus building
4. The early socialization of consciousness
5. Participation in ruling-class goals
6. The inability to serve working-class interests

The Scope of Ideological Action. The first distinctive aspect of the mass media's ideological role is their coverage in the broad field of culture. No other ideological apparatus of the capitalist state can achieve the breadth of the media's psychological influence. This is especially true of the electronic media.

Whereas the schools, family, political parties, churches, trade unions, and so on are ideological mechanisms for smaller groups, the mass media reach millions simultaneously in a variety of social conditions. Their penetration has been very effective. Whether through local transmission systems or international technologies such as satellites, the mass media have attained a truly global reach.

The superiority of the cultural influence of the media in comparison with other ideological means at the disposal of the class in power is confirmed not only by sociological analysis but by the very behavior of various fractions of the ruling class. The entire system of ideological formation, comprising schools, churches, political parties, and so on, turns to the mass media as the superstructural extension of each specific cultural task to be performed, whether educational, political, or religious. Thus, every ideological apparatus of the modern state, according to its own level, strategy, and class focus, uses the mass media as technological extensions of its particular superstructural function. The ISA of education, for example, uses television and radio as an extension of its work through such programs in Mexico as "Telesecundaria," "Tele-introduction to the university," "Tele-literacy for adults," "Radio Instruction for Youths," or "Literacy radio for adults." Film education is also used as a cultural reinforcement.

Trade unions, political parties, and churches all make use of media technologies and institutions to diffuse their respective dominant discourses to a much broader audience than they would otherwise have access to, as do judicial, professional, and cultural organizations. Such groups struggle in their respective fields to conquer and then conserve a consensus that allows them to reproduce themselves as dominant institutions.

Moreover, simultaneous transmission and sequenced dissemination allow these media to carry on the same operations outside their own sphere of production and domination: hence the so-called dephasing and cultural synchronization that permit the most remote and isolated superstructures to be intimately but unilaterally connected with the historic center of dynamic capitalism. It is this process of mass communication (and especially the electronic media), and not other, more traditional cultural institutions, that has provided the main ideological apparatus of the multinational state. Through the communication ISA the capitalist states of the center have created the greatest hold over human consciousness in contemporary history, the better to promote their cultural project of increased capital accumulation.

Thus, the mass media are used by the state as technological and collective extensions of an array of diverse institutions of domination. These media have integrated heterogeneous ISAs of the capitalist state and civil society, since it is through them that the main cultural trends of the ruling class are channeled and reflected. This has turned the media into the principal means for consensus building, but they are also the point at which the secondary contradictions of the ruling class are most evident.

The Capacity for Continuous and Rapid Legitimation. Another characteristic of the media that has placed them in the cultural vanguard of the capitalist state is the capacity for continuous circulation of messages of the electronic media and the rapid but symbolically disjointed circulation of messages of mechanically based media.

Both qualities are important for purposes of structural legitimation, particularly for capitalist social formations in acute crisis (as is true of so many Latin American societies). They permit a national and international consensus favorable to the structural reproduction of the capitalist mode of production.

These qualities of the media, along with their mass diffusion, help make them the most rapid technical means of maintaining the direction and structure of the diverse social groups required for the reproduction of the dominant social relations of the capitalist bloc. Every day the mass media tie together, whether instantaneously or periodically, many different areas of consciousness where a variety of social agents work. They create and recreate, over and over again, the field of thinking and behaving that the task of social domination requires in changing circumstances. The ruling sector uses these media for the vital cultural task of creating ideas about "the nation," "the fatherland," "history," and, in a word, social participation. Day by day the image of a society is passed along to all levels of society.

Intellectuals in the dominant media specialize in creating a world view and lifestyle models that affirm the presence of capitalism through media discourse. Two kinds of media productions play a fundamental role in reproducing the subjective conditions that the reproduction of capitalism requires: these are the discourse of news and the discourse of advertising.

The news discourse operates under the twin ideological covers of "objective information" and "relevant cultural product." Thus, the awareness of the social agents in news works is permanently attached to the cultural demands of a political order promoting the daily reproduction, expansion, and legitimation of national and international capital. Their activity and behavior is constantly oriented in this direction.

The discourse of advertising, on the other hand, uses the slogans "satisfaction of basic needs" and "consumer choice" to constantly and unobtrusively promote the accumulation of capital. This is accomplished through the rapid circulation and the easy mass consumption of goods produced under the conditions of exploitation. This discourse is favored by contemporary capitalism in its task of mass circulation of goods because it permits through a degree of collective influence the consumption of capital as a relation of value that generates value. It also helps to fetishize goods so that the inequalities of the production process are obscured. In both cases advertising helps to reproduce the fundamental relations of capitalism: the subordination of the working class to capital within the social relations of exploitation.

These two areas of discourse are today the cultural centers of greatest structural relevance because through them the mass media quite unconsciously reinforce, on a daily basis, the dominant relations of stability and reproduction/transformation required by capitalism: that is, the corresponding relations of capitalist exploitation and social subordination.

The media's ability to reach mass audiences rapidly and with a persuasive message allows the ruling class to transmit its dominant ideology. Besides this, the media provide it with the hegemonic power to achieve social mobilizations to protect its dominant interests, especially through various political programs. Thus, the dominant class can create and continually apply an ideological strategy of recreating and readapting the dominant culture. This explains its success in overcoming the periodic crises generated by its principle of inequality and its innate tendency toward irrational development.

These characteristics of the mass media oblige the current ruling class and its fractions to utilize and control them. It is only through their ownership and financing of the media that the dominant class can control the cultural direction of society. Not to do this would jeopardize their own existence by threatening continued social consensus.

The Capacity for Social Mobilization and Consensus Building. Another characteristic that helps to make the mass media the principal means of cultural struggle in modern society is their ability to create collective consensus and consequently to mobilize society. It is true that the ISA of education has certain advantages over the media in creating an ideological awareness in students: the dynamic persuasiveness in the teacher/student relationship and the learning model of repetition and evaluation of the dominant value system. Yet education is less flexible, and the media's power of socialization and mobilization is so broad and can be launched so rapidly that they hold a unique place in the global complex of communication and information.

The ideological effect of the mass media is not necessarily more complete and effective than that of the school; nor are the media all-powerful or automatically effective. Yet the media create a collective sense of reality and history that reinforces the main social consensus. Consequently, it is from the apparatus of the mass media that modern civil society takes its basic direction.

The social initiative of the media is carried out in two fundamental ways: (1) creating the economic demand for the reproduction of the national capitalist production through the consumption of goods, which maintains the momentum for the generation of capital; and (2) creating the political/cultural demand for the survival of capitalism by creating the consensus that turns the subjective order of consciousness to the current task of accumulation of capital. The persuasive ability of the media have made them the principal means of socialization and consensus building of contemporary capitalism.

The Early Socialization of Consciousness.   A fourth characteristic that distinguishes the mass media from other cultural mechanisms is their increasing role in the multi-socialization of children from their earliest years. This aspect of the mass media has complemented socialization by the family since early in the twentieth century and predates the impact of the school. Advanced technology has strengthened the tie between the social and ideological processes of socialization.

Until the end of the nineteenth century, children were socialized through two primary networks: the family and the school. Cultural instruction by the family is limited to a rather narrow range of topics, unconnected with the interests and objectives of those groups who transform the social and economic structures of society. When children enter the network of socialization composed of the social relations of schooling, their cultural arena broadens to include those interests. Because in capitalist societies the apparatus of schooling is generally under the control of the ruling class, education means that students will identify with the interests of that class.

At the end of the nineteenth century and the beginning of the twentieth, children began to undergo a new process of socialization that emerged from the first mass media: film (1895), radio (1920), and television (1936). Depending on their social class, children generally began this process somewhere between the ideological phase of early family life and that of school, and media socialization continued for the rest of their lives. From their earliest years they incorporated an innovative and extensive cultural panorama that linked them with the heterogeneous interests at the heart of the superstructure of society. In this dependent kind of socialization, people's consciousness is linked through the mass media to the varied interests—economic, political, and cultural—of the distinct class fractions of financiers, merchants, bureaucrats, industrialists, farmers, locals, and foreigners who constitute the spectrum of this dominant social formation. Thus, in capitalist society, from the very earliest years to maturity, people's consciousness is shaped by the mass media according to the needs of national and transnational capital.

Participation in Ruling-Class Goals.   The mass media permit broad participation in ruling-class projects and goals. Other institutions of hegemony—church, school, labor unions, family, and so on—usually express the interests of the particular class fractions that sustain them. The mass media express internal ruling-class disagreements to a greater degree than do other ISAs.

In a dependent capitalist society, such as those of Latin America, the bourgeoisie, whether from commerce, industry, finance, or the bureaucracy, national or foreign, advance their ability to participate in the superstructure through the use of the mass media. The reason for this is that once the material infrastructure is installed (e.g., transmitters, a captive audience, increased signal coverage), all that is required for these class fractions to transmit and promote their dominant ideology on a massive scale is access to media time and space so that they can broadcast and impose their own class interests as general needs and priorities of society as a whole.

This openness to all the interests of the ruling classes is not as easily found in other ISAs. All of these hegemonic apparatuses reflect a variety of interests, but their responses to these interests vary according to their development over time. Thus, each apparatus—the school, the family, the church, the political system, and so on—responds more readily to the class that historically created it and in some fashion reduces or limits the participation of other class fractions. But this is less true of the mass media, because, given the current structure of their cultural hegemony, their very high operating expenses (especially those of the electronic media) demand the economic and, consequently, the political and cultural participation of all the dominant class fractions, both national and foreign, to support their functioning.

This openness of the mass media to all dominant class fractions involves the participation of the ruling class, both foreign and national, in the construction and readaptation of the apparatus of legitimation to serve them in maintaining and reproducing the distinct types of capital that support the social structure. As a consequence, in carrying out their function, the mass media reflect the power relations among the diverse fractions of the ruling class who operate at the heart of capitalist society. The mass media are dependent upon the fractions of the dominant class and thus have been raised to the highest levels of ISAs in the current evolution of capitalism.

The Inability to Serve Working-Class Interests. The mass media in a hegemonic capitalist society are almost totally closed to the interests of the working class. The high cost of access means that workers have little real possibility of influencing the production, transmission, or cultural impact of these media and even less of disseminating messages in the working-class interest.

The workers' principal influence in the direction of the mass media comes from the organized pressure of those who work within these institutions and have the right to unionize and to strike. In response to this possibility, however, the management of this cultural superstructure keeps the work force highly propagandized and controlled through reformist actions and slick public relations (that is, a subtle manipulation of the image of capitalist enterprise). In this way the mass media are kept firmly in the hands of the ruling sector. The mass media, therefore, transcend their role as mere technical means of social relations and become the major cultural links for all people in the transformation of society. Mass communication constitutes the principal factor of the cultural superstructure by which world capitalism daily extends its social reach.

The Reproduction of the Labor Force

A third function of mass media has until recently not been mentioned by Marxists or critical communication researchers. Although it still has very little structure, it is daily gaining a more organic place in capitalist reproduction and the cohesion of society. This is the mass media's role in the training and reproduction of a qualified labor force. Marxist tradition views the school as the unique means to reproduce qualified workers. In fact, since the 1950s in the central capitalist countries and since the 1960s in the periphery, the information system for the masses is being affected by the global phenomenon of mass communication.

The twentieth-century school has had to modernize in response to two challenges: the new exigencies of capital accumulation in its modern phase of concentrated value, and the political-cultural crises periodically provoked by the inequality of capitalist society. Among the school's more relevant efforts has been the use of mass media as its principal technical extension. Through the media the capitalist school system has been able to amplify its basic functions of socialization in the dominant ideology and the preparation of the labor force.

This move demonstrates that the ISA of education, despite its traditional inertia, has not abandoned group instruction in ideology. The mass media used for the reproduction of a qualified labor force are the same media whose special properties we have just reviewed: their broad scope of ideological activity, capacity for rapid legitimation, power for mobilization and consensus building, multi-socialization of the young, and openness to ruling-class, but not working-class, interests.

The ruling-class intellectuals charged with guarding the smooth running of civil society have decided that the mass media and especially television can help solve a set of educational problems: the demand for higher education qualifications created by advances in the productive forces; the inadequate preparation of teachers through the traditional education system; the inability of schools to accommodate the growing number of students as a result of rapid population growth; and the periodic need to teach a new ideology more adapted to distinct social circumstances.

Among the many educational media projects implemented, the experiences of the United States and the peripheral capitalist states of Mexico, Brazil, Argentina, Peru, Chile, Ecuador, Honduras, the Dominican Republic, Colombia, and India are noteworthy. In each of these cases the media were used in different ways to extend the school into the area of mass information.

In summary, the historical circumstances of advanced capitalism have led to the educational use of the mass media, and in the future it will use these same technologies, along with the school, to reproduce a qualified labor force. The potential for further extensions of the mass media into education is constantly increasing as a result of the rapid development of the electronics, computer, and space industries.

The use of the mass media in the formation and reproduction of the labor force makes two vital contributions to capitalist development. First, it converts mass media technologies into indispensable tools for the reproduction of capitalist production, and, second, it reinforces the dominant role that they already play as ideological apparatuses of the capitalist state.

Some Tentative Conclusions

From this analysis of the triple function of the cultural apparatus of the mass media in the production and reproduction of capitalism, we may draw certain conclusions.

First, the triple structural role of the mass media strengthens the capitalist bloc in two basic ways. The economic-cultural integration the media promote helps both in the reproduction of the productive process and in the political legitimation of the goal of capital accumulation.

In the first case the mass media's acceleration of the circulation of goods makes the creation, transmission, and impact of mass culture more coherent with their clients' demands for consumption. They place in a single functional and reciprocal relation the production and consumption of material goods and the production and consumption of cultural goods. They operate as intermediaries between the necessities of production and circulation involved in the contemporary productive process and the cultural practices of mass society.

The recent trend toward using the mass media in the reproduction of a qualified labor force has converted them into instruments of a new structural unity: they have linked the need for the preparation of an increasingly specialized labor force with the instructions of mass culture in its "educational role." In these two functions, the economy and the culture are organically joined to serve the needs of the dynamic accumulation of capital.

In the second case, the mass media constantly reinforce the historic capitalist bloc through their broad coverage and the great speed with which they link the political needs of capital with the goal of cultural legitimation. Through them one of the principal trends in contemporary capitalism—public opinion—is promoted. This then becomes one of the main forces in building consensus for the political and economic mobilization to meet the requirements of capitalism. The capitalist state is able, through the media, to impose its most relevant cultural goals on nature, on people's consciousness, and on the political participation that capitalism requires in each historical stage in order to direct and reproduce its hegemony.

The many classes and dominant class fractions are able to pursue their own interests and ideological tasks by taking full advantage of the material and social characteristics of the most technically advanced mass media. Today every dominant sector attempting to maintain its domination and impose its own particular conception of society must have continual access to the apparatus of the mass media.

These media become the principal means of consensus of the contemporary capitalist state and reflect the basic interests that are indispensable for the reproduction of the dominant sector. They operate as the historic beacon of the ruling class, illuminating the needs and priorities of the power bloc for all. Still, at times the media reveal the secondary contradictions within the ruling class itself and the conjunction of forces at the heart of each historical situation that will change the group in power.

Each dominant class in history has had to control the primary apparatus of hegemony in order to remain in power. The feudal mode of production controlled the church and its practical ideology; the mercantile mode of production controlled printing and its diffusion; the premonopoly capitalist mode controlled the school; and contemporary capitalism is now obliged to control the mass media and such information technologies as satellites, computers, and telecommunications. At present the ruling class can get along without controlling the church, the school, and other lesser networks of socialization, but not the mass media. If it did not control the media, society would lose its political direction and the ruling class its power.

The three structural properties of the mass media and the specific nature of their operation have converted the media into the principal ISA used by contemporary capitalism to support its cultural goals for civil society. Thus, they have become more and more an organic function in the mode of monopoly capitalist production and can be changed only with a general change in the social structure.

Second, this discussion confirms that the current debate about the New International Information Order (NIIO) and national communication policies is not a simple disagreement about some cultural institutions that are distinctive because of their modernizing function in current society. Rather we are talking about transforming the three central functions of the mass media in the internal structure of capitalist society. The NIIO would transform the present dominant communication structure in the following ways:

1. In the economic sector of capitalist society, a change in mass culture would affect the circulation of goods and thus the general dynamic of production and the material bases supporting society. The goal of the NIIO is therefore also a new national and international economic order.
2. The distribution of political power would also be affected, bringing about a realignment of areas of influence of national and international power. This again means that the NIIO would be accompanied by a new kind of practical politics.
3. The other obvious effect of the proposed democratization of the mass media and the cultural process in its broadest sense would be on the dominant style of consensus building. Here too the NIIO would replace the prevailing form of consensus manipulation and create a new "moral direction" for society. In a word, what is needed in the debate over the NIIO and new communication policies is a struggle for the creation of a new society.

III. THE EFFECTS OF TRANSNATIONALS ON CULTURE

7 *Noreene Janus*

Transnational Advertising: Some Considerations on the Impact on Peripheral Societies

Advertising is a product of a particular society. [It] is the offspring of capitalism. The study of advertising is therefore the study of an economic system in its symbolic forms. (Inglis, 1972, p. 1)

The transnational expansion of U.S. advertising took place primarily in the 1960s and 1970s. During these decades virtually all large U.S. agencies were forced to set up international networks or be squeezed out of what is today a $14.8 billion world business (*Advertising Age*, April 19, 1982, p. M-7). By the late 1970s these global agencies derived 50 percent or more of their gross income from overseas markets. Furthermore, in most of the large consumer markets of the world they came virtually to control advertising, buying up or driving out local competitors. As a result of the setting up of global advertising networks, one may now speak of a standardized international approach to agency operations and advertising style.

Today this drive to expand is anything but finished. Faced with weak currencies and depressed economies at home, U.S. and European agencies have renewed a desperate search for overseas mergers and purchases. Although "inflation rates soar and currencies plummet, Latin America continues to be the growth spot for advertising" according to *Advertising Age*:

While European networks are mature (gross income in Europe declined 3.7 per cent in 1981) Latin America and Asia-Pacific regions are ripe for expansion. The numbers agree: gross income in Asia increased 11.3 per cent in 1981 while income in Latin America grew a whopping 104 per cent not accounting for inflation. (April 19, 1982, p. M-8)

As a result of such rapid expansion, several Latin American countries are now included among the twenty largest advertising markets of the world. Brazil, Mexico, and Argentina now rank with the United States, Canada, and European countries in total advertising expenditures (*Advertising Age*, April 19, 1982, p. M-16).

Although the global expansion of advertising, as part of the general process of transnationalization of the economy, requires a global analysis integrating core and peripheral countries, it is clear that the impact of marketing varies considerably. The social, cultural, political and economic consequences associated with the growth of transnational advertising are profoundly different in Third World countries and require a separate analysis. The consumption patterns promoted by advertising, if excessive in industrialized countries, are inaccessible in poor countries. Transnational strategies of needlessly differentiated products and costly packaging often make these products exorbitantly expensive. Moreover, they often replace local products that are cheaper, more durable, and more nutritious. Furthermore, the lifestyles promoted in advertising include implicit and explicit agendas for social relations, political action, and cultural change. In peripheral contexts, where extreme economic inequality and political repression often create highly polarized societies, advertising helps to mask these profound contradictions with the message that the free enterprise system is the answer to society's problems.

It is in these same peripheral societies that the above-mentioned issues have begun to be discussed and new holistic analyses have emerged. The principal elements of these analyses include (1) the economic context of the expansion of advertising; (2) the transnationalization of local mass media; (3) the transnationalization of consumption patterns; (4) the social, cultural, and political consequences associated with the growth of advertising; and (5) the limits of the effectiveness of transnational advertising activities, and strategies for resistance and change in the broad range of social sectors in peripheral societies. Each of these points will be briefly discussed below.

The Economic Context

Transnational advertising emerges within specific types of economies. Certain economic functions of advertising provide the logic for the cultural, social, and political shifts associated with its growth. Advertising has fulfilled several important functions in conditions of monopoly capitalism: (1) it allows competition to take place at the level of marketing rather than at the level of production; (2) it helps to accelerate the turnover of capital, yielding higher profits; (3) it artificially stimulates demand, enabling the system as a whole to avoid crises of realization. Within the process of the transnationalization of Third World economies, advertising encourages the consumption of light consumer goods, which tend to be those associated with high levels of advertising and high profit levels, and it raises barriers to entry in many industries, thus obstructing competition and promoting concentration.

The Promotion of Nonessential Products

While apologists for the free enterprise system claim that advertising informs the population about a broad range of goods and services, a closer look reveals that only certain specific types of products are advertised. This narrow range of product types is further restricted in the case of television, where an even more limited number of firms are represented.

In virtually all parts of the nonsocialist world, the most widely advertised products tend to be soaps/detergents, tobacco, over-the-counter drugs and remedies, perfumes, deodorants, toothpaste, prepared foods, beer, and soft drinks. The striking fact is that this range of products varies little from Panama, Trinidad, and South Korea to Austria and the United States. That Third World countries produce and market some of the same product categories as the United States has been interpreted by supporters of the dependent capitalist forms of development as a sign of growth. A U.S. international advertising consultant, discussing Brazil's rapid growth, points out that "sales of cigarettes, automobiles, detergents, and cosmetics could be considered good barometers of a country's economic development" (*Advertising Age*, March 5, 1973, p. 45). In fact, rather than expressing the level of development in a given Third World country, the production, marketing, and sales of these product types express the kind of development model it has chosen.

These products are not randomly selected from the vast range of products produced in capitalist economies. They are, rather, products with many characteristics in common. The industries represented tend to show high profit margins and high advertising-to-sales ratios. These conditions allow them to raise barriers to entry, perpetuating monopoly conditions. Comanor and Wilson (1974) studied forty-one industries in the United States and found that six of these (perfumes, cereals, drugs, soaps, beer, and soft drinks) had advertising-to-sales ratios in excess of 6 percent and an average profit rate of 11.9 percent (65 percent greater than the average return for the other industries studied) and that the forty-one industries, when considered as a whole, presented high barriers to market entry.

In Third World countries the products with high barriers to market entry tend to be those that have experienced the greatest penetration of transnational capital. In Mexico, as may be seen in Table 1, the industrial sectors with the highest average advertising expenditures are, in most cases, those with the greatest relative share of transnational capital.[1] This confirms the

---

1. These figures have been analyzed at two-digit categories, which conceals even higher levels of transnational penetration in some industries. Such variations are apparent when the statistical analysis is carried out at four digits.

Table 1. Industrial sectors with highest advertising costs as percentage of production costs: Mexico, 1970

Industrial Sector	Advertising as % of Production	% of Transnational Capital in Industry
Perfumes, cosmetics, and related products	6.9	70.4
Soft drinks and related beverage concentrates	4.5	30.0
Soaps, detergents, and other cleaning products	4.0	50.6
Pharmaceutical products	3.8	54.2
Tobacco products	3.2	96.8
Shoes, clothing, and knitted articles	1.4	1.3
Electrical and electronic appliances	1.3	50.1
Various chemical products	1.2	41.3
Other manufactured products	1.1	35.1
Publishing, printing, and related industries	1.0	7.8

Source: Prepared by Instituto Latinoamericano de Estudios Transnacionales from industrial census, Mexico, 1971.

relationship between advertising and the transnational expansion of industry.[2] The global expansion of U.S. advertising agencies has helped promote the transnationalization of Third World economies.

Barriers to Entry and Increased Concentration

Advertising is a force toward monopoly. Levels of advertising expenditure are set high so that only the most successful firms can afford to compete. In the United States advertising expenses are associated with increases in concentration in manufacturing, due partially to the influence of television advertising. Such advertising is apparently a powerful force in the promotion of consumer goods and systematically favors large firms that can afford expensive television advertising time. This relationship may also be observed in peripheral countries.

Thus, advertising helps many firms sell products with higher-than-average rates of profit and prevents other, smaller firms—often national ones—from entering the market. The ultimate result is greater transnational penetration of the economy as a whole. This penetration includes not only industry but the advertising and mass media sectors as well (Janus, 1980).

The Transnationalization of the Mass Media

The transnationalization of consumption and other elements of culture reflects the general transnationalization of the economy, which includes not only the

2. For further discussion of the history and strategies of transnational expansion by U.S. advertising agencies see Janus and Roncagliolo (1979).

production of goods but also the advertising industry itself and the mass media. In general, the mass media have become increasingly dependent on advertising revenues, and transnational advertising as a proportion of total advertising has also increased. It is important to note that the transnationalization of media advertising seems to be increasing at a faster rate than the transnationalization of the economy as a whole. The relation of transnational to national advertising is examined by Tunstall (1977). He explains that since 1945 there has been an enormous overseas expansion of American companies manufacturing consumer goods, which has produced a sort of "multiplier effect." In such fields the advertising-to-sales ratios are higher than in industry overall. Therefore,

if incursions of American, mainly consumer goods, companies account for 10 percent of a Latin American country's national product, the advertising which accompanies those products may account for, say, 30 percent of total advertising. Moreover, this will mainly be *national,* not local advertising; American companies might thus account for 50 percent of all advertising in *national* media. (Tunstall, 1977, p. 55; emphasis in original)

There are several ways to measure the relative share of transnational advertising in the major mass media of Latin America. The method used here is the identification of the product advertised. A study of twenty-two large Latin American newspapers found that, excluding the three government-subsidized papers, from 20 to 50 percent of all advertising space was purchased by transnational firms, and that the average paper devoted 31 percent of its advertising space to the products of global firms (Brockman, 1978). Similarly, in a study of twenty-five of the largest women's magazines of six Latin American countries, it was found that an average of 59.7 percent of their advertising space was devoted to transnational products (Santa Cruz and Erazo, 1980). An analysis of broadcast media in Mexico reported that of the 270 commercials transmitted by a popular radio station on an average day in 1971, 84 percent were for transnational products. Similarly, of the 647 commercials transmitted by the five channels operating in Mexico City, 77 percent advertised global products (Bernal, 1974).

More significant than the relative amounts of media time and space used for advertising is the power relationship that advertising encourages. Since as much as 80 percent of newspaper revenues may come from advertising (Schmid, 1978)—100 percent in the case of radio and television—advertising decisions can make or break the medium. A clear example of how dependence on advertising may be used to control media contents comes from South Korea. In 1974 its largest daily newspaper, *Dong-A Ilbo,* which was often critical of President Park's regime, suddenly lost the advertising support of twenty major clients following pressure on advertisers from the secret service (*Advertising Age,* Jan. 27, 1975, p. 67).

In Latin America there have been numerous cases where this power has been used to punish major newspapers. In both Caracas and Lima, advertisers removed their advertising from *El Nacional* and *El Comercio,* respectively, and placed it in competing papers. This type of action is especially effective when relatively few advertisers account for a large percentage of the medium's advertising revenues.

However, the use of advertising to control media contents is not limited to those sporadic cases in which advertisers cancel or threaten to cancel their contracts. Other forms of control may be exercised in more subtle ways and on a daily basis.

Catalan (1981) analyzed a broad sample of Chilean news magazines during the Pinochet regime. He found no correlation between a magazine's circulation and its advertising revenues. The magazines that he classified as oppositional, even those with high-income readers, received lower advertising revenues. Specifically, the banks, financial institutions, and insurance companies, all firms backed by important economic groups in the country, gave most of their support to the progovernment magazines. They advertised in oppositional magazines only when they employed a strategy of advertising in *all* news magazines. Catalan concludes that in Chile advertising is used as a political tool within the context of an authoritarian regime, restricting free competition for advertising revenues and thus restricting real pluralism in the media.

The heavy dependence of Latin American media on advertising leads to several questions. Are there viable forms of alternative financing that would avoid political and economic control by dominant interests? What is the role of the state in upholding the commercialization of the mass media, and how do these commercial media affect national strategies for dealing with transnational interests? How can real political and economic "freedom of the press" be achieved?

But the use of the media as advertising channels has profound implications that transcend the issue of freedom of the press. Commercial media help to commercialize virtually all areas of social life.

The Transnationalization of Consumption Habits

The patterns of production determine, to a significant degree, the patterns of consumption. Since production is increasingly determined by transnational firms, it follows that these same firms must increasingly support consumption habits compatible with their production wherever their products are manufactured and distributed.

This shift of consumption habits and the associated cultural changes brought about by advertising are recognized not only by the critics of advertising but by the advertising industry itself. The industry, however, stresses the educational value of advertising as a mechanism for bringing backward peoples into the modern world. Stridsberg, an expert in international advertising, explains that

in what is called its pioneering phase, advertising's function is not to rob sales from competitors or gull the unsophisticated, but to teach new consumption behavior. . . . It shows people how to use products and gives them confidence to try . . . better foods, new ways of keeping clean, use of tools, a raft of objectives and techniques which the village schoolmasters fail to get across. (Stridsberg, 1974, p. 76)

However, the transnationalization of consumption and the creation of a new consumer culture is not the harmonious process the advertising industry would like it to be. Local cultures do not always passively accept the new customs that are imposed upon them. There is, rather, a perpetual confrontation between transnational expansion and local cultural expansion. Although in many cases this confrontation merely reflects different cultural traditions, it is also true that the new products offered to the local populations are frequently more expensive, of poorer quality, or less nutritious than traditionally used products. Product acceptance often requires that the manufacturing firms make use of the transnational advertising agencies, which have over the past decades developed sophisticated techniques for overcoming customer resistance.

The shift of local consumption habits toward the logic of transnational production, therefore, often requires heavy investment in advertising.[3] Many transnational firms clearly recognize that production and distribution in foreign markets may be difficult to achieve. *Business International* describes one transnational firm's strategy for marketing its product in Latin America:

Because of the nature of the market in Latin America, international companies have found that production and sales of some items require special effort on both the consumer and supplier ends of the business. One such firm is Gerber Products Company, which this year began making baby food in Venezuela. Gerber has had to work at getting consumer acceptance for the product. . . . In Latin America, using processed baby food represents a major cultural change from the practice of preparing such food at home. Moreover, food prepared at home is usually more economical. To gain consumer converts, Gerber promotes its products as a service to parents. (*Business International,* 1972, pp. 284–85)

Similarly, Willatt admits that customer resistance to the product served as the principal element guiding Nestlé's long-range strategy for selling instant coffee in Latin America.

---

3. The sale of many products depends to such a great extent on advertising that advertising expenses may exceed production costs. Bernal (1974) found this to be the case, for example, in the Mexican tobacco industry.

In Brazil and other coffee producing countries of Latin America, a major function of marketing is to overcome local prejudice against instant coffee—to counteract the theory that instant is an inferior substitute for the ground variety which plays such an important part in the national economy. . . . This involves a three-stage strategy in any new market. The first stage to establish is to sell instant coffee as a convenience item saving time and trouble; the next stage is to establish it as "real coffee." The third and final stage is to convince the consumer that it is comparable in every way to ground coffee. (Willatt, 1970, p. 31)

Perhaps the most striking attempt to reorient consumption habits took place in postwar Japan. Until the late 1960s it was commonly accepted among U.S. manufacturers and their advertising agencies that Japan was an exceptionally difficult market for foreign firms to penetrate, and especially for manufacturers of processed food products. Pepsi Cola executives encountered every possible obstacle in their attempts to break into the Japanese market, and only by tremendous perseverence over twenty years have they been able to increase their sales substantially (Link, 1969). Similarly, both General Mills and General Foods complained that "changing eating habits in Japan isn't easy (Ward, 1978). Kellogg's, the U.S. manufacturer of breakfast cereals, found getting the Japanese to abandon their traditional breakfast of rice, fish, and seaweed a major cultural effort.

Nevertheless, by the end of the 1970s things had changed. After twenty years of constant struggle, the transnationals have succeeded in changing Japan's consumption habits. In a study carried out by the Japanese Ministry of Agriculture and Forestry, it was shown that more than 50 percent of the country's teenagers now prefer Western food. Rice consumption per capita has declined, and the "Japanese are now willing to forego the freshness they have always relished for the convenience of frozen and fast foods." Furthermore, "the Japanese seem to be developing a taste for red meat" and "bread is increasingly taking the place of rice on restaurant menus" (Ward, 1978).

The best-known example of the use of advertising to create homogeneous markets for the products of transnational corporations is that of infant formulas. Abbott Laboratories, American Home Products, Bristol Myers, and Nestlé each market an infant formula among the rural and urban poor of developing countries. Although the incorrect use of such products has been shown to cause serious health problems among infants, the advertising "suggests that it produces healthier babies. The newspaper advertisements frequently show a well-dressed woman in front of a pleasant, clean house, bottle-feeding a content plump baby" (Greiner, 1975).

The role of the mass media in achieving these cultural changes is of fundamental importance. When McDonald's fast-food chain expanded to Europe, it accompanied the opening of new stores with heavy media campaigns. This was because "Europeans often find it difficult to accept 'fast foods' [and we

use] TV, radio, . . . and cinema in Germany to show them that fast food is
fun" (Mussey, 1977, p. E-1).

Social, Political, and Cultural Changes

The shift of global consumption patterns according to the logic of transnational production is part of a larger process of cultural change. Product consumption is the material basis for the promotion of a standardized global
culture. As Cathelat remarked, "Advertising creates not only commercial
products but also *civilization*" (1976, p. 231). The study of these cultural
changes and the role played by advertising is basic to future work on the subject of advertising in peripheral contexts.

Historically, each society has been associated with a prototypical human
being consistent with the values and norms of that society. The characteristics
of this type of human being are those that have become so diffused that they
form part of the common sense of daily life within that society. The prototypical human being in the stage of monopoly capitalism is the consumer.
Consumption is the critical human link that allows demand to keep pace with
production. In addition to their role as producers of goods and services, workers must be transformed into active consumers. The mass media and advertising are part of the general socialization process used to create consumers.

The evolution of advertising style and contents reflects its increasing role in
the creation of consumer culture. Cathelat has traced the development of advertising from early informative messages to mechanistic conditioning and reinforcement of behavior and, later, to psychologically "suggestive" advertising. Research on individual attitudes and psychological reactions based on
symbolic disequilibrium evolved into a later form of advertising that is the
dominant form today: *projective advertising*. This form seeks to inscribe the
commercial word within the dominant social discourse, which includes culture, values, and lifestyles (Cathelat, 1976, pp. 92–114).

Assumptions about the consumer vary within the different phases of advertising's development. Consumer decisions are assumed in the first phase of advertising to be rational, whereas in the phases that follow they are assumed to
be irrational. The fourth form, projective advertising, is of special interest
because it represents a sharp change from earlier forms. Whereas the three
earlier types of advertising address the consumer as if consumption decisions
were endogenous or independent of the social environment, projective advertising assumes that the individual is a social subject and that consumption is a
social act. This form of advertising seeks to affect group-held attitudes and
social norms as well as individual interests. The target is the group dynamic
that governs the social collective and that maintains an equilibrium between
the individual and social pressures. This type of advertising is especially

suited for the promotion of lifestyles. It attaches social codes, modes of thought, and self-images to the product. Moreover, it reflects a culture based not on a fixed model of human nature but rather on the relationship between individuals and their society at one specific point in history.

The lifestyle that is promoted globally by transnational advertising is specific to U.S. society at a particular stage of its development: the postwar era of unlimited growth. For the "Global Shopping Center" to become reality it is necessary to create the "World Consumer" (Barnett and Muller, 1974). The dissemination of a lifestyle specific to advanced capitalism in the United States is significant because it occurred at the precise historical moment that it became possible to propose a "lifestyle" for Third World consumers that was unconnected to concrete economic realities. It was also a period when consumer psychology had provided the necessary tools for overcoming customer resistance and global communication had provided access to all but the most remote areas. An "international" lifestyle was possible only when these preconditions had been met.

An important part of the drive to create a globalized lifestyle is the global advertising campaign, which is a product of the interaction between developments in the three above-mentioned areas: the international expansion of Madison Avenue advertising agencies, the growth of global communication systems, and advances in consumer psychology. The "global advertising campaign" involves the creation in one country of a common theme or message that is applied in all countries where a particular product is made or distributed. It is generally produced by the agency office closest to the firm's international headquarters. It assures the transnational advertiser of increased efficiency, quality control, a uniform company image in all markets, and a substantial reduction in agency fees. The success of these global messages requires the use of images and actions with international significance. Advertising executives stress the existence of certain universal consumer characteristics. Arthur C. Fatt, when head of a large agency, claimed that despite obvious language and cultural differences, people of the world have the same basic wants and needs—that "people everywhere from Argentina to Zanzibar want a better way of life for themselves and that the desire to be beautiful, to be free of pain, to be healthy, etc. is universal" (Ryans, 1969).

Similarly, Helena Rubinstein uses a theme developed in the United States for its Latin American markets on the grounds that "women are the same the world over; there's not a woman alive who doesn't wish to look more beautiful" (*Advertising Age*, Jan. 13, 1969, p. 3). Revlon, Campbell, Marlboro, Union Carbide, and Coca Cola are among the transnational firms that have successfully used global campaigns. The uniform product image that these firms disseminate often exploits the appeal of "the American Way of Life." Kellogg's, for example, in promoting breakfast cereals in Japan, advertised them as "The American Breakfast"; its cereal boxes featured a picture of young, American-looking adults (Ward, 1978).

What is being promoted here is consumer ideology as part of the "collective consciousness"—the ideas, beliefs, feelings, and sentiments common to the collective "organism" (Cathelat, 1976). Gramsci treated the subject of collective consciousness at length, including its relationship to political action. He emphasized that the collective consciousness is an unordered, inconsistent, and even contradictory collection of thoughts and feelings. He also pointed out that the collective consciousness or "common sense" varies in different social classes and contexts. Each social class has its own world view. The various world views are, however, all oriented and directed by that society's dominant ideology. The dominant ideology of our times is consumerism, and its particular strength may derive from the fact that it helps to order the unordered elements of the collective consciousness.

The study of advertising as the creation of collective consciousness leads to the discussion of advertising as a language.

Advertising as the Most Dynamic Language

Advertising is not just a heterogeneous, randomized collection of words and images but rather a homogeneous system of mass communication based on a specific linguistic and iconic code. And because commercial advertising language is also used to describe other types of communication, it has been termed a "supralanguage" (Cathelat, 1976, p. 239). As a supralanguage it has gradually come to replace other forms of traditional communication, such as that found in political or religious systems. The power of advertising lies in its ability to influence other forms of communication and in its broad range of uses. The commercial language has become the dominant language of daily life.

Since advertising dominates modern everyday language, it is intimately linked to consciousness. The link between language and the very existence of humanity is its role in the development of thought and consciousness. Coward and Ellis explain: "Language and thought are inextricable: thought conceptualizes through language and it is not a matter of one being the instrument of the other but of one engendering the other; language makes thought possible; thought makes language possible" (1977, p. 79).

Language, however, is not just or even primarily words. It includes the experiences that form part of the individual's preconscious level and that provoke the use of language. Communication does not begin with symbols and images but rather with the evolution of a culture and the creation of meanings that each social subject within a society attaches to these symbols and images. Advertising works to alter a product's associations for consumers rather than the product itself. These associations take place prior to the use of language.

As Cathelat explains: "The transmission of the advertising message implies an authentic communication prior to the level of consciousness and language. And the quality of this preconscious communication depends on how much the advertising claim is consistent with the forms of interaction between the social group and the social subject" (1976, p. 220).

The social role of advertising, as a specific language, is the transmission of symbols and images with certain specific connotations that are formed prior to consciousness. The area of interest, then, is not only the use of these symbols and images but also the context into which commercial language is inserted. The "circulation" of advertising claims among persons or groups is less important than the whole process by which these groups attach meaning to the symbols used. The influence between language and culture is mutual: language promotes culture, and the culture provides the language. Similarly, advertising creates a consumer culture, but, at the same time, the cultural environment limits the advertiser's use of language.

However, advertising's role in the production of culture is not mechanical nor predictable. There is no assumed correspondence between the advertiser's use of certain symbols and images and the social impact of this communication. Similarly, the rate of social change from traditional societies toward consumer societies is not controllable even by the transnational firms. The reception of the commercial message is subject to many variables that are difficult to measure either individually or socially. The contradictions within any social organization and individual prohibit the advertiser's control over the impact of advertising.

Furthermore, the symbols and images communicated are subject to reinterpretation or "resemantization" by the receiver. That is, the audience may create a meaning different from that intended by the creator. Resemantization takes place at the preconscious level prior to language use.

Advertising and Social Control

Industrialization transforms both material and social relations. The mass production of goods must be accompanied by the creation of an appropriate mass consciousness: a "consumer consciousness." Workers must be transformed into consumers, replacing the struggle for economic and political participation with the struggle to participate in real or imagined lifestyles (Ewen, 1976, p. 19).

Advertising is a vital link between material and social relations, creating new forms of consciousness and new social relations by neutralizing potential areas of social protest. Advertising is a form of social control. It is a potent force counteracting currents of social change and promoting uncritical acceptance of the values of consumer society.

Advertising has become an important extension of the bourgeoisie of core countries in their political objectives in peripheral countries (Roncagliolo, 1979, p. 22). It permits a greater degree of class domination insofar as it helps to create consensus around a political and economic project. Toward this end, the captains of industry have become captains of consciousness: "Beyond standing at the helm of the industrial machines, businessmen understood the social nature of their hegemony. They looked to move beyond their nineteenth century characterization as captains of industry toward a position in which they could control the entire social realm. They aspired to become "captains of consciousness" (Ewen, 1976, p. 197). The growth of advertising today must be studied within the context of social struggles, particularly the struggle between classes. In addition to providing market information, advertising promotes an ideology that masks the work process by attenuating the class bases of dissatisfaction. It does this by showing the leisurely lifestyle of the dominant social class while avoiding the conflicts or contradictions associated with material relations. Advertising was used to defuse workers' movements in the United States during the 1920s and 1930s. This link between advertising and social control is well described by Ewen. During the 1920s

it was seen as necessary to meet the challenge not merely with direct force, but also with a change in the social and cultural dimensions of industrial life. Commensurate with the widespread demand for industrial democracy within working class communities, corporate strategies addressed the need to undermine the subversive potential that these communities held. . . . In the 1920s, with the development of consumerism, advertising and the growing utilization of mass communications on the national level, the American corporate order began to shape and publicize an affirmative social order for itself. . . . The corporate ideology of the twenties contended that the consumer society would meet and neutralize the political opposition to capitalism. (1976, p. 198)

The use of a specific language is crucial to the role of advertising as social control. This is especially clear in Third World contexts, where levels of social and political consensus are often low and conflicts are common. One example of the use of advertising language for social control comes from the Pepsi campaign used in Brazil. When transferred from the original U.S. context to Brazil, the theme "Pepsi Generation" was changed to "Pepsi Revolution." The creators of this campaign thought that the word "revolution," which has specific connotations in the Brazilian context, would be associated with a desire for change, the expression of which has been repressed since 1964. Since the object of the campaign was to promote a shift away from Coca Cola and other soft drinks toward Pepsi, and the major consumers of soft drinks are young people, the use of the word "revolution" was aimed at promoting a change in consumption as a substitute for a change in society. During the 1970s advertising in the Third World has employed terms generally associated with social and political change, such as "democracy," "national loyalty," "liberation," and "personal freedom," to stimulate the consumption of light consumer goods. The use of terms that shift the meaning of social change toward the sphere of consumption is based on the use of language and the relationship of language to consciousness discussed above.

Another important way in which advertising undermines social protest is analyzed by Victoroff (1978). He suggests that the real strength of advertising may only be explained in the context of a society that is in the process of social disintegration with regard to traditional religious and political values (1978, p. 41). Advertising fills this void by creating social consensus around a strong ideology that promotes social integration. This function of advertising is especially important in view of the present loss of legitimacy affecting the global capitalist political project and the efforts of various public and private institutions to recreate this legitimacy. Thus, the growth of advertising must be analyzed in the context of the so-called "crisis of democracy."

The use of advertising as a powerful "supralanguage" raises several important questions. How does advertising operate to create consciousness? To what extent has commercial language replaced or influenced traditional languages? How do illiterates, defined in the traditional sense, "read" advertising and become "literate" in the codes used by commercial language? What is the "educational" role of advertising in peripheral contexts? In those sectors of the population with no access to formal schooling, what is the impact of advertising as mass communication? Does advertising help to bring certain precapitalist formations into the modern capitalist system by providing new forms of consciousness in addition to promoting the exchange of material goods? To what extent does access to advertising language substitute for access to the goods and lifestyles proposed? And to what extent can the proposed "democracy of consumption" replace demands for economic and political democracy in the periphery?

Limits to the Impact of Advertising

Many analyses of advertising start from the assumption that with the appropriate strategies and techniques, advertising can sell anything to anyone. This assumed omnipotence has serious implications for peripheral societies struggling to achieve cultural sovereignty and autonomous democratic development.

What are the contradictions of advertising? In the attempt to reach broad sectors with high purchasing power, advertising also reaches large numbers of poor people who cannot buy the lifestyles proposed. The means of ideological "distribution" are still very inaccurate. Do the marginalized poor resent being shown a world they are not part of? Does the resentment lead to an awareness of the type of economic system that requires advertising? Does advertising affect all levels of consciousness in the same way? Or are consumption patterns independent of political action?

What elements of daily life are resistant to advertising that promotes certain lifestyles? Does political practice serve to mitigate the effects of advertising? Does the development of political consciousness in one area of daily life lead to awareness in other areas? Will consciousness of the unequal class access to consumption bring about an understanding of capitalist development? What are the effects of transnational advertising on the process of creating political consciousness, and what are the areas of potential mass awareness of this issue as part of a larger phenomenon of social change in nondemocratic regimes? And, finally, what types of resistance—whether incipient and unorganized or deliberate and planned—are emerging from peripheral contexts? These are the major questions to be answered in future studies on advertising.

References

Barnett, R., and R. Muller (1974). *Global Reach*. New York: Simon and Schuster.

Bernal, V. M. (1974). *Anatomía de la Publicidad en Mexico*. Mexico City: Nuestro Tiempo.

Brockmann, M. (1978). "La Publicidad y la Prensa: Análisis Cuantitativo de una Semana en los Diarios Latinoamericanos." Mexico City: Instituto Latinoamericano de Estudios Transnacionales.

Catalan, C. (1981). "El Mercado de Revistas de Actualidad y la Inversión Publicitaria: El Caso de Chile." Paper presented to the seminar on "Economía y Comunicaciones en America Latina," sponsored by the Instituto Latinoamericano de Estudios Transnacionales, Santiago, December.

Cathelat, B. (1976). *Publicité et Societé*. Paris: Payot.

Comanor, W., and T. Wilson (1974). *Advertising and Market Power*. Cambridge: Harvard University Press.

Coward, R., and J. Ellis (1977). *Language and Materialism*. London: Routledge and Kegan Paul.

Ewen, S. (1976). *Captains of Consciousness*. New York: McGraw-Hill.

Greiner, E. (1975). "The Promotion of Bottle Feeding by Multinational Corporations: How Advertising and the Health Professions Have Contributed." Cornell International Monography Series, no. 2. Ithaca: Cornell University.

Inglis, F. (1972). *The Imagery of Power: A Critique of Advertising*. London: Heinemann.

Janus, N. (1980). "The Making of the Global Consumer: Transnational Advertising and the Mass Media in Latin America." Ph.D. dissertation, Stanford University.

Janus, N., and R. Roncagliolo (1979). "Advertising, Mass Media, and Dependency." *Development Dialogue*, 1.

Link, L. J. (1969). "U.S. Food Companies Find Eating Habits in Japan Not Easy to Change." *Advertising Age*, July 28.

Mussey, B. (1977). "McDonald's Brings Hamburgers (with Beer) to Hamburg." *Advertising Age*, May 23.

Roncagliolo, R. (1979). *Publicidad y Cultura en la Era Transnacional.* Mexico City: Instituto Latinoamericano de Estudios Transnacionales.

Ryans, J. (1969). "Is It Too Soon to Put a Tiger in Every Tank?" *Columbia Journal of World Business,* March–April.

Santa Cruz, A., and V. Erazo (1980). *Compropolitan: El Orden Transnacional y Su Modelo Feminino.* Mexico City: Instituto Latinoamericano de Estudios Transnacionales.

Schmid, A. (1978). "The North American Penetration of the Latin American Knowledge Sector—Some Aspects of Communication and Information Dependence." Paper presented at the Seventh International Peace Research Association Meeting, Oaxtepec, Mexico.

Stridsberg, A. (1974). "Can Advertising Benefit Developing Countries?" *Business and Society Review,* 11, Autumn.

Tunstall, J. (1977). *The Media Are American: Anglo-American Media in the World.* New York: Columbia University Press.

Victoroff, D. (1978). *La Publicité e l'Image.* Paris: Denoel/Gonthier.

Ward, B. (1978). *Advertising Age,* supplement on marketing in Japan.

Willatt, J. (1970). "How Nestlé Adapts Products to Its Markets." *Business Abroad,* June.

8 Alberto Montoya Martín del Campo and
María Antonieta Rebeil Corella

Commercial Television as an Educational and Political Institution: A Case Study of Its Impact on the Students of Telesecundaria

Telesecundaria (TS) is Mexico's most important experiment in the use of the mass media for educational purposes. TS was started under the Díaz Ordaz regime in 1968, and since then it has been an important means of providing secondary education to youths throughout the country and especially in rural areas. The TS system has undergone a significant expansion since its inception, having in 1982 an enrollment of approximately 130,000 students. TS is a type of formal schooling that utilizes television as a basic component of the teaching-learning process. The curriculum followed by TS is the same one approved by the Ministry of Education for general secondary education. The students in the classrooms receive televised lessons (thirty per week, six every day, seventeen minutes each), followed by activities coordinated by classroom teachers and supported by written texts that provide additional information. The teachers remain with the same group of students for all the subjects taught, whereas in general secondary schools teachers are specialists in the various disciplines. This disadvantage is compensated for by the use of television.

In the coming years, Mexico's national system of telecommunications will be using its own satellite. This technological change will make secondary education possible throughout the nation, including its most remote areas. At the same time, Mexico's Ministry of Education foresees an increasing demand

143

for secondary education. In the next decade 20,000 schools will be needed, of which 9,000 are now in existence.

The expansion of TS as well as its increasing importance as a far-reaching low-cost system led the Consejo Nacional Técnico de la Educación, the main advisory organization of the Ministry of Education, to carry out an evaluation of it. The general objectives of the investigation were to contribute to a better understanding of TS's operational characteristics in the context of other types of secondary education and the educational role of commercial television, and to point out possibilities for its qualitative improvement (Montoya M. del C. and Rebeil Corella, 1981b; for a summary of results see *Educación*, 1981).

A series of eight interrelated studies were carried out in order to produce a more comprehensive view of the system. Different aspects of TS were analyzed, including the teaching-learning process, its unitary costs, the content and pedagogical structure of the televised programs, its historical evolution, its relationship to educational demand and the supply of other types of secondary instruction, and its relationship to the nation's use of the media for educational, as opposed to commercial, purposes. Another study analyzed the educational and political impact of *commercial* television on TS students (Montoya M. del C. and Rebeil Corrella, 1981a). In this paper we discuss the main theoretical and methodological points of this last study, as well as the results of the general survey.

Why was a study of the impact of commercial television deemed necessary? For one thing, TS students constitute a social group whose exposure to television is twofold: they receive their formal school courses through television, and they watch other types of television programs in their spare time. They are thus incorporated into both the public-formal and the private-informal educational systems. Moreover, to take a more social approach to the issue, the use of the communications satellite will expand not only TS and cultural television, but commercial television as well. This means that Televisa (Mexico's private television monopoly), whose role is that of an enterprise producer and transmitter of messages, will also have access to complete communication coverage of the nation.

For over thirty years, Televisa has been transmitting material whose content was designed with commercial criteria in mind. These messages have not only "entertained," "informed," and "persuaded" the viewers, but have gone beyond these apparently neutral activities. Television conveys conceptions of the world that influence people's understanding of, as well as their feelings about, their social environment. In other words, commercial television is carrying out (and is about to expand) an educational and a political activity among its audiences. The purpose of this paper is to discuss some of the theoretical propositions behind this statement and to provide some empirical evidence obtained from a survey of TS students. It is most probable that similar results could be obtained from other Mexican adolescents with the same socioeconomic background as TS youths.

Theoretical Propositions

A review of the literature from the functionalist perspective on the effects of mass media leads to the following reflections: (1) there is a need for a critical and comprehensive view of the issue, given the functionalists' lack of analysis of the political determinants of cultural institutions, and (2) a more comprehensive view of the phenomenon should establish the structural context of the economic and power relationships in which individuals are found, and the social contradictions that affect their lives. Individuality is developed in the context of social relationships.

A truly scientific analysis can be built upon these basic conceptions. This will lead to an inquiry into the social origins of the activities carried out by the mass media of information, the classist education they transmit, and the biases in the messages they produce.

Redefining the Source of Information

Empiricist conceptions of information sources remain at a descriptive level and therefore fail to provide true explanations of the effects of television. The real sources of information are never discussed, and the great majority of empiricist studies are devoted to relating the content of television programs to specific behaviors (Montoya M. del C. and Rebeil Corella, 1981a).

From a more structural perspective, sources of information can be characterized on three categorical levels: (1) the informational schemes developed by television programming; (2) the nature of television as a cultural and political institution; and (3) the class practices and structural agent behind the cultural project of commercial television.

At the first, most immediate level are the *informational schemes,* which are formed by the different kinds of programming developed by television (news, musicals, westerns, advertising, sports, comedy, etc.). These messages have peculiar characteristics in terms of content and syntax, formats and styles. These cultural categories are in turn acquired by the receivers through an informal process of education, shaping their world view, values, interests, tastes, and motivations.

At a second, more abstract level, the source is *commercial* television as an institution in itself. In Latin America, and in Mexico in particular, television developed as a private enterprise following the U.S. model (Pasquali, 1975). This fact in itself determines the role television plays in society and the interests it serves because it defines its relationships with particular social classes and the cultural tasks to which it is directed. However, communication enterprises have evolved into more specialized types: those which are mainly involved in the production of messages, and those which mostly transmit readymade programming. Much of Mexico's commercial television is of this second type, leaving the production of programs and advertising to other enterprises, many of which are transnational corporations.

The third, most abstract level of analysis examines the social classes that shape, finance, support, and direct the activities of this cultural institution. Social classes carry out their ideological work through intermediate agents, such as television. Therefore, television has a double dimension; on the one hand it is an agent of social class interests, and on the other it is a particular kind of cultural institution. This political-cultural character permeates all the activities of commercial television.

Power Relationships and the Information Source

Power relationships in societies with high and structural levels of inequality are maintained through physical and symbolic violence and through the creation of acquiescence, even consent, by the subaltern social classes to a exploitative social order (Gramsci, 1977, p. 204).

Television plays a major role in the day-to-day recreation of hegemony through its various forms of messages. It educates the dominated classes by communicating beliefs, understandings of social reality, and values. These ideas and feelings about the world and life create acquiescence on the part of the oppressed to the structural system of domination. The passive approval and consensual participation of the dominated is a prerequisite to the smooth operation of a classist way of life.

Television as an Educational Apparatus

It has been over sixty years since Mexico's Ministry of Public Education was established. It has been over thirty years since what could be called the Ministry of *Private* Education was initiated with the foundation of commercial television. The then-new communication technology fostered the creation of an educational institution *sui generis*.

Formal education is carried out in classrooms according to a specific program and curriculum, and employs standard materials, evaluation mechanisms, and means of certification, all organized to meet specific objectives. Informal education through television, on the other hand, usually takes place in a private environment, the home, in a one-way (noninteractive) information process in which the receiver can not change his or her role. This informal education is nonsystematic, fragmented, and nonprogressive, and there is no official certification for those who receive it on a day-to-day basis over many years. Nevertheless, its cultural impact on society is highly significant.

In 1977 approximately 50 percent of Mexico's households had a television receiver. By the end of the 1980s, this figure will have increased dramatically because of the operation of the satellites. Homes, then, are the perfect class-room for the "electronic teacher" whose influence on today's and yesterday's generations runs parallel to that of formal schooling. Moreover, this electronic school requires a much smaller number of workers than does the formal schooling system. In 1977 a total of 4,215 employees were on the Televisa payroll (Noriega and Leach, 1979, pp. 93–100), while the Ministry of Education, in 1981, had 800,000 employees, 600,000 of whom were teachers. This enormous difference is obviously due to technology. Television, with lower costs and an enormous influence in society, is perhaps more pervasive than schooling in countries with low levels of formal education.

Furthermore, a rather large number of social institutions determine the content of classroom instruction. Even though the formal curriculum reflects the dominant ideology, there is at least a public definition of its goals and a political arena where social contradictions can be expressed. Commercial television in Mexico, on the other hand, is a private enterprise that arbitrarily designs the messages to be transmitted. It exercises a monopolistic position as a sender of messages, responding only to the economic-political interests of the national and transnational corporations that finance it (Montoya M. del C., 1981).

Commercial television has become in Mexico a vehicle for the transmission of North American culture, constantly eroding national identity and local cultures. Televisa classifies audiences as "urban," "national middle class," and "Americanized middle class": peasants and Indians are nonexistent in this scheme. The enterprise's own records show that during 1976–77 40 percent of its programming was produced outside Mexico. Foreign messages particularly dominate channels 5 and 8, whose audiences are primarily children and adolescents. This figure does not take into consideration the bulk of advertising and news supplied by transnational corporations, nor the fact that many "nationally" produced programs are copies of U.S. originals (e.g., "Fiebre del 2," "Increíble," "60 Minutos," "Plaza Sésamo," and "Dallas").

The Individual and Commercial Television

The best way to understand individuals and their opinions is to understand them as being linked to a particular set of social relationships that have an objective existence on their own. Individuals cannot be understood as isolated totalities linked to each other by communication and forming a society in their accumulative aggregation. On the other hand, individuals are not mere reproductions of society. They develop their own activity: learning, knowing, judging, loving, deciding, acting, working, and participating in some way in their society. Thus, a multiplicity of internal and external influences and, therefore, contradictions merge within a person to create a dynamic uniqueness and yet similarities with other human beings.

The issue of television's impact involves simultaneous realities in people's lives: the influence of the communication apparatus, individual activity, plus relationships among people. Individual learning and subjectivity are a product of a person's direct and indirect experiences: that is, those a person lives through and those that are communicated in some way. Individuals should be understood as historically culturized by the social situations that surround them: their workplace, schools, unions, political parties, family, even the new cultural institutions of mass information. In recent decades, however, the greatest part of reality known to individuals has been increasingly provided by the indirect experiences offered by the mass media, as C. Wright Mills noted in *The Power Elite* (cited by Beltrán and Fox, 1980, p. 311).

Television messages are social products themselves. The television spectator does not view "reality" but a reconstruction or interpretation of reality. The media select the issues, codes, and linguistic-semantic categories under which social reality is defined, perceived, and presented to television viewers. Audiovisual language has the peculiarity of creating an illusion of being "before" objective reality. Nevertheless, these messages are concrete and material expressions of ideology and instruments for producing class domination.

The Appearance of Educational Messages

Television programming appears in an enormous variety of forms. A review of various investigations into the contents of television in Mexico shows certain constant themes (Menasse et al., 1977, pp. 213–48). Mexico's imported weekly serials, for instance, whether comedy, police, or adventure programs, continually portray problems and situations pertaining to the North American reality. A day-to-day exposure to such messages might be expected to provoke an inclination toward the American way of life and a desire to live in a similar manner.

Information and news programming in Mexico is also a vehicle for the creation of a cultural and emotional atmosphere conducive to the spread of North American interests. Not only do they cover the political, economic, and social life of the United States in abundant detail, but they represent conflicts in other nations, and conflicts between the United States and the rest of the world, from the point of view of U.S. interests. In recent times Televisa has openly allied itself with the U.S. Department of State and challenged Mexican foreign policy, particularly with regard to Central America. Mexican television audiences learn to see North American interests as their own.

Advertising is another fundamental area of transnational influence. Most of the commercials on Mexican television are produced by transnational corporations. Advertisements demonstrate goods of all kinds, surrounded by luxurious environments and associated with "important" foreign personalities. Materialism and individualism are their main motivational support (Janus and Roncagliolo, 1981). Soap operas are also an important part of the television curriculum. Their messages are perhaps the most Mexican in origin. The main plot is invariably the social mobility of middle-class people. The already rich suffer, as in "Dallas," and the poor either do not exist or eventually find their way to love, power, and money. The characters embody individualistic values that lead them to success (that is, economic success). These programs provide models of behavior and of conflict resolution for their viewers.

Given these theoretical propositions, the specific objectives of the TS study included the following:

1. To assess TS students' opinions about U.S. society, as portrayed on television serials, in comparison with Mexican society
2. To assess TS students' knowledge and understanding of current world events
3. To assess TS students' ability to distinguish real life from soap operas

Methodology

The analysis of mass media effects necessarily involves the researcher in two related fields of study: the psychological and behavioral reactions of individuals (that is, *social* individuals); and those dimensions of reality portrayed by the mass media in structurally determined messages. The point at which these two dimensions of reality converge constitutes a mass media effect.

The indivisibility of these two aspects of reality calls for a two-step methodological procedure. It is necessary both to pick out and make explicit the media content that is hypothetically influencing the individual subjects of the study and to define the psychological dimensions of such effects. In no way do we imply that all changes in individuals are due to the impact of the media. However, we do propose as a general hypothesis that the contents of commercial television are making a definite contribution to the social formation of individuals, in this case the students registered in the TS program.

The Effect Agent

The effect agent—the content of television programming—should be considered from two points of view: the dimensions of social reality that, given their relevance in the lives of individuals, *should be* and *are being* portrayed on television, and the dimensions of social reality that for some reason or other *are not being* reproduced or transmitted through television. The latter category cannot be ignored: the source's selection of messages should not be taken as given or as neutral. Thus, *ignorance* is also considered as an effect of television.

A list of current world issues was created according to the following main criteria: they had to be relevant, well-known social issues of which Mexican adolescents, and Mexicans in general, should have some knowledge and about which they should have some opinion. At the same time, a series of media content investigations were reviewed in order to establish the aspects of social reality that were actually being represented through the mass media, and television in particular (Beltrán and Fox, 1980, pp. 104–5; Herner, 1979, pp. 185–202; Kaplún, 1976). From this procedure the following list of categories emerged:

1. The American way of life
2. Violence
3. Political and economic reality of
   Mexico
   Relations between Mexico and the United States
   Relations between Mexico and Latin America
   Relations between Latin America and the United States
4. Living conditions in Mexico
5. Consumerism

The Effect Level

Psychological processes in individuals are very difficult to assess. A long tradition of research on perception, attention, attitudes, behavior, and so on has produced a body of knowledge on the mechanisms of learning (Bandura, 1977, pp. 22–55; McGuire, 1968, pp. 136–41). The basic intent of this study is to get a closer look at the *results* of the informal learning process provided by an individual's exposure to television.

In this study, an effect of commercial television is defined as the degree to which an individual knows about (or lacks knowledge of), understands (or lacks understanding of), is interested in (or is not at all interested in), and has an opinion on (or does not have an opinion on) some fact, person, or situation of social relevance for his or her own life. This definition of the effects of television considers both knowledge and ignorance as results of the ideological work of television, since this institution has the potential to facilitate both conditions. In this sense, then, an effect can vary depending upon the intensity of a person's exposure to the medium during his or her lifespan.

In order to clarify the psychological levels of effects, five processes were chosen to be researched: (1) knowing (defined as the act of learning about a fact or situation, as well as possessing information about it); (2) understanding (the interpretation that TS students provide about a fact or situation); (3) aspiration (the desire that TS students manifest to be someone else or to possess something other than what they have); (4) identity seeking (the involvement of TS students with some circumstance, person, or way of life to the degree that they experience it (or him/her) as a part of their own life experience); and (5) opinion forming (the value judgment that TS students make about a particular person, fact, or situation).

Table 1. Effect Agents and Effect Levels

Effect Agents	Effect Levels				
	Knowledge	Understanding	Aspiration	Identity Seeking	Opinion Forming
Commercials			Aspiring to be like people portrayed in ads or to possess what is advertised	Identifying with the way of life and values reproduced in ads	Expressing an opinion in favor of owning certain merchandise
News, Information	Knowing or not knowing about economic and political life of Mexico and other countries	Interpreting certain international situations from the U.S. standpoint; misunderstanding Mexican problems			Expressing an opinion in favor of United States in its international relations
Soap Operas	Recognizing the characters of soap operas		Aspiring to individualistic values	Identifying situations and problem resolutions in soap operas as characteristic of real life	Expressing opinions in favor of the forms of conflict resolution featured in soap operas
U.S. Police, Fiction Serials	Knowing about the North American way of life	Interpreting fictional situations on the basis of American way of life: e.g., rationalizing violence	Aspiring to live in America or act according to the American way of life	Identifying with the North American way of life	Expressing opinions in favor of the North American way of life and violence

Selection of Television Programming

Television messages can take a wide variety of forms. The selection of programming for this study was based on the theoretical propositions stated above and on other media research. This study assessed the effect of advertising, soap operas, news and information programs, and police and fiction serials. Table 1 is a summary of the main points discussed above as well as some of the hypothetical propositions that guide the data analysis.

Research Design

The research design of this study was that known as "ex post facto": observations were done *after* the subjects had been affected by what is considered to be the source of influence. In this case commercial television exposure (the independent or classificatory variable) was assessed after TS students had been viewing television for an unknown amount of time and had been the subject of many other social influences. A multiplicity of impacts occurred with no control on the part of the researcher, and any of these might be the source of certain effects that were attributed to television. In view of this possibility, the results of the study were always related to the following variables: (1) amount of daily television exposure; (2) program selectivity; and (3) the socioeconomic background of the students.

Instruments and Sample

Questionnaires consisting mainly of multiple-choice items were created for the study. Items in them were tested several times with different samples and were redesigned accordingly.

A sample of 528 TS students was drawn according to the following procedures:

1. Random sample of six states: Distrito Federal, Guanajuato, Oaxaca, Tabasco, Veracruz, and Puebla
2. Urban/rural-stratified sample of TS schools within the six states (eight schools were selected)
3. Grade-stratified sample of TS students (sixty-six per school; twenty-two in each grade)

Data from 480 students were analyzed (48 answer sheets were canceled for various reasons, including mortality).

Results

Three general hypotheses guided the data analysis:

1. The content transmitted through commercial television contributes to the informal education (social formation) of TS students.
2. The content of commercial television orients TS students toward:
   Approval of the North American way of life
   Acquisition of fragmented and uncritical views of the economic and political life of nations
   Identifying as real the life models represented on television
   Approval of values portrayed in television advertisements
3. Commercial television's impact on TS students is conditioned by their family's income, their parents' education, the basic work activity of the family, their grade in school, their place of residence, the time and type of television exposure, program and channel selectivity, the source's credibility, and other media exposure.

TS Students: A Socioeconomic Profile

Before going further into the evidence on the effects of television on TS students, it is important to describe this group of 480 adolescents. (A comparison of the sample's socioeconomic profile with that of the 1979 census of TS shows a great similarity between the two groups of students; thus, the sample is not atypical of the universe of TS students.) Their ages generally ran from twelve to sixteen, although some were slightly older (TS students as a whole are older than their peers in other forms of secondary education). The majority (53 percent) were male. In most cases the father was either a peasant or a factory worker; the mother was a housewife, a small-scale merchant, or a domestic. Usually both parents were illiterate or had finished only a few years of elementary schooling. Many of the students did not work; those who did were either peasants or domestics. Many of them got no pay for their work (they may have been employed by their own fathers); however, those who were paid received around 1,000 pesos a month ($12.00). Monthly income for 80 percent of the TS students' families was less than 3,500 pesos ($42.00). Sixty percent live in small towns or country villages; 80 percent owned the house they lived in. It was common for two to six people to live in a one- to four-room house. Seventy percent of these families had access to only two or three public services.

Television and Other Media Exposure

The data analysis shows that these adolescents practiced a number of activities after school: work, homework, sports, and television viewing. Sixty-eight percent said that they watched television between one and four hours daily. The mean television exposure was 3.6 hours daily. This was considerably more time than they spent receiving classes through Telesecundaria, since TS programming lasts only two hours a day.

These TS students were continuously exposed to other media as well. For instance, 73 percent of them read magazines daily and almost all of them listened to the radio daily. Newspapers were read by 38 percent of them at least once a week. Movies, however, did not seem to be a favorite pastime: they said that they rarely went to them. They liked Mexican films. As far as radio programming was concerned, 69 percent preferred modern music stations. The magazines that they read the most were *fotonovelas* and those containing adventure stories. In newspapers they preferred the sports section, followed by the international and national news sections.

The television channels they watched most often were channels 2, 5, and 13. Channels 2 (owned by Televisa) and 13 (owned by the state) have the widest range. Channel 5 also belongs to Televisa, and its programming is mainly American. The programs they watched most often were of the comedy type (e.g., "Chavo del 8," "Hogar Dulce Hogar"), followed by musicals (e.g. "Siempre en Domingo"), Mexican films, science fiction serials ("Batman," "Wonder Woman"), and finally sports and soap operas.

It seems clear that these TS students spent a good part of their spare time in front of the television. From the channels they selected, it can be inferred that they watched programs like soap operas and films that are not intended for young audiences. Moreover, a large percentage of them watched channel 5's foreign programming.

TV Commercials and the Students' Aspirations

The evidence shows that although the students wanted whatever was advertised, they did not believe that everyone was able to buy these goods. An increase in hours per day of television exposure did not affect this belief, which was more pronounced among the sons and daughters of urban factory workers than among the sons and daughters of peasants. However, the value reasoning used in some advertisements (e.g., that people who drink a certain kind of brandy are more distinguished than others) was more influential for those students who spent five or more hours a day watching television. Yet those who watched less than five hours a day could clearly distinguish the fancy scenarios (mostly foreign) in advertisements from Mexican reality.

Soap Operas and Students' Perception of Real Life

A considerable amount of media research has been devoted to melodramatic stories, such as those found in *telenovelas* and *fotonovelas*. Descriptions of their contents are fairly consistent. The central plot is a love drama involving a girl, a boy, and his economic success. "Good" characters are always rewarded in the end; "poor" ones generally obtain love, and the "rich" usually increase their possessions and achieve love. Money, an absolute value, a must for happiness, is obtainable through personal sacrifice, education, or a stroke of luck. Women are always subordinated to men, and a woman must be pretty and young in order to be rewarded in the plot. The setting and the plot are generally devoid of community or civic life, and characters live in isolation from their social context.

Individualism and Economic Success. An overwhelming majority of the students affirmed that personal economic success was very important to them. A contingency table was drawn up in which the independent variable is the amount of daily exposure to *telenovelas* and the dependent variable is desire for abundant economic success. The results show that those who were most determined to look after their personal economic interests were also those who spent the most time tuned in to *telenovelas* ($\chi^2 = 6.77$, df $= 2$, p $= .05$). Furthermore, these students attributed economic success both in *telenovelas* and in real life to personal effort and sacrifice.

Telenovelas and the Representation of Reality. The evidence shows that the TS students surveyed tended to identify soap opera situations with those of real life. Only 11 percent said that soap operas fall short of adequately representing real life, and 14 percent said that they are very limited versions of real life. Furthermore, almost half of the students stated that the emotional problems dealt with in *telenovelas* are the most important issues of life. Media messages are not a natural and spontaneous product of reality but are socially determined. *Telenovelas,* their characters' isolation from social organizations, and their individualistic solutions to problems constitute facts that are accepted uncritically by young spectators.

Soap operas were clearly a favorite among these adolescents. According to 70 percent of them, *telenovelas* are very helpful in portraying the serious problems of the country! Asked whether the conflict resolutions of soap operas could be used as guides for one's own life, 80 percent responded that this was definitely so. Thus, *telenovelas* can be considered true "schools of life" for these students.

Socialization to Foreign Cultures

The loss of national values and culture is a long-standing problem in Mexican society that has accelerated with the introduction of television. This is specially true for the new generation that loves Elton John, dances the Hustle, wears jeans, and wants to own a Honda. Among social institutions, commercial television is perhaps the foremost promoter of this phenomenon. Some studies (Esteinou, 1981; Esparza, 1981) have revealed how television's content is determined by monopoly enterprises, most of them transnational corporations. For this reason television broadcasts an overwhelming number of foreign messages that acquaint and familiarize viewers with foreign ways of life.

The TS students surveyed tended to identify with the characters in foreign serials rather than with Mexican ones. The students were divided into two groups: those who said they preferred the privately owned channels (Televisa) and those who preferred the state-owned ones. Those who watched more Televisa identified more with the American characters ($p = .05$).

When it came to choosing a place to live—Mexico or the United States—it is not surprising that the majority of them said they would rather live in the United States. Country selectivity was put on contingency tables with three different variables: commercial television exposure, privately owned television exposure, and exposure to police and other U.S. series. The results show a tendency to prefer U.S. residence among those who spend more hours watching television. This tendency is even more marked among those who prefer Televisa channels and is maintained among those who more frequently view foreign police and other series. (See Table 2.) It is noteworthy that pri-

Table 2. Desired residence

Exposure to Privately Owned Channels	United States		Mexico	
	(No.)	%	(No.)	%
No exposure	14	44	18	56
Exposure to 1	101	51	98	49
Exposure to 2	89	65	48	35
Exposure to 3	17	61	11	39
Total	221		175	

$\chi^2 = 8.87$ df = 3   p = .03

vately owned channels are the main sponsors of such foreign programs as "Kojak," "Chips," and "Six Million Dollar Man."

Perhaps the most alarming results are the ones related to the students' aspirations toward the "American way of life." Half the students in the sample agree with the proposition that "the American way of life should be established around the world." Those who feel this way are also those who prefer to watch Televisa's channels. Moreover, this aspiration is more popular among those who are in the third grade of TS than among those in the first and second grades.

In other words, commercial television does seem to make a difference in the students' approval of the universal spread of American culture. This influence runs parallel to formal schooling, since higher-grade students are even more attracted to American life than lower-grade ones.

National and International Reality in Televised Information

Most of the news programs around the world are produced by American agencies, which control information production and dissemination and represent the underlying economic and political interests of the United States. Several mechanisms are used routinely in the interpretation of historical reality through U.S. eyes. Among them is fragmentation: the process in which reality is broken into pieces and events are taken out of their social context.

These mechanisms not only distort one's view of society but create barriers to understanding. This means that audiences will have to reintegrate the fragments into the whole picture and then proceed to clarify the causes of the problem. Many people will never obtain a good idea of what is going on. For example, although the Mexican economy is penetrated by foreign investment, many Mexicans do not know what transnational corporations are, or what their impact is on their own lives.

The Credibility of the Source. Table 3 provides clear evidence about the students' selection of the most credible and informative medium. Television appears to be the main informant of this audience.

Table 3. Choice of information medium

	Most Informative Medium		Most Credible Medium	
	No.	%	No.	%
Television	285	59	265	55
Radio	93	19	85	18
Newspapers	75	16	83	17
Magazines	12	2	29	6
No answer	15	3	18	4

N = 480

We also tested for the credibility of individual reporters among TS students. Over three-fourths of them mentioned as the most trustworthy those who appear on privately owned channels (Zabludobsky, Ochoa). Only 18 percent named the reporters from state television. Furthermore, not only are these reporters to be trusted, but some are better known than some of the foremost decision-makers within the president's cabinet. Television as a medium is highly credible, and Televisa newsreaders are considered very trustworthy. The process of ideological hegemony requires that people have faith in classist institutions and the personalities associated with them.

Internal Problems. Television may produce knowledge as well as ignorance. Food production shortages are among the social problems facing Mexican society. The agricultural crisis should be known to all citizens. It started in 1965 and has spawned a stream of related problems, one of which is the need to increase imports of food in order to meet the demand. This, of course, has affected the lives of many people, especially those working in rural areas. Yet news programs have failed to provide an adequate portrayal of the issue or to address its structural causes. This can be seen in the responses of students, particularly those who spend more than 3.5 hours a day in front of their television sets. For instance, for 67 percent of them the food shortage problem is nonexistent, even though the great majority of TS students are the children of workers and peasants.

Among Mexican news programs, "24 Horas" (also seen in the United States through the Spanish International Network, an affiliate of Televisa) is the most widely seen. Broadcast by a privately owned television network, "24 Horas" is noted for its partial and fragmented portrayal of reality and its support for the Reagan administration's policies in Central America. Frequency of exposure to "24 Horas" was used to predict TS students' understanding of the food production issue. As can be seen in table 4, those who watch this program more frequently are also those who tend to blame "lazy" or "unmotivated" small-scale peasants for low production and overlook the structural causes of the problem and conditions beyond the small producers' control, such as insufficient returns from their produce.

Table 4. Opinions on food production problems

	Problems Attributed to Individuals		Problems Attributed to Outside Sources	
	No.	%	No.	%
Exposure to "24 Horas"				
None	33	43	43	57
Occasional	96	46	115	54
Frequent	52	56	41	44
Very frequent	46	62	29	38

N = 455.

$\chi^2 = 8.07$ df = 3   p = .05.

Transnational Enterprises.   As was mentioned before, anyone living in a dependent country should be able to identify transnational corporations as one of the United States' prime means of extending its economic and political dominance over Latin America. Given the importance of this fact, it is to be expected that at one time or another it will appear in news programs. In fact, only 57 percent of TS students have heard of transnational corporations, and a smaller percentage (31 percent) are able to define them adequately. Moreover, they are unable to identify as transnationally produced some goods advertised constantly on television. Many affirm that "Pronto" and "Sabritas" were produced by Mexican companies.

Asked where they learned about transnationals, many (40 percent) mention television as their source. Others say they know about them from newspapers, books, or parents. Most students who mention the latter sources are able to describe a transnational corporation correctly. However, 70 percent of those who say they have learned about them from television fail to do so.

International Issues.   One of the most relevant events of 1981, from the point of view of Latin American history, was the on-going civil war in El Salvador. Since the Nicaraguan revolution ended, and particularly under the Reagan administration, the United States has increased its direct intervention into Central America. These subjects were covered daily in Mexican news programs, and by April of that year TS students should have had some idea of the situation in El Salvador.

They were first asked what was going on in El Salvador. Most of them responded either that the country was carrying on a war with another country, or that El Salvador was following its normal course of development. Only 33 percent knew that El Salvador was undergoing a civil war. When asked what policy was being followed by the United States in the then-acute crisis, only 35 percent were able to describe it as it was: "Direct intervention through the provision of armaments and military advisors." The rest responded either that the United States was not intervening at all or that it was helping El Salvador

Table 5. U.S. motives for intervening in El Salvador

	No.	%
The United States is interested in the violent uprisings in El Salvador because it wants:		
To support Salvadoran development	165	34
World peace	112	23
To protect small and weaker countries	83	17
To control social movements in Latin America in order to protect its interests	91	19
No answer	29	6

N = 480

by sending food and medicine. They were then asked to identify U.S. reasons for intervening in social uprisings in Latin America. Their answers can be seen in table 5.

These responses speak for themselves, revealing the misinformation to which these adolescents are exposed and their confusion about these issues, many of which affect them directly. In many instances their view of reality is a reflection of the messages of commercial television.

General Conclusions

The conclusions of the study may be summarized as follows:

1. Television as a social institution has a political and cultural character. Because of its relationship with social classes and its influence on people's thinking and behavior, it cannot be considered neutral. The daily formation of consensus, or acquiescence to the dominant way of life, is the most important overall effect of television.
2. Commercial television in Mexico constitutes the ideological expression of monopoly national and transnational capital. Being highly dependent on those interests, it has not developed a national cultural project. Rather, Mexican commercial television is dependent on U.S. interests for technology, financing, and programming. The cultural and political sovereignty of Mexican society is threatened by foreign values, ideas, and influences. With the imminent introduction of satellites, which will allow the extension of television to the entire nation, the further "culturamericanization" of new generations is an undesirable but likely outcome.
3. Television educates. It does so in multiple ways and in conjunction with many other institutions shaping people's individual characters. Its influence cannot be separated from the entire social context.
4. Commercial television has had an impact on the youths participating in the study. They were more exposed to its influence than to that of Telesecun-

daria. They like the American way of life and want it for the rest of the world. Many of them would like to live in the United States. They are educated in the individualistic and materialistic values of capitalist society. They are taught to strive for material possessions, and they have learned the lesson. Television is for them a trustworthy and informative medium. While ignoring crucial problems of Mexican society, they learn about Latin American history through the eyes of the U.S. Department of State and the transnational news agencies, whose voice is reproduced and magnified by Televisa for Mexican audiences.

Misinformation and ignorance are among the effects of commercial television. Individual subjectivity so educated is an objective support for the maintenance of specific power relationships. The democratization of Mexican society requires the democratization of all institutions. Among them, television must be a priority.

References

Bandura, A. (1977). *Social Learning Theory.* Englewood Cliffs, N.J.: Prentice-Hall.
Beltrán, L. R., and E. Fox de Cardona (1980). *Comunicación Dominada.* Mexico City: Instituto Latinoamericano de Estudios Transnacionales/Nueva Imagen.
Educación (Mexico) (1981). Vol. 7, 4th ser., no. 38.
Esparza Oteo, L. (1981). "La Política Cultural del Estado Mexicano Hacia la Televisión." In *Televisión y Enseñanza Media en México: El Caso de la Telesecundaria.* Mexico: Consejo Nacional Técnico de la Educación, Secretaría de Educación Pública.
Esteinou Madrid, J. (1981). "La Contribución de los Medios de Comunicación en el Proceso de Reproducción de la Fuerza de Trabajo." In *Televisión y Enseñanza Media en México: El Caso de la Telesecundaria.* Mexico: Consejo Nacional Técnico de la Educación, Secretaría de Educación Pública.
Gramsci, A. (1977). *Pasado y Presente.* Mexico: Juan Pablos Editor.
Herner, I. (1979). *Mitos y Monitos: Historietas y Telenovelas en México.* Mexico: Universidad Nacional Autónoma de México/Nueva Imagen.
Janus, N., and R. Roncagliolo (1981). *Publicidad, Comunicación y Dependencia.* Mexico: Instituto Latinoamericano de Estudios Transnacionales.
Kaplún, M. (1976). "La Radiotelevisión Latinoamericana Frente al Desafío del Desarrollo." Paper presented to the seminar on "La Radio y la Televisión Frente a la Necesidad Cultural de América Latina," Quito, CIESPAL.
McGuire, W. (1968). "The Nature of Attitudes and Attitude Change." In G. Lindzey and E. Aronson (eds.) *The Handbook of Social Psychology,* vol. 3, pp. 136–41. Reading, Mass.: Addison-Wesley.
Menasse, R., et al. (1977). "Un Estudio Sobre la Publicidad en la Televisión Comercial Mexicana." *Revista Mexicana de Ciencias Políticas y Sociales,* 86–87, pp. 213–48.

Montoya Martín del Campo, A. (1981). "Los Condicionantes Nacionales y Transnacionales de la Información en México." In *Aportes de Comunicación Social*. Mexico: Coordinacion General de Comunicación Social, Presidencia de la República.

Montoya Martín del Campo, A., and M. A. Rebeil Corella (1981a). *El Impacto Educativo de la Televisión Comercial en los Estudiantes del Sistema Nacional de Telesecundaria*. Mexico: Consejo Nacional Técnico de la Educación, Secretaria de Educación Publica.

Montoya Martín del Campo, A., and M. A. Rebeil Corella (eds.) (1981b). *Televisión y Enseñanza Media en México: El Sistema Nacional de Telesecundaria*. Mexico: Consejo Nacional Técnico de la Educación, Secretaría de Educación Publica.

Noriega, L. A., and F. Leach (1979). *Broadcasting in Mexico*. London: International Institute of Communications.

Pasquali, A. (1975). "On the Instrumental Use of Mass Media in America for Purposes of Dependence." Paper presented to the New World Conference, San Antonio, Texas, Nov. 4–8.

IV. ALTERNATIVES FOR LATIN AMERICAN CULTURES

9 *Maximo Simpson Grinberg*

Trends in Alternative Communication Research in Latin America

The exposition and analysis of the prevailing tendencies in the area of alternative communication raise various difficulties. First of all, one must insert this analysis into the global context of information and communication structures, structures of a fundamentally monopolistic nature that operate in a variety of sociopolitical settings and at national and transnational levels. This contextualization goes beyond my immediate objectives here; indeed, I take it for granted that this context is known to those interested in the issue of alternative communication. Yet I cannot avoid at least touching upon the main lines of investigation into the relationship between communication and society, and communication and democracy, that prevail among Latin American critical researchers, since alternative communication proposals are a specific expression of their conclusions about these relationships.

The broader areas of critical research in communication alternatives currently include the cultural or consciousness industry; the transnational nature of information/communication structures; the new technologies, both the so-called light ones and those that tend to increase social control by the dominant classes; the North–South information imbalance and, consequently, the problems derived from the phenomenon known as cultural imperialism. Other problems that have gained researchers' attention in recent years—some of which originate in the above-mentioned problems—concern the "free flow" of information, the manipulation of news and its political and ideological implications, and the problem of national sovereignty, which is threatened by the development of telematics in general and satellite communication in particular. To these one must add the review and study of the juridical aspects of international communication and investigations into property and control structures and the economic role of the mass media in the circulation and reproduction of capital.

Turning from this brief and obviously incomplete list, we now find ourselves facing two questions that cannot be ignored if we wish to grasp the structure that underlies all the diverse conceptualizations of alternative communication. First, from what political and ideological position is the status quo in social communication being questioned? Second, what is meant by democratization in communication?

The range of positions is wide, but I will try to summarize them here. The prescription of some critical researchers can be summarized briefly: the promotion of national policies for communication power at the international level and the direct or indirect reconcentration of this power in the hands of each nation. Other scholars would add internal democratization as a goal of those national policies. For example, Roncagliolo and Avila state: "Beyond the definition of communications there is a general social policy. And in this sense the central alternative is: authoritarianism or democracy. . . . Due to that fact, maybe it is time to stop proposing simply national policies of communication, in order to start designing policies of communications' democratization, with explicit adjective and purpose" (1982, pp. 9, 10). Along similar lines, Juan Somavía notes that advocating true freedom in information flow implies "replacing the current oligopoly with a plurality of communication sources." This in turn entails "stating that in the Third World, the states have the basic responsibility of stimulating and promoting alternative information structures and styles in the framework of national communication policies, without transforming the information into a control device of the government over the rest of the society" (1977, p. 8).

The range of communication research encompasses both technocratic-authoritarian ideologies centering on considerations of national information sovereignty and structural modernization and positions that one could refer to as technocratic-populist, with a marked bias in favor of strengthening the communication power of the state and its control over social communication. There are, on the other hand, researchers who stress such concepts as pluralism, access, and participation. Others talk about the right to information,[1] which they define as a social good, and the receiver's rights in communication

1. A national debate over the regulation of the right to information took place in Mexico under the Lopez Portillo administration (1976–82). Researchers, journalists, government officials, and representatives of social, political, and cultural organizations participated in this enormously important event. The only precedent in Latin America was the debate that took place in Peru after the press reform promoted by General Velazco Alvarado's administration in 1974.

processes. Still other scholars, while assigning a central importance to the democratization of property systems, note the urgency of transcending the old juridical distinction between public and private in order to move forward to the incorporation of communication as a *social right:* "Communications, and the right to communication, belong to the same category. The communication activity must bow to democratic social demand, in which the real control over information comes from the organized receivers and the social producers of the messages" (Roncagliolo and Avila, 1982, pp. 10–11).

It is noteworthy that within what is usually known as the Latin American left, the basic positions are clearly opposed: there are those who put "nationalization," "statization," and "socialization" in one conceptual bundle,[2] promoting in fact the state control of the media, and those who place themselves at the opposite extreme—that is, who state the need for a radical decentralization of communication power among the majority sectors of the population.

Among "critical" researchers who encourage the "socialist" statization of communication structures one finds a combination of scientific and ideological assumptions that have not been analyzed in depth. I refer to the synthesis of Leninism, neobehaviorism, and cyberneticism based on categorical extrapolations—very typical of the North American school—from behaviorist reductionism and cybernetics to the historical and social analysis of Leninist Marxism. An extreme example is the work of Camilo Taufic, whose book *Periodismo y Lucha de Clases* (1973) has been very well received by diverse schools in Latin America. Starting from the above-mentioned foundation, Taufic gives no emphasis to a radical change in the structures of property and control of the media, or to mechanisms for generating more democratized messages that would promote multidirectional flows of communication; rather, he proposes a simple change of contents, on the assumption that the receiver is passive. And this change of contents is envisioned as the result of a direct or indirect statization of the media, which are assigned a determining role as the generating sources of social consciousness.

Concerning the concept of *democratization* in the communication field,

---

2. In Sweezy's words: "This is mistaking the juridical categories with the production relationship. . . . Both in Italy and in France, for example, the state, directly or through state corporations, owns a great deal of the means of production (obviously, it is not *private* property, but with the same certainty it is a *capitalist* form of property)" (1971, pp. 9–10). For his part, Castoriadis rejects Lenin and Trotsky's assertions in favor of the principle that what determines the socialist nature of state (or nationalized) property is the nature of the political power: "What grants or denies a socialist nature to the 'nationalized' property is the structure of the production relationships. . . . The soviet power, as the working-class power, does not live on its own; on its own it tends to degenerate, like any other state power. It can only live and consolidate itself in a socialist sense by taking as a foundation the fundamental alteration of the production relationships, that is, the access of all producers to the managing of the economy. It is precisely what did not take place in Russia" (1976, p. 168).

certain assumptions should be made clear. For the right and the authoritarian left—influenced implicitly or explicitly by neobehaviorist conceptions—the democratization of communication structures is usually identified with universal access to the discourse of power. For the right this is to occur through the promotion of new technologies and the multiplication of options by the same social classes that benefit from property and media control and are, consequently, the organic transmitters of the predominant social discourse; and for the authoritarian left, through the articulation of a pseudo-decentralization of Leninist inspiration. An example of the latter process is the employment of "popular correspondents" by a highly centralized press under the strict control of the political-state apparatus; another example is the formal concession of the media to social organizations that work as quasi-state entities and that, theoretically or practically, are just "transmission leashes" of the power apparatus. (I develop this topic in *Leninismo y Comunicación,* forthcoming.) This was the system proposed by Armand Mattelart and the First National Assembly of Leftist Journalists during the Chilean Unidad Popular administration of Salvador Allende, which proposed as its ultimate goal the "straightforward statization" of the mass media (Mattelart, 1974a, p. 102). A different position is examplified by the thoughts of two already-quoted researchers: "All that leads to the problem of policy subjects. The organic feature of a democratization policy is precisely that the state apparatus stops being the only policy subject" (Roncagliolo and Avila, 1982, p. 12).

These differences lead us to examine both the diverse Latin American historical experiences and the options that researchers propose in relation to the following issues: (1) the real nature of the means of production,[3] (2) the articulations between the means of material production and the means of communication production, with their respective production relationships;[4] and (3) the articulations between the state, the political society, and the civil society. In the last case the researcher will stress or omit the distinction, essential in any system, between plain social communication and state social communication.

For the analysis of communication structures and the designing of genuine

3. The key to identifying the predominant means of production in any given social formation is the analysis of the true production relationships, which include procedures for making decisions about the goals and organization of work and the final disposition of the economic surplus.

4. As for the production relationships themselves, Castoriadis (1976) notes that their nature is determined by the management means of production—that is, "the organization and cooperation of the physical and personal conditions of production, the defining of production goals and methods." The class content of production consists, among other things, of the "monopolization of the means of production by a social class" and the "constant reproduction of that same monopolization." It seems clear that this analysis is applicable to the field of communication production, where property and media control and the means of *management* determine the nature of the transmitter-receptor relationship.

alternatives, we start from the analytic principle that the nature of the predominant communication system in a given social formation is determined by the interation of two factors that are vital to its makeup. These are the predominant means of social production and the political system—that is, the specific articulation that has been established between the state, the political society, and the civil society. From the interaction among these factors, the basic features of the predominant communication system and the possible margins for alternatives emerge.

All this means that research must not stop at the critical analysis and rejection of the current communication structures, or the application of alternatives to only one economic and sociopolitical system. The design of alternative communication models is not possible if scientific study is replaced by a simple dogmatic position or if the analysis of a vast and conflicting area of reality is overlooked.

Without positing an automatic relationship between the above-mentioned positions and the nature, role, and validity of the so-called communication alternatives, it is nevertheless clear that there is a relationship between researchers' political positions and the kinds of alternative communications proposed. And it could not be any other way, because the starting point for the formulation of alternatives is located precisely in one's conception of the relationship between communication and global society.

Conceptualizations: Two Predominant Tendencies

Approaches to the phenomenon of alternative communication—whose origins date back to the 1960s—are varied. First of all, diverse adjectives are attached to the phenomenon, such as "popular," "participatory," "indigenous," "self-governing," and "emancipatory." Each of these expressions stresses a certain aspect of a complex reality. Their common denominator lies, in my opinion, in the sense that this form of communication constitutes an alternative to the dominant discourse of power at all levels. In some cases alternative communication—a concept that I use in a generic and nonexclusive way—is defined in opposition to the mass media, giving it an eminently nonprofessional and self-governing quality (to which the expression "participatory communication" is also related). In others the expression refers to every communication phenomenon that implies an opposition to the dominant discourse of power. And whereas alternative communication is usually envisioned as an *answer* to mass communication, it is sometimes noted that it is not always an action tending toward change, an answer to a situation of ideological and cultural domination, but may simply represent the persistence of communication forms of a generally participatory nature that predate the mass media in cultures where communitarian forms of social relationship once existed. Alternative communication, in this case and in some others, would be a social resistance phenomenon.

Other topics—such as the relationship between alternative communication and so-called consciousness-raising education (or conscientization); the insistence of some experts on the self-generation of messages as the distinctive sign of alternatives; the use by the critical communication group of decodification and the analysis of the state's role in the promotion of options; and the distinction drawn by some scholars between alternative communication and counterinformation—cannot be given sufficient scope in this paper, although an epistemological analysis of these positions would provide a panorama of the prevailing conceptualizations on the subject of alternative communication.

The different approaches outlined above can be traced, directly or indirectly, to two fundamental currents that I will discuss here and to the new tendencies outlined below (see "New Experiences and Theoretical Inquiries"). The analysis of these two positions is essential for a global comprehension of the nature and significance of alternative communication in Latin American societies. I am referring first to the conceptualization of alternative communication as an exclusive antidote to transnational capitalist structures; and second to the approach that subordinates the alternative nature of certain communication experiences to their insertion within strategies for structural change worked out by self-designated political-ideological "vanguards." These are not, however, two genuinely differentiated lines of thought: in some cases we can see that the supporters of the "vanguard" theory have the same theoretical and political presuppositions as those who hold the first-mentioned position. In this area of knowledge, as in others, the lines are interwoven, and no rigid delimitations can be established without becoming arbitrary. However, it is both possible and necessary to explicate the conceptual core of these two lines because of the enormous consequences that such starting points have for the development of alternative communication in Latin America.

Alternative Communication as a Response to Transnational Structure

Within the first line of thought, research in alternative communication is based on a previous analysis that emphasizes the fundamentally transnational nature of the communication structures in Latin America. This analysis is, as has been said already, a common denominator of most research, and abundant literature witnesses to its importance in specialized areas of communication. Both independent scholars and those working in private and university research centers, within political and social movements, and in intergovernmental organizations and other professional groups such as UNESCO and the Federation of Latin American Journalists have dealt for years with the transnational nature of communication structures. Thus, there is a great deal of accumulated knowledge about various aspects of transnational structures, and works in this tradition range from denunciations of news manipulation to detailed studies about transnational control of social communications, in both the technical-economic and the political-ideological spheres.

Researchers in this group consider alternative communication an *answer* to the transnational, unidirectional, and authoritarian character of the mass media. Those who take the most extreme position consider the technological structure of the mass media an impassable barrier to their democratic and participatory use. Others assume that this antidemocratic character is not inherent in the technology but derives from its monopolistic use on behalf of the dominant classes and from their market rationality—that is, not from the technology but from the communication *model,* a transnational model exported by the central countries to the peripheral areas. Diego Portales states: "Alternative communication is a project opposed to the unrivaled predominance of the transnational communication model. This is, so to speak, its genetic impulse" (1981, p. 65). For his part, Fernando Reyes Matta answers the question about the nature of alternative communication by saying: "This concept encompasses all forms of communication that emerge *as an answer to the dominant system,* whose power centers lie in the Western capitalist countries and whose expression is a permanent transnational-type expansion" (1981, p. 65; emphasis added).

In a line of reflection that both enriches and complements this research, some see mass communication not as an irreducible antithesis to genuine communication, but as a *support* for alternative communication within a global democratization process. And if alternative communication is defined in terms obviously opposed to commercial, industrialized communication, Portales makes it clear what "alternative" means:

this approach would result in a communication system strictly *marginal* to the society. It might be feasible for certain traditional societies not significantly penetrated by transnational ideology, technology, and communication: this may be the case for tribal societies that attempt a modernization or transformation radically different from the model offered by modern capitalism. But the same does not happen with those societies whose traditional structures were destroyed by transnational penetration and replaced by structures that were modern and underdeveloped at the same time.

The Latin American case demands a conceptualization different from the alternative communication model—one in which the technological advances of modern communication are assumed, but turned to radically different objectives than those pursued by transnational communication. (1981, p. 66)

The distinctive features of alternative communication, positively defined, would be, according to Portales, social organization of property, artisan production of messages, multidirectional and horizontal flows of communication, and widespread access of social sectors to the creation and transmission of messages favoring change (1981, p. 66).

Finally, Portales proposes the following synthesis of functions. Their importance is obvious:

Our hypothesis is that alternative communication is able to surmount the ideological barriers imposed on it by transnational domination only if it fulfills these requirements. First, it must be able to relate both horizontal and vertical communication flows; and second, it must succeed in integrating both the artisanal and industrial production formats. (1981, p. 67)

An alternative model of communication, Capriles states, if its point of departure is the here and now of social existence, cannot ignore the presence of major institutional-industrial structures, the vertical and unidirectional relationships they impose, and the predominantly bureaucratic nature of their functioning (1981, p. 153). Reyes Matta agrees and postulates an active alliance between journalists and audiences to promote a change in society and communication systems. There would have to be a coordinated effort by journalists, political groups, unions, working-class neighborhoods, and organizations of professionals to thwart the influence of transnational messages. For that purpose, he argues, actions are to be contemplated both inside and outside the system. Reyes Matta proposes a working hypothesis that enjoys support in the research literature: "The *fair* position is to advance, not in parallel lines, but toward a juncture where alternative communication would be able to unite fully with mass communication and, through the latter, reach wide social sectors, delivering the richness of a message whose source is located within the grassroots' agitation, debates, and struggles" (1981, p. 107).

The Political-Intellectual Vanguard Theory

A great number of researchers seem to be situated around a position that is explicitly or implicitly based in the so-called vanguard theory. The conceptual defining core of this position is the leading role awarded to the political-intellectual elites as trustees of the theoretical and historical knowledge that they must transmit to the masses so that they can fulfill their revolutionary mission.

According to this line of thought, the soundness of communication experiences, other than those within the transnational power structures, depends on their insertion in a totalizing strategy. Thus, no "partial experience" should be regarded as an alternative strategy, because communication must be considered "one of the most important aspects to be developed in the heart of a political organization," an organization that must, of course, be the vanguard of a wide political-social process. In such a framework, the promotion of alternative communication praxis involves "a challenge for the political cadres and the research groups from militant organizations" (Graziano, 1980). Graziano continues:

when stating the problem of an alternative communication, we are pointing at the same time to two different ways in which such a problem is solved: first of all, a view from the opposition that implies the development of alternative modalities of communication *with* the masses, of *ideological transmission,* of media choice and message generation; and, second, a vision of power formed in a coherent and systematic project for the use of the media in a revolutionary process. (Graziano, 1980; emphasis added)

And, forthwith, a definition of alternative communication is proposed. This definition is noteworthy for the demands and limitations that it implies. Graziano suggests that the term should be used "for those dialogic relationships in *the transmission of images and signs* that are inserted in a transforming praxis, acting on the social structure *as a whole*" (1980, p. 38; emphasis added).

Beyond the contradictory mention of "dialogic relationships" in this vertical context, this approach, as we have already seen, disparages all spontaneous praxis that does not *consciously* promote a radical change under the sponsorship of a political organization charged with designing and carrying out the above-mentioned "totalizing strategy." Hence "*with* the masses" and the expression "ideological transmission" in the passage quoted above: this is an instrumentalist approach to the communication process. It would create communication channels *with* the masses, but not promote communication *of* and *for* the masses, independent of any political apparatus and the political control of the vanguard. It also involves a neobehaviorist conception of communication according to which the core of all communication is a unidirectional transmission of messages—in this case "liberating" messages—with the goal of creating in the masses an adequate level of consciousness.

In all this, there is an echo of Kautsky's and Lenin's ideas about the inability of the proletariat (and thus of the oppressed and exploited majorities in general) to attain by itself a socialist consciousness, without the intervention of an illustrious elite. Lenin supports his position by quoting from a well-known Kautsky paper:

The vehicle of science is not the proletariat, but the *bourgeois intelligentsia:* it was in the minds of individual members of this stratum that modern socialism originated. Accordingly, the old Hainfeld programme quite rightly stated that the task of Social-Democracy is to imbue the proletariat [literally: saturate the proletariat] with the *consciousness* of its position and the consciousness of its task. (Lenin, 1969, p. 40; emphasis in Kautsky's text)

For an even sharper irony, compare the famous "Circular Letter" of Marx and Engels to August Bebeland and others (Sept. 17–18, 1879): "In one word, the working class is not capable of achieving by itself its emancipation. To that end, it needs to place itself under the direction of 'cultured and possessing' bourgeois, because only they have the 'time and possibilities' to come to learn what can be useful for the workers."

From a similar perspective, followers of Gramsci promote the dialectical interaction between the intellectual element, always in a leading role, and the popular element as the axis of a new, historic, revolutionary bloc that would find its support in a Leninist party transformed into the "modern prince." The source of this conception can be found throughout Gramsci's works, and especially in "The Modern Prince," an essay that compares the historic role of Machiavellianism and the "praxis theory," an expression Gramsci uses to refer elliptically to Marxism.

Concerning the basic question of *for whom* Machiavelli wrote, Gramsci reflects that the Florentine politician tried to educate politically "those who are not in the know," the revolutionary class of his time, the Italian "people" and "nation." He crowns his reflection with this assertion: "Machiavelli wished to persuade these forces of the necessity of having a leader who knew what he wanted and how to obtain it, and of accepting him with enthusiasm. . . . This position in which Machiavelli found himself politically is repeated today for the philosophy of praxis" (1971, pp. 135–36). But this praxis philosophy is not embodied in a providential person but in the Leninist party, as can be noted from the context of his discourse:

> The modern prince, the myth-prince, cannot be a real person, a concrete individual; it can only be an organism, a complex element of society in which a collective will, which has already been recognised and has to some extent exerted itself in action, begins to take concrete form. History has already provided this organism, and it is the political party—the first cell in which there come together germs of a collective will tending to become universal and total. (1971, p. 129)

About the historic task of this party-prince, our author states, in a well-known paragraph, that it

> must and cannot but be the proclaimer and organiser of an intellectual and moral reform, which also means creating the terrain for a subsequent development of the national-popular collective will towards the realisation of a superior, total form of modern civilisation. (1971, pp. 132–33)

It is a position that resembles Lenin's, but more finely elaborated, just as Gramsci's reflections elaborate the Leninist thesis about the relationships among intellectual elite, vanguard party, and proletariat. Starting from this approach and from the Gramscian conception of the organic intellectual, some researchers believe that "popular emancipating communication" implies that intellectuals who have undergone a political conversion that causes them to identify with the interests of the masses must make an effort to place themselves "within the subordinate classes' social place and cultural perspective." According to Gimenez, however, the intellectual "does not disavow his condition, nor does he abdicate his leading role in his contact with the people" (1978, p. 29). The intellectual's role, Gimenez notes, is not exhausted in the task of "lending voice to those who have no voice." It implies above all and primarily his intervention in educating and leading the people, actively contributing so that the subordinate classes will attain a critical consciousness about their own cultural horizons. . . . His characteristic efficacy is to urge the popular classes toward political and social freedom, deeply respecting their self-identification system, their cultural initiative, and their right to be different. (1978, p. 30)

A Few Critical Observations

The "response" approach to alternative communication has made very significant contributions to the understanding of communication problems in Latin America and the conceptualization of an alternative. The prevalence of this approach, entered on criticism of the transnational model, is explained historically by the heavy weight of transnational communications in Latin America and other Third World countries within a global context of political and economic domination. Nevertheless, there are limits to its power to capture the changing Latin American reality and the richness and scope of alternative communication.

Indeed, as can be seen throughout this chapter, the exclusive and excluding manner in which this approach has been promoted by many researchers has further limited its usefulness. These limits are inherent in its own definition, tied as it is to a single model. Other political-social contexts in which alternative communication has arisen as an answer to authoritarian relationships—not necessarily or solely transnational ones—have been left out of the analysis. Thus, for explicit or implicit ideological reasons, and for political reasons often of articulation, researchers of this school have by and large excluded the study of the alternative experiences that emerged in the so-called regimes of transition to socialism (for example, during the Chilean Unidad Popular administration). To this omission may be added the absence of serious work on the nature and structure of social communication in Cuba, as well as the options of a one-party state and a party-state monopoly of the mass media, which are possible in the Cuban context.

These exclusions have both theoretical and practical consequences for the formulation of options for change that are not a simple monopoly transfer from a dominant social class to a new power elite, leaving unchanged the asymmetrical relationship between sender and receiver. Real alternatives are precisely the opposite: the promotion of a radical change in communication relationships, with all that implies in terms of message ownership, control, manufacture, and diffusion systems.

It is appropriate to note that the *negative* definitions of alternative communication, developed in opposition to the transnational model, generally find a complement in *positive* definitions that present alternative communication as the paradigm of communication democratization. Capriles puts it this way:

"It would be the *conditio sine qua non* of all possible democracies: the permanent dialogue, the spontaneous and relevant participation, never arbitrary or conditional, generating collective decisions and the socialization of production and its fruits" (1981, p. 151). However, in many cases such statements fail to confront the reality of Latin American communication systems and processes, which by general agreement (often implied and not stated) have been excluded in advance from the analysis or are discussed in casuistic language.

Although researchers notice the incongruity of nominally promoting processes of democratization while endorsing—by action or omission—authoritarian regimes, some reflections and investigations are being published that imply a "redefinition of the commitment" (Gonzaga Motta and da Silva, 1982) of the communication workers concerning their role in promoting change. Such a redefinition requires an analysis of reality that enables us, equipped with deeper knowledge and aware of the contradictions and surprises that are furnished by historical events, to come up with alternative formulas consistent with a democratic and pluralist viewpoint on social and communication structures.

From this perspective, alternative communication is not only an antidote to transnational structures but also a proposal that questions the *concentration* of communication power independently of the reasons that are given to legitimate this situation. This stand takes into account communication structures—symmetrical or asymmetrical—as an expression of power relationships, and understands society itself as a communication macrostructure.

In a previous work describing the various dimensions of alternative communication, I tried to typify certain situations and contexts in which options arise:

at a particular moment the option of acting as a direct or indirect media monopolizer faces the state; in other cases, this becomes an option for both private and state channels; in still other instances, the option is particularly available to private interests, whether national or transnational, either in a totally autonomous way or encouraged by state or semi-state organs, when the state contains . . . isolated bastions of the majorities' interest; sometimes the state is the one that assumes, directly, the property and control of a medium,[5] as a way of confronting national or transnational private interests; finally, as has happened in Spain and Chile,[6] the alternative arises facing both the capitalist monopoly and the popular and leftist press. (1981, p. 116)

5. The state's intervention, in order to be truly democratizing, cannot consist of holding, directly or indirectly, the property and control of the media but instead must promote the real *decentralization* of communication power. I do not thereby reject the state's right to have its own media, but there must be a clear distinction between the state's media and the communication structures of civil society, as has already been said. Otherwise we will find a simple monopoly transference, with a civil society suffocated by the power apparatus in the name of the civil society itself.

6. See, for example, the press of the industrial sectors of Santiago, which arose during the Popular Unity administration of Salvador Allende (1970–73); and the independent bulletins writ-

In line with this effort to place the concept in its historical context (an effort that may also help make it more widely applicable), let me risk proposing a provisional definition of alternative communication that keeps in mind the different contexts in which the option emerges:

we will say that we can call any medium an alternative medium that, in a context characterized by the existence of privileged sectors that retain the political, economic, and cultural power, in all possible situations—from a one-party system with statized economy (Cuba) to the capitalist regimes of parliamentary democracy and the military dictatorships—*implies an alternative to the dominant discourse.* (Simpson Grinberg, 1981, p. 122; emphasis in original)

Concerning the definitions of alternative communication that revolve around the hegemony of political and intellectual elites, I would like now to consider, first, the theoretical problem and the practical questions it raises.

Lenin's conception of the processes of consciousness formation reveals an incongruity that Rossanda has pointed out by asking this question: "How can one pretend to be Marxist and state that consciousness has an origin other than the social being?" (1981, p. 8). Yet history offers various examples that, taken in isolation, would enable one to demonstrate both the capacity for self-emancipation of the exploited classes and the important role of the elite as bearers of fertile ideas that, interacting with the popular classes' daily praxis and "inherent ideas" (Rude, 1981) result in a level of consciousness that works as the motor for political-social processes. Movements of a spontaneous nature have arisen from the popular classes' short-term economic needs and their immediate objectives, both in capitalist societies and the so-called preindustrial ones. (For illustrative examples see Rude, 1981.) A dramatic example that touches Latin Americans closely is the case of the Spanish revolution of 1936–37, in which the so-called vanguard implacably drowned in blood the radical initiatives of workers and peasants for contravening the interests and strategies of the vanguard.[7]

Anyone who goes over the rich bibliography on the vanguard-mass relationship and the intellectuals' role in the revolutionary process will notice that the emphasis placed on self-emancipation versus the need for a vanguard varies, often according to the particular circumstances in which the analysis takes place.[8] For example, there is a clear shift in favor of the intellectual elite between Marx and Engels on the one hand and Lenin on the other.

---

ten by workers from Barcelona, which filled "the informational and two-way communication vacuum, which the partisan community had not been able to do, and at the same time helped to satisfy the demands for topics of everyday life" (Vidal-Beneyto, 1979, p. xxv).

7. See the excellent summary in the second part of Chomsky, 1974.

8. Fay questions the historical basis of the Lenin-Kautsky thesis: "Lenin takes from Kautsky the false idea that the spontaneous movement cannot overcome the trade-unionist phase—that is, the deviations compatible with the capitalist regime. That is not Kautsky; it is Lassalle! We have

I would like to underline the consequences of the vanguard theory and its use for the legitimation of power and the suppression of popular autonomy in the course of political-social processes. The key to the suppression of popular autonomy (which has as one manifestation authoritarian communication structures) perhaps lies in the combination of these theoretical biases with the domination relationship that the vanguard establishes with the social majorities once state power has been seized—domination relationships that tend to reproduce themselves beyond the subjective will of the leaders. The theoretical duality involved in formulations about the inevitable historic mission of the proletariat and the legitimation of the vanguard that represents it and acts as its superconscience has a correlate on the level of communications: both social and cultural organizations and the mass media are, from this point of view, simple "transmission belts" of the vanguard, regardless of whether it is in opposition or in power.[9] In most cases this is, as historical experience demonstrates, an instrumentalist conception of alternative communication, whose final goal is the strategic control of popular movements. Alternative communication, however, in its widest sense, implies the exercise of *direct communication democracy,* free from control and without any need for gifted interpreters of the collective feeling. Such a definition would contradict the vanguard theory and its practical hegemony.

Other researchers, on the contrary, stress the autonomy and legitimacy of popular communication: "Deep down, what is at stake is the learning and the practice of a new kind of relationship between people and social classes, between the people and the government as a state corporation" (Díaz Bordenave, n.d., p. 9). In other words, what is at stake is *the learning of new power relationships* that, born on the basis of social life itself, imply at the same time the demystification of communication power, symbolized in our societies by the

here a kind of continuity without critical filtering because it was inspired, in 1902, by a few examples of struggles in Russia that go back to 1896.

"However, there had been, and later there were even more, [contrary] experiences, especially the silk weavers from Lyon, who spontaneously, in 1834, adopted as a goal the overcoming of the capitalist framework, the June 1848 journeys, the Paris Commune of 1871, the 1905 revolution and the 1917 revolution in Russia, the 1918 and 1919 soviet revolutions in the Hungarian and Bavarian republics. These movements, notwithstanding their spontaneity, did not have a trade-unionist nature; they pointed toward historical objectives, overcoming the capitalist framework." Fay, 1981, pp. 38–39).

9. Point 7 of the resolution adopted by the First Cuban Communist Party Congress on the mass media established that: "IN ORDER THAT ALL MASS DIFFUSION ORGANS can fully carry out their role in the political-ideological, moral, and aesthetic education of the population, so that they will be able to efficiently carry out their mobilizing role for the great tasks of socialist construction, it is essential for them to act as vehicles of the Party, of the Communist Youth Union, of the mass and social organizations, and the workers, individually considered" (quoted in Goutman, 1979, p. 52).

mass media. And for that, one has to start from a theoretical and political perspective that goes beyond the strategies elaborated by sectors or groups that pretend to be the gifted agents of the historical situation. One must attempt to view the process of change from a point of view that transcends a merely partisan one in order to arrive at a conceptualization of power that, in both a latent and manifest sense, situates it within the domain of everyday life and both inside *and* outside the state apparatus. From this perspective, alternative communication would attain a significance that would not depend upon its formal insertion into a political movement with defined goals for global change. Alternative communication thus forms outposts for new social relationships and, specifically, establishes constitutive practices in a wide variety of processes that often—because of their "heterodox" characteristics—fall outside the limits of orthodox vanguard perception and theory.

Finally, some reflections on Gramsci. His works, in which one observes a great intellectual keenness, have served as the foundation of some of the positions outlined above. But because of their fragmentary nature, interpretation is often uncertain. The work of Gramsci poses a balance between coercion and consensus and therefore leads to the most diverse readings. Rossanda notes what she calls Gramsci's two stages: the Gramsci of the *Advice,* sovietist and anti-Jacobin, and the Gramsci of "The Modern Prince," who stressed a decade later "the vanguard, the prince, the only one capable of interpreting reality, liberating his still unformed potential." Thus, she states, we observe him "closing in an opposite direction of the 'direct democracy,' the dialectic between class and conscience" (1981, p. 10).

Some brief reflections on Gramsci will, in my opinion, help us get to the core of this controversy. In the first place, there is the question of leadership formation:

is it the intention that there should always be rulers and ruled, or is the objective to create the conditions in which this division is no longer necessary? In other words, is the initial premise the perpetual division of the human race, or the belief that this division is only an historical fact, corresponding to certain conditions? (1971, p. 144)

This question refers to the division of labor in class-based societies and the probability of its future elimination, but it can also be applied to communication because, historically, the strict division between sender and receivers is an expression of that class-based division of labor. But the vanguard, which does not place a limit on its domination, intends to retain its role as the only sender for historically valid social discourse.

In another passage Gramsci questions the existence of "pure" spontaneity, comparing it to "pure" determinism. He notes that the unity between "spontaneity" and "conscious direction" is "the real political action of the dominated classes," and thus provides a critical reflection worth quoting:

There exists a scholastic and academic historico-political outlook which sees as real and worthwhile only such movements of revolt as are one hundred per cent conscious, i.e. movements that are governed by plans worked out in advance to the last detail or in line with abstract theory. But reality produces a wealth of the most bizarre combinations. It is up to the theoretician to unravel these in order to cover fresh proof of his theory, to "translate" into theoretical language the elements of historical life. It is not reality which should be expected to conform to the abstract scheme. (1971, p. 200)

New Experiences and Theoretical Inquiries

Looking at recent works on alternative communication, we find a common denominator: the attempt to overcome the stereotypes and taboos that for many years have been barriers to an understanding of reality and to formulate alternatives. This suggests that we should consider carefully what the fundamental research tools might be for the study of alternative communication.

The problem is to capture the social communication reality of a continent that is peasant and pluricultural. Leftist theories that identify the proletariat as the *only* universal class with a clearly defined historic destiny neglect the great masses of Latin Americans, whose only certain destiny would seem to be in the subordination to the labor aristocracy and vanguard elites that have claimed—and still claim—to represent them. Second, it is necessary to abandon—without rejecting its tremendous importance—the fascination with the mass media and the uncritical faith in its omnipotence in the formation of the collective consciousness (as found, for example, in certain works of the Frankfurt school), and to look within, to our rural communities and urban centers, to study popular experiences of different kinds and to understand what they are like and how their channels and autonomous communication networks operate. It is also pertinent to ask what the relationship is between the discourse of the dominant system and its audiences, how and to what extent this system gravitates to the conceptions and attitudes of individuals and groups, and at what levels the critical decodification of audiences takes place. This type of inquiry has broad implications because it shows us the significant changes that are taking place within society.

Research about the participatory communication networks that *predate* the mass media is of primary importance. We must consider not only cultures with different forms of communitarian activities, but also the problem of multigenesis and the real meaning of alternative communications. From such a perspective, alternative communication cannot be conceived of *only* as an answer to transnational structures, but will be seen also as a manifestation of the "persistence of certain cultural expressions" (Díaz Bordenave, n.d., pp. 2–3). In fact, the persistence of cultural forms opposed to the industrial-developmentalist model of the national bourgeoisies (and of most Marxist and neo-Marxist projects), as well as the existence of the great popular political-social movements themselves, indicates the limits of the mystifying, persuasive power of the mass media. A belief in the omnipotence of the mass media ignores not only the relative autonomy of popular cultures, but also the importance of praxis as the source of the collective consciousness. Luis Gonzaga Motta notes that, to date, most studies have accepted "the Marxist axiom that the dominant class's ideas are, in any epoch, the dominant ideas." Yet, he adds, "The popular classes too live their contradictions at the level of day-to-day life, and they respond dialectically to attempts at manipulation" (1981, pp. 12–13). This analysis does not, of course, suggest idealizing the grassroots sectors, but it stresses their creativity and their ability to resist the imposition of social and cultural guidelines.

Starting from similar concerns, Alcira Argumedo suggests a rethinking of the Marxist concept of alienated consciousness, which to a great extent shares a conceptual core with the paternalistic position that it was intended to refute. This rethinking would promote new theoretical research in an area that to date has been crystalized in stereotypical repetition; the importance of this concept for the evaluation of alternative communication does not need emphasis:

> We talk about *alienated consciousness* in the sense of accepting as adequate and valid the vision of the world and the domination established by empires in successive historical stages. . . . But the history of the colonial or neocolonial domination in all three continents through four hundred years shows that the "peaceful" times of apparent acceptance of the domination, or, for us, of a lack of manifestation of latent dissent, have been the exception and not the rule for dominated peoples. And this historical distortion of information—the phenomenon is not new—has led even certain progressive sectors to see the history of domination as built on an "alienated" consensus of the dominated. (Argumedo, 1981, pp. 12–13)

Some have already begun to question the real nature of systems that are assumed to be socialist and of the communication structures that are proposed as an alternative. Others stress the need to look for a third option among what Argumedo calls "the two paradigmatic models": the transnational capitalist model and the Soviet model. Along similar lines we find researchers like Ana Maria Nethol contesting the liberal models widely adopted in Latin America, yet noting that "the communist model was, and still is, authoritarian in its political theory and practice" (1981, p. 1). Díaz Bordenave similarly stresses the need to formulate "a different development model from the ones arising from liberal capitalism and state communism, and propose to our people a democratic socialism with a communitarian base, self-governing and participatory" (1982, p. 18). Nobody could ignore the importance of such statements, especially when taking into account that the double discourse of a great deal of our critical communication writing—liberator versus authoritarian—is only an echo of the false polarity rejected by these authors.

Against this background it is only natural that the political and professional commitment of the communication researcher is being redefined—a commitment that has often been mistaken for an unconditional adherence to the real or apparent power apparatus of the people. In a critical analysis of national communication policies promoted by UNESCO and its manifestation in Brazilian society, Gonzaga Motta and Ubirajara da Silva state:

The commitment of the professionals and scholars in the communication field should be to Brazilian culture, and especially to the grassroots expressions of it that historically have been left out. Resistance to domination, present in these popular expressions, cannot be eliminated because it is in people. *And the commitment, defined this way, is not opportunistic because it lasts through changes in government.* (1982, p. 27; emphasis added)

These statements, applicable to Latin America as a whole, suggest that there is a trend among researchers to shed theoretical blinders and to observe and understand the social communication reality of the majority. Research to date, according to Marques de Melo, has been devoted mainly to the study of the communication behavior of the dominant classes (1980, p. 11). Precisely because of that, it is encouraging to see that the study of nonconventional channels and workers' critical decodification is being pursued, as is the analysis of information exchange structures, in both rural and urban areas; to these we must add the interest in the forms of popular culture that arise from workers' movements and the so-called urban movements (see, e.g., Bosi, 1972; Gonzaga Mota, 1981; Limeira de Melo, 1981; Lins da Silva, 1982).

In accordance with such concerns, Gustavo Esteva has drawn attention to the need to investigate the theoretical and political value of citizens' movements and organizations. Common features include the practice of self-governance and a propensity toward direct action, both of which contribute to "an alternative rationality that is not a simple logical result, but an alternative social praxis" (1982, p. 46). Manuel Castells observes: "A new spirit is spreading through the crisis-ridden world . . . : neighborhood associations, parents' associations, neighborhood committees, consumer organizations, user organizations, participation organizations, cultural clubs, social centers, an endless number of citizen expressions that struggle, organize, and develop a consciousness, attempting to transform the material base and the social form of daily life" (1977, pp. 9, 33).

One way of becoming immersed in this movement is by analyzing the workers' and unions' press and the subordinate classes in general terms. Even though this analysis is in its initial stage, three fundamental research lines can be detected: the analysis of *current events,* the *case* analysis, and *historical* studies encompassing diverse stages. Lins da Silva (1982) has suggested a wide range of topics for study in the first two categories. Concerning historical studies, of great importance in my opinion, I would like to note two contributions to this long-neglected area, the works of Brazilian and Mexican authors: Albino Rubim, *Sobre la Prensa de las Clases Subalternas (1880– 1922)*, and Guillermina Bringas and David Mascareno, *La Prensa de los Obreros Mexicanos (1870–1970)*. But historical studies are not limited to studies of the press but encompass other aspects of popular communication, as is shown by Luis Roberto Alvez' investigation of communication and resistance in the Brazilian colonial culture, both of which he specifically links with inquisitorial techniques (1980).

All these studies stem from a concern that I have already referred to: the need to study the current extent and impact of native communication systems that predate the coming of the mass media to Latin American countries.

In fact, in all historical cultures, from the indigenous to peasant ones and the poor sectors of the urban zones, there have been participatory communication forms simply because in such cultures there were forms of participatory activities like, for example, the Quechuan *minka*, the Brazilian *mutirão*, the Haitian *convite*, and other kinds of cooperation. (Díaz Bordenave, n.d., p. 2)

In talking about the relationship between alternative communication and social change, we need to note that these forms of alternative communication are not a mere survival of earlier forms that have tended to be displaced by liberalism and capitalist industrial society, but a phenomenon whose effect points to the future: they, along with peasant associations, the cooperative movement, neighborhood associations, unions, and the ecclesiastical base communities, "are the ones that really practice democracy in our society and are redoubts of democratic communication" (Díaz Bordenave, 1982, p. 19).

The self-governing experience of the Bolivian miners' radio stations is a truly unique phenomenon, not only in Latin America, but perhaps worldwide because of its political, cultural, social, and historical dimensions. This experience is linked directly and indirectly with controversies about the autonomy of the worker and popular communication vis-à-vis the so-called vanguard. The initial investigation indicates that this field might be fertile for others as well (Lozada and Kuncar, 1982). Another important area of research studies concerns alternative communication among women, a phenomenon that gained little attention until recently.[10]

In the Mexican case, research has touched on a number of diverse topics, including the newspapers of workers and unions (see Jose Luis Gutierrez Espindola's research on the magazine *Solidaridad* [1981]; indigenous and peas-

10. The Women's Alternative Communication Unit of the Instituto Latinoamericano de Estudios Transnacionales has published several papers of great interest, including a 1982 series on the magazines *FEM* and *María, Liberación del Pueblo* (Mexico), *Nueva Mujer* (Ecuador), and *Mulherio* (Brazil), and on Radio Enriquillo (Dominican Republic). A very broad paper on the topic is Santa Cruz (1982).

ant radio stations, some of them subordinated to the National Indian Institute of Mexico (e.g., Correa, n.d.; Velazco, n.d.); discourse of the workers' press (Poloniato, n.d.; Tomasini, 1981); the rescue of collective memory through historical drama and other means of expression (Escobar, 1982); and processes of cultural reevaluation among indigenous populations (Rendon and Cifuentes, 1982). Another interesting research line is centered on the relationship of popular education processes and urban recovery movements (Quintana, 1982), a problem on which many research studies have focused. Finally, it is appropriate to mention activities linked to popular access to communication technology (Ehrenberg, 1982; Gumuscio Dagron, 1981). The significance of these kinds of activities and the corresponding research studies cannot be overstated, especially if we take into account the fact that the marrow of alternative communication is the decentralization of communication power, which implies a decentralization of the technological know-how.

An important research area that I have purposely left until last is alternative communication in transitional regimes. This area is only beginning to be explored, but it is of enormous theoretical and political significance, even though it contains some timid and fragmentary research and some that dodges the central problem: theoretical models of society—explicit or implicit—and the political communication practices that derive from them. We will focus here on the communication policies and alternative expressions that arose at two historic moments: the Unidad Popular government of Allende in Chile (1970–73) and the revolutionary regime of Velazco Alvarado in Peru (1968–75).

In the case of Chile, some authors, because they start from a functionalism and neobehaviorism of the Leninist type, cannot extract from the facts the pertinent conclusions. Consider, for example, Armand Mattelart's pioneering and illustrative work on the alternative press in the industrial belts in Santiago, Chile (1974b). Even though his approach is basically anecdotal, Mattelart's dialogues with the industrial belt workers have enormous value because of their political and ideological implications. The importance of this thematic material rests on the facts that are narrated, independently (as in other cases) of the evaluation and interpretation that the author offers about them. Still, it is paradoxical that a defender of the "socialist" state monopoly of the media would stress the problems and conditions from which diverse alternatives arise, not only in opposition to the right wing, but also in opposition to the official or semiofficial press of the Allende regime. In the problems expressed by workers in this context, we can observe the radical contradiction between the power exercised by certain paternalistic vanguards and the cultural and social communication autonomy of the working masses.

Another researcher, Claudio Aguirre Bianchi, also reviews the alternative press during the Unidad Popular administration (1979). In this work of great substance, the author's analysis centers on the criticism of functionalist-behaviorist theories and the formulation of what he calls a "draft for a subversive theory" of social communication. Aguirre Bianchi's reflections are valuable because of the particular context in which he is working and the kind of information he supplies. He provides the finishing touch to initiatives that arose, he says, "as a reaction to a certain degree of bureaucratization at some government levels—middle-level administrators and political chiefs responsible for the enterprises incorporated into the Social Property Area (1979, p. 267). He concludes:

As an answer to a bureaucratization of the elite, a kind of workers' populism arose. In confrontation with these tendencies, some new situations emerged. Although no sector really controlled the state apparatus, at the popular base a new state of things was forming, new organizations were seeing the light, and people were starting to think about new policies. (1979, p. 268)

What interests us here is the suppression of grassroots communication phenomena because of decisions alien to workers, who in fact represented—as Aguirre Bianchi notes—a duality of power and an obstacle to the centralizing tendencies of the state. The team that put out the workers' youth magazine, *Compañero,* published by Editora Nacional Quimantú, gave journalism classes to many young workers:

The goal of this publication was to contribute to the mobilization and the participation of young people through a process of permanent questioning of the young workers' daily lives. When *Compañero*'s experience was beginning to bear fruit, it was interrupted because of political differences within the Unidad Popular front about the main question: the mobilization process and its meaning. (1979, p. 259)

Here we have a topic that calls for much more penetrating analysis: alternative communication as an expression of the duality of power in transitional governments: in other words, an emerging conflict, latent or open, between the centralization and the democratization of communication power.

In the Peruvian case we find as a result of the national press reform contradictions that point in the same direction: the conflict between democratization and centralization, between the bureaucratic-state apparatus and popular participation. This case leads one to reflect on two important points: the concept of socialization (as opposed to simple direct or indirect statization) and the nature of the relationship between sender and receiver as a determining factor in any genuinely democratizing project in communication structures. About this, the authors of a major research project on the phenomenon say:

The process of communication itself was not greatly altered regardless of the expropriation. If we start from the simplest communication model, one that considers the existence of a sender, a message, and a receiver, we can say that the sender was, in some way, the government with its respective colorations. (Peirano et al., 1978, p. 212)

Within this picture the authors refer, although briefly, to a phenomenon that another researcher calls "the alternative within the alternative" (Gargurevich, 1981, pp. 191–214): the development of a parallel journalism "within the reformed press." This gave way, they note, to the emergence of two *antagonistic* projects—the government's and the one promoted by sectors of the radicalized petit bourgeoisie "who assume strictly popular interests" (Peirano et al., 1978, p. 214).

Needless to say, such cases are extremely significant because they point to a new research area that has been ignored—as I have already noted—by most scholars: the alternative communication effect that arises within processes of economic and social-political transition. Even though Peirano and his colleagues (1978), in their study on the Peruvian case, seem to reject the so-called "third way," in fact their observations on the false socialization and the monopoly on social discourse by the state implicitly point toward a global criticism of the two paradigmatic systems and the need to expand the alternative communication concept beyond mere opposition to transnational capitalist structures.

The circle of our exposition closes with the convergence of our initial concerns about the concept of alternative communication itself, and the limits imposed on the study of the phenomenon, and our concerns about the relationship between alternative communication and global democratization projects, which led us to question once again the relationship between communication models and models of society. The convergence of the interest in the varied expressions of popular communication and in alternative phenomena within change processes indicates a clear change in the conceptualization and the orientation of research studies on the topic of alternative communication.

References

Aguirre Bianchi, C. (1979). "Medios Alternativos de Comunicación y Formaciones Sociales de Conciencia." In J. Vidal-Beneyto (ed.) *Alternativas Populares a las Comunicaciones de Masas*. Madrid: Centro de Investigaciones Sociológicas.

Alvez, L. R. (1980). "Comunicação e Resistencia na Cultura Colonial: Brasil, 1590." In J. Marques de Melo (ed.) *Comunicação e Classes Subalternas*, pp. 132–43. São Paulo: Cortez Editora.

Argumedo, A. (1981). "Comunicación y Democracia en las Propuestas de Nuevo Orden Mundial de las Comunicaciones y la Información." Paper presented to the Seminar on Communication and Democracy, sponsored by the Latin American Council of Social Sciences, Santa Marta, Colombia, March 17–20.

Bosi, E. (1972). *Leituras Operárias*. Petropolis: Vozes.

Capriles, O. (1981). "Venezuela: Política de Comunicación o Comunicación Alternativa?" In M. Simpson Grinberg (ed.) *Comunicación Alternativa y Cambio Social*, vol. 1: *América Latina*, pp. 149–66. Mexico City: Universidad Nacional Autónoma de México.

Castells, M. (1977). *Ciudad, Democracia, y Socialismo*. Mexico City: Siglo XXI.

Castoriadis, C. (1976). *La Sociedad Burocrática*, vol. 1. Barcelona: Tusquets Editores.

Chomsky, N. (1974). *Vietnam y España: Los Intelectuales Liberales Ante la Revolución*. Mexico City: Siglo XXI.

Correa, E. (n.d.). "La Experiencia de Radio Tlapa, Guerrero [Mexico]." Manuscript.

Díaz Bordenave, J. (1982). "Democratización de la Comunicación: Teoría y Práctica." *Chasqui*, 1.

Díaz Bordenave, J. (n.d.). "La Comunicación Participatoria en la América Latina." Mimeographed.

Ehrenberg, F. (1982). "Acceso Popular a las Técnicas de Impresión." Mimeographed.

Escobar, R. A. (1982). "El Historiodrama Filmado: Cuatro Casos de Devolución del Habla al Pueblo." Mimeographed.

Esteva, G. (1982). "Políticas Estatales Alternativas en Comunicación y Cultura en América Latina." Paper presented to the Meeting on the State and the Cultural Industry in Latin America, Center for Economic and Social Studies of the Third World, Mexico, Aug. 9–11.

Fay, V. (1981). "Del Partido Como Instrumento de Lucha por el Poder al Partido Como Prefiguración de una Sociedad Socialista." In *Teoría Marxista del Partido Político*, vol. 3. 4th ed. Mexico City: Cuadernos de Pasado y Presente, no. 38.

Gargurevich, J. (1981). "La Alternativa Dentro de la Alternativa." In M. Simpson Grinberg (ed.) *Comunicación Alternativa y Cambio Social*, vol. 1: *América Latina*, pp. 191–214. Mexico City: Universidad Nacional Autónoma de México.

Gimenez, G. (1978). "Notas Para un Teoría de la Comunicación Popular." *Christus* (Mexico), 517, Dec.

Gonzaga Motta, L. (1981). "Comunicação Alternativa e Cultura da Resisténcia no Brasil." Paper presented to the Seminar on Communication and Democracy sponsored by the Latin American Council of Social Sciences, Santa Marta, Colombia, March 17–20.

Gonzaga Motta, L., and U. da Silva (1982). "Crítica a las Políticas de Comunicación: Entre el Estado, la Empresa ye el Pueblo." *Comunicación y Cultura* (Mexico), 7, Jan.

Goutman, A. A. (1979). "Los Medios de Comunicación en Cuba." In *Argentina, Cuba, Chile: Realidad Política y Medios Masivos*. Mexico City: Cuadernos del Centro de Estudios de la Comunicación, Universidad Nacional Autónoma de México, no. 4.

Gramsci, A. (1971). *Selections from the Prison Notebooks*. Trans. Q. Hoare and G. Nowell Smith. New York: International Publishers.

Graziano, M. (1980). "Para una Definición de la Comunicación Alternativa." Paper presented to the Twelfth General Assembly and Scientific Conference on Communication Research Studies (AIERI-IAMCR), Caracas, Aug. 25–29.

Gumuscio Dagron, A. (1981). *El Cine de los Trabajadores: Manual de Apoyo Teórico y Práctico a la Generación de Talleres de Cine Super 8.* Managua: Central Sandinista de Trabajadores.

Gutierrez Espindola, J. L. (1981). "Prensa Obrera, Nación, y Democracia: Crónica de la Revista *Solidaridad,* 1937–1980." Dissertation, School of Political and Social Sciences, Universidad Nacional Autónoma de México.

Lenin, V. I. (1969). *What Is to Be Done?* New York: International Publishers.

Limeira de Melo, C. B. (1981). "Experiencias Participativas Vinculadas con Movimientos Populares: El Caso Brasileño." Paper presented to the Seminar on Communication and Democracy sponsored by the Latin American Council of Social Sciences, Santa Marta, Colombia, March 17–20.

Lins da Silva, C. E. (1982). "Prensa Obrera y Sindical." *Chasqui,* 1.

Lozada, F., and G. Kuncar (1982). "Las Emisoras Mineras de Bolivia: Una Histórica Experiencia de Comunicación Autogestionária." Paper presented to the Seminar on Communication and Pluralism: Alternatives for the Decade, sponsored by the Instituto Latinoamericano de Estudios Transnacionales, Mexico, Nov. 22–26.

Marques de Melo, J. (1980). "Comunicação e Classes Subalternas." In J. Marques de Melo (ed.) *Comunicação e Classes Subalternas,* pp. 11–14. São Paulo: Cortez Editora.

Mattelart, A. (1974a). "Comunicación y Cultura de las Masas." In *Comunicación Masiva y Revolución Socialista.* 2d ed. Mexico City: Editorial Diógenes.

Mattelart, A. (1974b). "Prensa y Lucha Ideológica en los Cordones Industriales de Santiago: Testimonios." *Comunicación y Cultura* (Buenos Aires), 2, March, pp. 77–108.

Nethol, A. M. (1981). "Reflexiones acerca de la Teoría y Acción Comunicativas Dentro de los Procesos de Transición a las Democracias." Paper presented to the seminar on Communication and Democracy sponsored by the Latin American Council of Social Sciences, Santa Marta, Colombia, March 17–20.

Peirano, L., et al. (1978). *Prensa: Apertura y Límites.* Lima: Centro de Estudios y Promoción del Desarrollo.

Poloniato, A. (n.d.). "Jurado 13: Radio Novela Alternativa?" Mimeographed.

Portales, D. (1981). "Perspectivas de la Comunicación Alternativa en América Latina." In M. Simpson Grinberg (ed.) *Comunicación Alternativa y Cambio Social,* vol. 1: *América Latina,* pp. 61–80. Mexico City: Universidad Nacional Autónoma de México.

Quintana, V. M. (1982). *Educación Popular y Movimientos Reivindicatorios Urbanos.* Guadalajara, Mexico: Servicios Educativos de Occidente.

Rendón, J. J., and B. Cifuentes (1982). "La Lectura y Escritura de la Lengua Zapoteca: Un Proceso de Revalorización y Organización Cultural." Paper presented to the national meeting on Society and Popular Cultures, Mexico, Universidad Autónoma Metropolitana-Xochimilco, July 5–9.

Reyes Matta, F. (1981). "La Comunicación Transnacional y la Respuesta Alternativa." In M. Simpson Grinberg (ed.) *Comunicación Alternativa y Cambio Social,* vol. 1: *América Latina,* pp. 81–108. Mexico City: Universidad Nacional Autónoma de México.

Roncagliolo, R., and L. Avila (1982). "The National Communication Policies (NCP) in Latin America: Analytic Perspectives and Democratic Experiences." Paper presented at the meeting on the State and the Cultural Industry in Latin America, sponsored by the Center for Economic and Social Studies of the Third World, Mexico City, Aug. 9–11.

Rossanda, R. (1981). "De Marx a Marx: Clase y Partido." In *Teoría Marxista del Partido Político 3*. 4th ed. Mexico City: Cuadernos de Pasado y Presente, no. 38.

Rude, G. (1981). *Revuelta Popular y Conciencia de Clase*. Barcelona: Editorial Crítica/Grupo Editorial Grijalbo.

Santa Cruz, A. (1982). "Mujer y Comunicación: Nuevas Voces en la Búsqueda de una Democracia Auténtica." Paper presented to the Seminar on Communication and Pluralism: Alternatives for the Decade, sponsored by the Instituto Latinoamericano de Estudios Transnacionales, Mexico, Nov. 22–26.

Simpson Grinberg, M. (1981). "Comunicación Alternativa: Dimensiones, Límites, Posibilidades." In M. Simpson Grinberg (ed.) *Comunicación Alternativa y Cambio Social*, vol. 1: *América Latina*, pp. 109–29. Mexico City: Universidad Nacional Autónoma de México.

Simpson Grinberg, M. (in press). *Leninismo y Comunicación*.

Somavía, J. (1977). "Prologue." In *The New International Information Order*. Mexico City: Instituto Latinoamericano de Estudios Transnacionales.

Sweezy, P. (1971). "Czechoslovakia, Capitalism, and Socialism." In *La Transicióñ Socialismo*, Medellín, Colombia: Zeta Limitada.

Taufic, C. (1973). *Periodismo y Lucha de Clases*. Santiago: Editora Nacional Quimantú.

Tomasini, M. A. (1981). *La Propaganda Política Mexicana en 1976*. Mexico City: Cuadernos del TICOM (Taller de Investigación en Comunicación Masiva), Universidad Autónoma Metropolitana-Xochimilco, no. 8.

Velazco, A. (n.d.). "Radio Huayacocotla: Una Experiencia de Comunicación Radiofónica Alternativa en México." Manuscript.

Vidal-Beneyto, J. (1979). *Alternativas Populares a las Comunicaciones de Masas*. Madrid: Centro de Investigaciones Sociológicas.

10 *Fernando Reyes Matta*

Alternative Communication: Solidarity and Development in the Face of Transnational Expansion

With the capitalist model of development, stimulated to the utmost in its transnational phase, has come a form of communication that universalizes and transnationalizes culture. Critics of this model have tried, in one way or another, to counter the two essential features of transnational communication: its verticality and its atomizing effect on society.

The search for a new kind of communication has taken on a special significance in recent years, especially in Latin America. These new approaches are more than communication projects; they embody a change in perspective, in consciousness. At the same time, they are antagonistic to the development model and the communication system generated to serve it. Hence, " 'alternative' is, in this confrontation, the *other,* the different, that which does not abide by the rules imposed by the dominant system" (Chapa and Angel, 1980).

Definitions of "alternative communication" are still unclear. Marginal communication, group communication, popular communication, and horizontal communication are encompassed by the widest definition of alternative communication, which must refer as well to the relationship between alternative communication and the dominated: the oppressed sectors of society at the national level, and the dominated countries at the international level.

Once the problem is located on this wider plane, it is necessary to accept phenomenological diversity. The alternative reply is born of the various viewpoints from which oppression is perceived and described. As a result, alter-

190

native communication takes diverse forms, which emerge from the need to express the particular world view of a social group, class, country, or region. The choice of form is part of a process whose goal is participatory communication in which each receiver is a potential sender, the interaction of participants maintains life in the social fabric, there is for individual and collective creativity, and, in sum, the social being recovers his or her voice.

Alternative communication has been presented as different from existing forms without describing the degree of difference:

From this lack of precision is born ambiguity. One cannot, for example, speak properly about alternative communication when referring to a change or reform intended simply to make a given system of social communication more functional. In this field, as in others, not every novelty is really alternative. In a first attempt to describe the problem that we are looking at, then, we would say that any proposal for communication that pretends to be alternative presupposes, as a negative condition, the fundamental rejection of the communication structure in force. (Rey, 1980)

Various studies, especially in Latin America, have documented the behavior and effects of the dominant system. The rejection of the system arises from this knowledge. However, this rejection leads to different perceptions about strategy and tactics. One points toward profound change and the other toward constructive activity in the medium of real history in which we must move.

The strategy is to make communication a participatory process—a process of dialogue and widespread creativity. This strategy does not merely oppose the dominant system but lays out its own historical project, whose goal is to build new ways of life and holistic development for individuals and social sectors.

Tactics, on the other hand, require a constant search for spaces and forms for alternative communication, for opportunities to express proposals for social revitalization and solidarity, all within the limits imposed by the reigning system. Possible areas of action include looking for opportunities to present the alternative message in existing media, creating alternative media and media forms, and creating the conditions for a "critical consumption" of what the dominant structure delivers. These interrelated actions together reveal the possibilities available in the alternative communication process.

Alternative communication has roots that stretch beyond the reaction to the transnational expansion of modern capitalism to experimental popular journalism. This form of journalism, practiced in European countries and in the periphery, especially Latin America, worked to mobilize the people and create the consciousness that drove people's rights movements. In the Latin American case, journalism was a tool in the struggles for independence at the beginning of the last century. Latin American journalism was only later deformed by massive industrialization of the media to serve the interests of various clans and economic power groups and to create an economic and information power structure from which came the "established press." The established press viewed itself as working by the standards of the centers of power in the Western world. It distorted the historical development of journalism in Latin America and transformed a journalism of ideas, of opinion, of positions, into a tool of dominant groups. The lingering respect for the journalism of ideas, opinion, and commitment is one of the lodes that alternative communication has discovered and claimed as its own to exploit.

Though this historical background is important, alternative communication is primarily a phenomenon created to fill the communication needs of the large social sectors that, in developed as in developing countries, are marginalized by the dominant communication and development model. This is the essential meaning of alternative communication: it is a reply to a model of communication rooted in capitalism in expansion. Capitalism becomes transnational as a means of taking over markets and accumulating profits. The peripheral countries constitute a reserve market for this expansion. In consequence, the reference point for the alternative perspective is that transnational model. Hence, we assume that an understanding of alternative communication requires us to pass over analysis from an exclusively communication perspective in favor of one that situates the phenomenon in the global questions that at economic, political, and cultural levels affect and define industrialized and peripheral societies alike.

Such a notion has been expressed, albeit in a partial way, in the studies and conferences on the subject. The partiality is explained by the diversity of analytic challenges that alternative communication presents. For some, the best expressions of alternative communication are the state communication monopolies. These have, in the European context, loosed a flood of alternative expressions (independent radio and television stations, social communication organizations, etc.) that complement political and academic proposals for the democratization of communication. This was the predominant theme in the 1978 meeting in Barcelona on People's Alternatives to Mass Communications (Vidal Beneyto, 1979). Different contributions have been made by those wishing to confront the power structure created by the big private communication systems. This was the framework of the twelfth Conference of the International Association for Mass Communication Research (IAMCR) in Caracas in 1980. The same antagonism marks the works of the Alternative Media Syndicate in the United States, whose practical work is richer than its theoretical development. Another contribution, at the conceptual level, comes from the most deprived peripheral areas, like Mozambique, whose experience has produced significant reflections in the last few years (Mattelart, 1981; Mattelart and Mattelart, 1981). All of this work orients, reinforces, clarifies, but it also maintains the analysis of alternative communication in a zone of predominantly local experiences. In this essay, too, the local experience is the primary point of reference. Yet we must, for the better understanding of the alternatives, take into consideration the features of the global phenomenon that is advancing toward the ideal of a global village with transnational culture. As Cees Hammelink has written, we are seeing the establishment and adjustment of a corporate village that bases its daily work on the synchronization of communication at a world level (1978).

As noted above, the primary reference point of alternative communication is the transnational model in its global expansionary phase. We must recognize that this model debilitates the full, integrated development and the political, economic, and cultural independence of the people of the Third World and of the industrialized world. Consequently, the analytic challenge here is to integrate diverse phenomena that are all partial replies, in different societies, to still other phenomena that have a common origin. From industrialized capitalist countries, from recently liberated countries, and from the Latin American societies especially affected by capitalism's transnational phase come replies, investigations, and contributions to a common discussion, whose participants never even realize that the discussion is a common one. The atomization syndrome is alive and well, hindering the work for "another development" begun in the experiments of the mid-seventies.

A series of international reports has attempted to give development a definition other than the one imposed by the capitalist expansion inherited from the Second World War. These have a common element: the attempt to recover diversity in the dialogue between societies and within them. The "What to Do" Report published by the Dag Hammarskjold Foundation; the RIO Report headed by the Nobel prize–winning economist Jan Tinberger; the contributions of the Third System Project, started by the International Foundation for Development Alternatives; and, more recently, the Brandt Report, whose aim was to salvage a development project capable of ensuring the whole world's survival—all, in one way or another, call attention to the necessity of making culture and the media areas of creativity, expression, and communication in which all sectors of society have the opportunity to be informed and to inform, to participate and to create the diversity that ensures the participation of the majority in the creation of society. As the Brandt Report says, "fundamental changes are not the result of bureaucratic work, but have their origin in a historical process that reflects what is being prefigured and gestated in the minds of people" (see Aguirre Bianchi and Hedebro, 1980).

The Historical Factors

Forms of alternative communication vary greatly from one setting to another, so any attempt to systematize their features and discover their common denominator necessitates a historical perspective on their circumstances and evolution. Alternative communication emerged in a context that in large measure has existed only since the Second World War. There are perhaps four historical factors that have determined this context, which in turn has defined the alternative dynamic as much at the level of media used as at that of content.

The Struggle Against Colonialism

With the end of the Second World War came the crystallization of forces whose aim was to break away from colonialism and recover the right to national independence. These forces had been growing in strength for decades, especially in North African and Asian countries. The 1960s saw the emergence of new countries that not only had to begin the difficult process of political organization, but needed as well to affirm a cultural identity. They were forced to reshape the communication system and make it their own mechanism of expression, using new languages and having different priorities in the transmission of information from those imposed by the colonial powers. This process is especially evident in those African and Asian countries that have looked back to their popular culture—their traditions and folk forms, their dances, theater, and song—and at the same time have used the instruments of modern communication for their own historical project. Thus, for example, the Mozambican Photographic Association speaks of its medium as a new cultural front:

Photography is a most rigorous document which permits the whole Mozambican people to re-live the armed struggle for national liberation, to know our heroes, to see our leaders in the direction of combat and in the organization of life. Photography is . . . an important instrument in the consolidation of national unity which shows the whole reality of our country, its beauties, its natural wealth, its cities, its mountains, rivers, and lakes, its vast plains, the fauna and flora, its beaches and islands. The understanding of the whole nation and the reinforcement of patriotic sentiment are decisive stimulants to the growth of each Mozambican's determination to value and transform the fatherland itself. ("La fotografía," 1981)

The search for cultural identity, the creation of messages in different languages and with different content from those imposed by the transnational communication structure, is accompanied by a growth in consciousness of how information and communication systems manipulate information about the new reality in the country. India was one of the first colonial territories to win its independence after the Second World War. The images of the new country in the Western press betrayed the press's inability to understand a subcontinent of 650 million people, of whom 80 percent live in villages, with daily newspapers in twenty languages and other periodicals in fifty. From this cultural diversity the nation of "shadow puppets" emerged as the world's principal producer of films, a fact almost unknown in Europe, the United States, and Latin America, and not widely known in Africa and Asia (Eapen, 1980).

Such developments are part of the struggle to affirm a cultural identity that colonialism, in one way or another, tried to alter.

National and International Reactions to Neocolonialism

Beyond the independence process, the decades after the Second World War have seen the emergence of a new phenomenon called "neocolonialism." By means of more sophisticated mechanisms than those of colonialism, especially economic ones, the neocolonization process has created conditions of growing dependence for new countries and for the Third World in general. In those areas of the world, the expansion of transnational corporations plays an essential role; informational and cultural domination follow. In some countries neocolonialism has been very evidently active in defining political processes. The documented case of International Telephone and Telegraph's intervention in the Chilean situation is one of the most obvious examples of this. Similar events have taken place in Jamaica, Nicaragua, Mozambique, Tanzania, and other regions of the Third World that have begun a process of change. A network of relationships is being created and expanded so that in regard to national debt, transfer of technology and of food, use of energy, and other factors, such countries' independence is only relative.

The movement of nonaligned countries has actively opposed this phenomenon. Its influence is recognizable in the proposals for a New International Economic Order, and it has affirmed the necessity of escaping from the cultural inheritances of colonialism. The declaration of the heads of state of the nonaligned countries at their conference in Algeria in 1973 is a key to understanding the interrelation of politics, economics, and culture from the standpoint of this movement of countries—countries that in spite of differences maintain a common position in regard to problems derived from colonialism and revived in neocolonialism.

Efforts of the nonaligned countries within the United Nations have been decisive in the progress of the international debate on communication and the affirmation of a "new world information and communication order" as a necessary condition for balanced and shared development. The movement has also taken steps to create alternatives within the world flow of information, including—a precarious move—the news agency pool and subsequent agreements to exchange radio and television programs.

Quality of Life and Humanistic Development

From the very interior of the societies that call themselves postindustrial has come a heterogeneous movement that has expressed itself in various ways. This movement defends "the quality of life," which is being attacked by the expansion of the transnationals on their own home ground. However, the movement's frontiers go beyond the environmental problems posed by industrial development. It raises questions in which many other movements find their roots: the movement for the authentic liberation of women; the movement for peace, and the profound rejection of the growing arms trade and the possibility of nuclear war; the movement in defense of democracy in the context of the information society and growing resources for state control through electronic technology; the movement for creative and autonomous use of free time; the movement for food grown and processed to promote human health and not to fill the commercial requirements of big companies. These and other issues created by accelerated development and an accumulation of profit that has led to opulence define a common platform on which people from many social groups ask whether life could not be lived differently, beyond the order defined by the market and the laws of cost and benefit.

In 1966, in his lectures in Mexico, Herbert Marcuse was already expressing anxiety about the evolution of life in industrialized countries:

The new needs and satisfactions that technological society offers, just as much as the new liberties, work against man's authentic liberation; they turn against man his physical and mental faculties, even his instinctive energy. The result? A profound frustration, a penetrating hatred beneath the relative felicity of the "opulent society," and a reaction expressed in a notable increase in the aggression that permeates technological society. (Marcuse et al., 1968)

Ten years later Dupuy and Robert speak clearly of "the treason of opulence" in a book full of categorical statements: "Medicine makes us ill, school makes us dull, communications make us deaf and mute, transport immobilizes us." Their analysis identifies the modern distortion of rationality in these terms: "The mode of industrial production violently alters the framework within which people live; the physical space and time of daily life, relations between people, and even their language are profoundly altered by the logic of commerce" (1979).

Fifteen years after Marcuse's lectures, Edgar Morin's *Pour Sortir du Siecle 2000* was published. It reflects on a world in the prehistory of the human spirit, "in the Iron Age of the planet." We have the greatest resources of information that humanity has ever known, says Morin, but "all events happen in a disorderly fashion, without meaning for us; they constitute *noise* in the purest sense of Shannon's theory; our lives swim in a medium of *background noise*, a whirlwind of events" (1981).

The years have increased the anxiety. These realities, questions, and challenges have given form to a press—represented by the French magazine *Autrement*—that tries to express the will of a world searching for alternative ways of life, a search that is cheered especially by the younger generation. Since the middle of the 1960s the underground press has traced an alternative itinerary in the heart of the dominant communication system. The *Nation*, the oldest, progressive political weekly in the United States, has been joined by publications like *Ramparts*, the *Village Voice*, and the *Guardian*, whose content and form depart from the rigid schemes resented by the younger generation. The Vietnam war mobilized youth, and so did the counterculture, disconcerting to capitalism, of the hippies and the other movements that followed them. Not one but many contradictions lie within the movements' programs, and more than one represents a regressive introversion that closes its eyes to the world. Still, at the end of all the questioning are new perspectives on alternative communication. Looking at the first half of the 1980s with Ronald Reagan in the White House, one can say that the alternative press network—alternative in various ways—in which mass organizations and community groups play a central role, is containing and struggling against a policy that puts peace in danger, cuts social benefits won over decades, and permits transnational corporations to take over the role of maintaining order in society.

One member of this alternative network is *Mother Jones*, a magazine based in San Francisco that covers subjects like the dangers arising from the disposal of nuclear waste in fishing zones and the dangers of video display terminals to their operators' health (both in the July 1981 issue). Other members are *Coalition* (published by the Coalition for a New Foreign and Military Policy), *Peace and Freedom* (Women's International League for Peace and Freedom), and *Community Jobs* (the Youth Project).

A look toward Europe reveals more examples of alternative publications. There the area covered by the alternative press has been enlarged by the development the communication media have undergone on that continent. The union press, the church press, the movement press (representing the groups formed since 1968), the ecology press, the feminist press, the press that promotes the consumption of natural foods (and opposes the nutritional manipulation of the transnationals)—all are well received. There are in addition publications that depart from the classic private information enterprise pattern, such as *Le Monde*, the most powerful example of an undertaking conceived by a journalists' cooperative. This overview shows that an alternative message is latent in the cultural atmosphere of industrialized society, although it does not correspond to an articulated or uniform process.

Reactions to Political and Economic Authoritarianism

Significant contributions to alternative communication have also come from another direction: the popular movements and mass organizations that arose to confront political authoritarianism (predominantly military dictatorships) and economic authoritarianism (the privilege and power of groups). In Latin America this resistance has been dramatically in evidence for decades. Since the Second World War, however, and especially in the last decade, Latin America has witnessed a recrudescence of both forms of authoritarianism.

They are no longer the result of "barracks plots" by generals or colonels but are more ideologically motivated. Of particular significance is the doctrine of national security, which serves as the basis for the persecution of "the internal enemy," who is identified with popular movements and mass organizations. The interrelation of these military tactics with the transnationals' expansionary strategies—given incentive by the economic philosophy of Friedman, Von Hajeck, and other theorists who advocate a free market without limits—has implications for the ability of the great majority of people to satisfy their basic needs. The state has been converted into a guardian who maintains authoritarian social control so that the economic mechanisms of the "free market" may act for the benefit of certain power groups. Political, economic, social, and cultural democracy suffers the oppressive consequences.

But it is precisely in the midst of this somber panorama that many forms of expression have emerged to respond to the needs of the "voiceless." From song, graphics, theater, the popular press, cinema, and to a certain degree radio (television only fleetingly) emerges a cultural reality that superimposes itself on censorship and authoritarianism in order to create an alternative to the dominant structures of communication.

Brazilian experiments in alternative communication have been especially strong and creative. Since the military coup of 1964, the popular forces have banded together. Christian base communities have played a central role, especially in São Paulo, a city with a high concentration of workers and people of low income. From this alliance of social movements communication forms with significant strength have emerged. The *nanica* press (from *nana*, "grandmother" or "nanny," "lullaby") is so called because although its circulation is small, it has great influence. It questions military authoritarianism and criticizes an economic model that sustains profound injustices. "*Pasquín* of the *nanica* press was the one to begin to demonstrate that there was a space," according to Chico Mario de Souza, one of the creators of the alternative record business in Brazil, "that we didn't necessarily have to accept the official communication vehicles, that we could create alternative media. After *Pasquín,* others began. The alternative book also appeared. Poets and committed writers threw themselves into the publication of their own books, with limited print runs of one or two thousand copies. Hundreds of books appeared, but the writers still aren't organized. On the other hand, having created a musicians' cooperative to make alternative records, we are advancing greatly; we make an impression in the press and in other media" (Rameda, 1980).

This view of alternative communication reveals its two essential facets: the expression of a culture both transformed and transforming, and cultural resistance to the transnationalization process. The latter is particularly evident in Latin America, the zone of greatest influence and expansion of the transnationals after the industrialized countries themselves. This brings us to the practically and theoretically rich attempt to recover the cultural values of the nation and to formulate a cultural identity in which the popular sectors, as mobilizers of resistance to that transnational capitalist project, can recognize themselves. "Culture is the field of battle, and there is a popular struggle against alienation. Even in advanced capitalist societies, the culture industry, at least the best parts of it, feeds on the popular movements that emerge among the people. In other words, when the culture industry attains good quality, it is because it is feeding on elements that first of all emerge from the people, even within capitalism. . . . Something similar occurs in our country," said the Peruvian Carlos Ivan Degregori, in a debate on culture and social class. He added, "In reply to the question, what is the popular, or what is popular culture, within this increasingly transnational reality, I would say: it is something perpetually recreated" (DESCO, 1980).

In Latin America, more, perhaps, than any other region, the traditional forms of communication (song, drama, crafts, poetry, pictures, dance) are closely interwoven with the possibilities offered by modern techniques of communication (film, photography, records, slides, audiocassettes, and even videocassettes). "Hermenegilda Cundergue Speaks to Her People" is a series of seven programs recorded on five cassettes intended as a critical orientation course on the media. In this Venezuelan production by the Jesús María Pellin Center, Hermenegilda is a black woman who broadcasts from her clandestine transmitter, "analyzing with humor and mischief and with the wisdom granted by the university of life various media and programs." This was one of the early experiments in "cassette forums," begun by Mario Kaplún in Uruguay and then brought to Venezuela (Kaplún and O'Sullivan, 1978). The forms of alternative media were made possible by the enormous expansion of the radio–cassette player, which is now most pervasive in the popular sectors. The need to market transnational products makes it possible to redeem some instruments for use in the communication and dialogue begun in the popular areas, even under dictatorships. Popular creativity can profit from the contradictions in the system, even when popular forces are in retreat.

Under these circumstances alternative communication has acquired in Latin America an essentially antiauthoritarian profile. Communication becomes a consciousness-forming process in the struggle to construct a social dialogue and a society in which participation is a basic axis.

Fundamental Characteristics

What characteristics emerge as constants from the diverse projects described above? What characteristics are essential for an alternative experience to provide a real alternative and not merely a diversion? In this search for the essentials, the Latin American reality is the point of departure of our analysis.

Languages and Oppositional Connotations

Alternative communication experiments are characterized by their oppositional and propositional character. They postulate forms and content that construct their "own language." This language is not easy to construct or to
discover. It is part of a collective consciousness, a popular imagination that
alternative communicators seek to discover, inserting themselves in a "commitment without prejudices" into the social reality of the great majority of the
people, who have been marginalized by the dominant communication:

All of reality is what *is* and what is *not*, containing not only the dominant, but also,
and fundamentally for us, the alternative. The dominant ideology is not reality, but
only part of it. For the same reason that the dominant signs are not the whole discourse, neither are they the macrotext that embraces everything. Nor is the social education that characterizes the messages of authoritarian structure the only one or forever
valid. . . . The objective of criticizing the dominant messages and elaborating alternatives is to achieve a process of transformation. (Prieto Castillo, 1980)

Alternative forms are bound, inevitably and necessarily, to the advances
made by Paulo Freire. Daily life is fertile ground for joint reflection. Understanding of alternative communication experiments, of what they say and
what they suggest, is rooted in daily life. Text and context reach their greatest
strength when the form of communication and the people share a common
reality. When in a festival of "Canto Nuevo" in Chile, a young group sings,
"Song with Everyone," the first verse says much more than it seems to: "All
the voices, all / all the hands, all / all the blood can / be song in time." Those
words become coherent with the lived experience of solidarity, of looks exchanged, of shared hopes. The Latin American element in the song, as well as
the consciousness of one's daily round, enables one experiencing oppression
to feel the possibility of not being alone. Does it not suggest something beyond the text of the play *Prometheus Bound* that was produced in Uruguay?

It is in the play of words and looks that the alternative language is created,
in the play of common commitments, of objective and subjective realities.
Identity is there, rooted in a time whose challenges are put into evidence by
the contradictions of every day:

There is no need to throw oneself into the search for identity; there is no need to go out
with a flashlight to see what we find. The problem of identity resides in being able
to recognize the strength we have and the conditions of exploitation in which we
exist. . . . The problem of identity is not a search for identity. The problem of identity
is to assume what we are, in order to be able to turn our hand to the history in which
we want to be, without being careless about what we are. (Orlando Plaza, quoted in
DESCO, 1980)

In that recognition of reality, those who work in alternative communication can identify themselves with the large majorities who see these forms of communication as their own.

The Orientation of Social Praxis

It is not possible to conceive of authentic alternative communication without a strong link to a social praxis that feeds and supports it. The quality of alternative communication depends upon the persistence of participation.

We must first define what we mean by marginal and oppositional communication. Marginality is not determined by the resources and the precariousness of the media of communication, or by their circulation. Even though it has been produced with the best will and the greatest "social sensitivity," a program, publication, or message can *put itself* at the margin of a social body that serves as its point of reference and starting point for dialogue. Marginality is seen in a neighborhood newsletter produced in isolation by a concerned local journalist, or in a television program made by a committed producer for transmission by an open cable station in any North American city. Marginality is determined by the position the communicators adopt. They can be in the middle of a process and make it a part of themselves, searching for the social weave, or they can put themselves at the margin, starting from their own vocations and supposing that their talent alone is sufficient to give an account of the social process, closing off the possibility of dialogue. The majority of alternative experiments emerge from a marginal situation, but aim at true alternative status.

With oppositional communication we are on another level of complexity. Some magazines and radio programs see their task as the rejection of certain political forms and antidemocratic programs, and they are backed by political organizations. There are many of these experiments in Latin America. But the difference between alternative communication and oppositional communication lies in the implicit attitude of the experiments toward the design of a strategic model for change. Alternative communication is part of a process and an attitude that aims to advance toward participatory social relations and solidarity, toward a reality where democracy has multiple and constant expressions, not only those that accompany occasional elections. The alternative takes in the oppositional.

Alternative communication, understood as a process, is fed by suitable contributions from marginal and oppositional expressions. But an alternative project's relation to society is what determines its existence and growth. Thus, alternative communication experiments are a consequence of a will to act that makes them the center and mobilizing force for a given kind of action, a given historical project for which they can be sources of information, orientation, or symbolism, and points of reference for identity, for atomized sectors wishing to reconstruct their social fabric.

The Strength of a Spiral Flow

Precisely because alternative communication requires a social framework that reinforces and orients and a shared language, communication experiments create dynamics very different from the vertical, one-directional flow of dominant communication forms. Theoretical contributions are important in that they fix a different perspective on the role of communication from that provided by the trade development model. But these contributions do not give an account of the whole process of growth and interrelationship that emerges each time as an essential aspect of authentically alternative communication. The interweaving and mutual support of diverse expressions and practices enable alternative communication and its messages to create a spiral flow of information: it starts from a basic pole or center and grows from there. Social organizations, popular needs, and moments of action constantly expand these expressions toward their goal, which is to answer back. The Grupo Experimental de Cine Universitario was born in 1973 in Panama. Its practice offers one of many examples of the relationship between communication and social reality. "The group shows its pictures principally to *campesino* organizations, unions, and students' and women's federations, that is, to all of those for whom the production was made and who have participated in it. The success of the group's work for the construction of a national cinema has opened the doors for it to state television" (Canclini, 1977). To go from the social bases to a medium capable of reaching a mass audience is a great achievement in the spiral of alternative communication. However, the important thing is not to lose—even under such circumstances—the essence of alternativeness: dialogue and participation. An advance has been made in Costa Rica, where new producers have also had a chance to reach the masses. "These half-hour films are broadcast once a month on television, followed by a discussion by specialists. In the future, so-called tele-clubs will be set up, in which debates will be organized at the end of the broadcast," wrote Peter B. Schumann in an article on political cinema in Latin America (quoted in Canclini, 1977). One of the films in this series was "Puerto Limón" (1974). It described an event that also inspired a play with the same name by the Tayacán theater group, which is one of the most active elements of the "Nueva Canción" movement in Costa Rica ("La nueva canción," 1981).

This dynamic of growth, interrelationship, and the search for support is not new, but it assumes a new aspect when it is part of a communication process whose goal is to become an alternative to the communication processes created by the transnational capitalist model. One can cite examples that already have a significant history, such as the Bolivian miners' radio:

One has only to glance over copies of miners' petitions for the last fifteen years to find, after each conflict with the government (the direct owner and administrator of the Bolivian Mining Corporation), in the first five points, immediately after "withdrawal of the army," "restitution of wages and salaries," and "freeing of detained workers," "*return of the transmitter to the workers. . . .*" How are the transmitters maintained? The workers maintain them in an admirable and evident demonstration of class consciousness and political vision, punctually delivering a proportion of their miserable salaries for the maintenance of *their* transmitter, the only one they have confidence in and the one they go to in search of reliable news, of opinion that is not only "committed," but relevant, from which they receive instructions in the hours of conflict and danger, when all of the workers' transmitters are integrated into a national chain. (Arrieta, 1980)

In this case the relationship between communication medium and audience is substantially different from the classic relationship of sender and receiver. The roles of sender and receiver are interwoven, while the production of information makes each listener an actor: sometimes he or she hears, sometimes tells, sometimes discusses what the radio said. And in this process the spiral grows.

The spiral in which alternative communication legitimates itself does not touch only its working-class audience, transparent in their commitment and fully opposed to the established order. A whole area of partial involvement, of questioning, can be found in the spaces created by the contradictions of the "established press" and the capitalist cultural-industrial model. In this, as in other cases, the alternative message helps to form a social body that generates a consciousness in which partial truths are harmonized in the perspective of a project for change.

This leads us to recognize the existence of a cultural environment related to the dominated pole of society, where not only creativity exists, but also a "reading" of the messages produced by the communication system allied to the dominant pole and the great transnational systems. Thus, the alternative spiral builds a dynamic of progress toward a time when the social and popular movements that are disadvantaged today will have hegemony. In some local experiments this may not be clearly seen, especially if one looks only at some of the phenomena— in both rich and poor countries. However, if we see them all together, it is clear that the principal model is in force, as is shown graphically in Figure 1.

The categories "dominant" and "dominated" recover for the analysis of communication its principal point of reference: communication is always part of a development model. Communication does not exist at the margin of history, apart from the tasks of human beings and society. It reflects the conflicts of power and the order that the hegemony of the powerful imposes on the rest of society. Yet history is never frozen, and models are never installed forever. Within that dynamic, vertical forms of communication—especially, but not only, the capitalist transnational ones—confront alternative communication

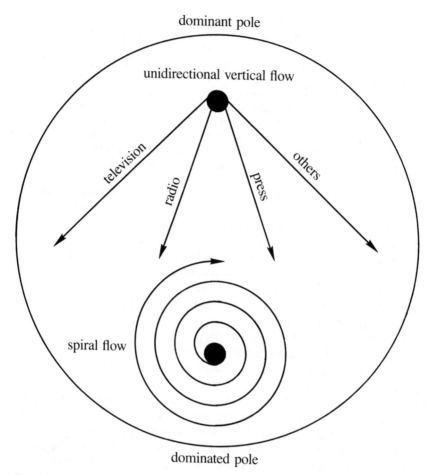

dominant pole

unidirectional vertical flow

television

radio

press

others

spiral flow

dominated pole

Figure 1. Communication Models

forms. This confrontation occurs as much within various societies as in contemporary international relations. "A subordinate relationship analogous to
that between the dominant and dominated classes," says Granados Chapa,
"exists too between countries. It is important, therefore, to meditate on the
fact that transnational culture and thus transnational communication exercise
dominion over national culture and communication, which, therefore, have to
become alternatives to the former" (Chapa and Angel, 1980).

The confrontation thus described at the global level is related to two great
development models. The transnational capitalist model atomizes social relations, promotes individualism, orders human relations according to hierarchi-
cal principles, depoliticizes democracy by turning it into a supposed democ-

racy of consumption, and distorts cultural diversity in order to implant a supposedly global culture that gives transnational expansion its legitimacy. The model of participatory development, on the other hand, recovers the benefits of production for the great majorities of society and searches for the kind of participatory relations in which pluralism is possible within a consensus of solidarity. This is a model of authentic and integral development of all of the facets of creativity, especially in political dialogue, understood as the essential expression of collective creativity in the chosen process of change.

Once the problem has been located in this macro-perspective, the *alternative* vocation of alternative communication emerges. It involves more than just "another" message, information going in the opposite direction from the dominant model. It creates the conditions for the influence or hegemony of new values of authentic democracy, open to the multiple creative capabilities of the individual and of society.

The spiral of alternative communication thus has a goal—to alter the inherited political, economic, and cultural structures up to the point at which national and popular sovereignty coincide. And after that, what? This question goes to the heart of historical experiences of change and of socialist movements. It cannot be avoided. What is in question is the creation of forms of communication marked by a process in which solidarity and participation are learned in a daily practice. These forms cease to be "alternative" when the conditions of the new society are reached; at this point the accumulated experience must give way to *participatory communication,* the superior expression of a society that sees itself and realizes itself as participatory. Participation, as a paradigm of individual and collective human development, is before us as an essential challenge. "I do not live in a perfect society, nor do I ask that you give it that name / if I have learned something about that, it is that women and men make it," concludes Pablo Milanés in one of his more recent songs.

Alternative Forms: From Micro to Macro

We now face the problem of forms. This is a field in which analysis has been a bit confused. Alternative communication has often been considered as a set of forms involving small audiences, rather than as a conceptual problem; in fact, "alternativeness" lies not in instruments but in the way they are used.

Alternative language is characterized by its high credibility and its easy assimilation and reinterpretation and by the depth of connotation of its messages. These characteristics of alternative language are reinforced, without a doubt, by the medium in which they are expressed, especially when the instruments used have not been incorporated into the industrial communicative process by the dominant system. Such is the case with urban murals, itinerant theater groups, wall newspapers, and other so-called marginal forms. But, in general, the media can be the same as those used by the dominant pole in its work of cultural domination: festivals, film, radio, records, cassettes, video, theater, the press, and even television. The difference between mass media that are servants of the culture industry and alternative media is the latter's accessibility to the sectors capable of creating an alternative language and impressing upon the media the alternative contents of their program for change. This perspective is as valid in industrialized as in peripheral societies. The diverse forms of alternative communication generally provide mass organizations and other civic organizations with syntheses of social phenomena, a different ordering of reality from that of the dominant media. At the same time they are sources of proposals for action. Syntheses and proposals are the tasks of alternative communication, from traditional or primitive cultural expressions to those created by the industrial system that are recovered by oppositional organizations for their own social and cultural aims.

The forms of expression within alternative communication are diverse. They can be found in practically all communication fields. An alternative itinerary emerges from the popular theater, song, popular poems, murals, and even certain crafts that use wool and pieces of fabric—as in the case of the Chilean burlap quilters—to transmit a significant message. All these expressions start from the participants' discussion of the conditions that affect them. The agenda goes on toward the more technical media—records, photography, film, and other fields.

Within that agenda there are some persistent problems:

1. The efficiency and influence of alternative communication
2. Economic viability
3. Political viability
4. The choice and emphasis of some instruments and forms as opposed to others that have been developed in the alternative field

None of these problems can be considered in isolation. The problem of economic viability is often bound up with that of political viability, since an oppositional expression may find a niche, even in the midst of restrictions, allowing its practitioners to survive and advance economically from that base. The most obvious cases are the alternative magazines that circulate in Brazil, Chile, and Peru and bring in at least enough income to continue to publish their alternative message. Yet when such magazines establish a significant presence inside their societies, they are suffocated by the very mechanisms that bind politics to the production process. Thus, paper is denied them, pressures are applied in the market, or constant censorship impedes them from increasing or even maintaining their circulation. At strategic moments, economic pressures great enough to make the continued publication of the magazine impossible are applied, as in the case of Uruguayan magazine *Opinar.* The police confiscate an issue when it is completely printed: all the expenses of printing have been incurred, but it is impossible to charge for advertising or recover the investment by sales.

However, economic and political viability do not mean the same thing for alternative expressions and the media of the industrial system. The influence of an alternative medium is conveyed not only through its circulation, but more especially through its content. One of the strengths of alternative communication is the novelty of its articles, messages, and programs, which are delivered to social sectors that are constantly exposed to massive industrial communication. To the extent that these messages are alternative, not only in form and political connotation, but in their essential approach to reality, they contribute a focus of attention in a whole universe of communication existing in a society in conflict.

This fact directly touches on a theoretical question constantly discussed in alternative communication experiments: the relationship between action and representation. With the assumption that alternative communication must be closely linked to a social praxis goes the tendency to think that communication is, in and of itself, action. The special contribution of a communicator committed to the alternative process is left aside. It is necessary to reiterate that the alternative communicators, the "cultural animators," have a special creative role. Discovering and advancing from the base of popular culture and collective consciousness, they have the specific mission of creating the synthesis and propositions that clarify the expressions of the social whole. Canclini is right to ask:

Is there not a certain utopian simplification in this effort by some contemporary artists to dissolve absolutely the representation of action? It is undeniable that, in one sense, this change is a positive one: the criticism of art as representation is the criticism of imaginary satisfaction as a substitute for real satisfaction, as a way of evading the changes necessary to obtain real satisfaction. But we do not believe that this emphasis on action—the logical objective of revolutionary art—should exclude the elaboration of symbols, which is indispensable in every culture. Only in a society in which relations between people were transparent could art and language in general be fully identified with action. . . . It was important that the falsified cinema of our countries learn to speak of our way of eating, of working, of the shantytowns and the urban youth. But the producers who went through this consciousness-raising process know today that film too is a language, that it has complex requirements if it is to reach people effectively, that the growth of political consciousness is deeper when reflection is wrapped in the myths, the pleasures, and the games that accompany the lives of all people. (1977)

Thus, the choice of instruments is determined not only by the political and economic prospects for their use, but also by the approach of the alternative creator. The communicators' attitudes are important—how they locate themselves in society, the standpoint from which they generate a message that may have alternative content. At the same time, it is important that they assume that it is fitting to act within a society whose popular imagination is formed by a multiplicity of presences—by both tradition and the cultural industry's constant bombardment.

As an alternative activity confronting the dominant model of communication, the process of the "other communication" must meet the fundamental challenge of creating interaction. One of the consequences of the dominant model of communication is atomization—atomization of creativity and of searches for expression by civil society, atomization of social relations and of joint reflections on the cultural situation. Alternative projects have to advance against a globalizing system of information and communication that tries to create homogeneous behavior patterns, superimposing on cultural diversity the historical project of a universal, transnational culture. This effort takes place on three levels: the international, the national, and even the local or community level.

On each of these levels there are poles of power creating a reality with roots in a single project: that of capitalism in its transnational phase. Within the several areas in which it acts, this project converts to its own uses independent expression and particularity, uses marked by the mercantile approach to the organization of society. Alternative communication constructs itself and explains itself in zones of action different from those of transnational culture. Influence and efficiency attained at one level will not necessarily be attainable at another level. Hence, it is important to develop an analysis of micromedia, of the media of intermediate development, and of alternative macromedia.

Micromedia

Micromedia products are particularly rich and diverse, since they develop in the face of concrete challenges, in specific circumstances in which a new language is constructed and the message is closely identified with and motivated by verifiable evidence. The influence of micromedia, in spite of the precariousness of resources, can therefore be extraordinarily significant.

The work of the Centro de Comunicación Popular in Villa El Salvador, in Lima, reveals the potential of this area of communication. Since 1974 this center has put into operation an audiovisual workshop, for the creation, projection, and discussion of scripts with themes proposed by the people of the community, using slides and cassette recordings; a song workshop, concentrating on the composition and public performance of Peruvian and Latin American folk music; a film workshop, for the projection of films and organization of film forums in the community, teaching the community residents to use the projectors and serving, too, as support for the meetings organized by community leaders; a publications workshop, for the production of leaflets, bulletins, and popular publications, among them the magazine *Crítica,* the only steady news source in Villa El Salvador that has increased its circulation from month to month; a theater workshop, for the creation of works with social content, subsequently produced and acted in the streets of Villa El Salvador by community residents who are members of the workshop.

It is interesting to observe the functioning of this structure in relation to the conditions it wishes to confront—to see the methodology of an effective communication process produced within the popular social sector. Miguel Ascueta, the director of the center, uses a specific example to explain the process:

If we are analyzing the problem of malnutrition in our families, the audiovisual workshop makes a script with slides; the publications workshop writes an article on the theme for publication in *Crítica,* the theater workshop creates a work on malnutrition, accompanied by songs from the song workshop, and the film workshop looks for a film on the subject, or helps the other workshops with their planning. All of this is put at the disposal of the inhabitants of the blocks and the residents' associations, of feminist groups, young people, parishes, so that the theme is not exhausted but is deepened. It is the community of which the Centro de Comunicación Popular is a part that decides what the most adequate solution to each problem is. We see, then, that the objectives of the center in using the media and techniques of communication in this way are to inform, to educate, and to mobilize the population. (1981)

The relationship between communication and education is most evident in this form of alternative communication. The categories run together when the approach is based in the "other development." These are precisely the categories that the dominant system tends to separate.

Media of Intermediate Development

A field of significant influence at the national and regional levels is constituted by the so-called media of intermediate development. These produce alternative expressions related to political projects that affect the great majority of people in each society, raise broad issues, and provide a forum for synthesis. In them, an alternative community at the national level finds its orientation, information, and motivation. They do not have large print runs or broadcast over a wide area, but they have the strength of their message.

In general, these media do not correspond to the mechanisms of popular action at the base. They are obliged to spread their messages within market structures, needing a substantial distribution at a national level. Perhaps the most concrete and tangible examples are alternative magazines. In the peripheral countries, especially in Latin America, and the industrialized countries alike, they meet a series of obstacles imposed by the economic system and the mechanisms of distribution.

Cuadernos del Tercer Mundo, with Mexican and Brazilian editions, was a pioneering effort with macroalternative aspirations, of which I will speak later. Other national magazines reflect similar forces: *Movimiento* in Brazil,

Diálogo Social in Panama, *Aportes* in Costa Rica, *Marka* in Peru, *Proceso* in Mexico, *Análisis* and *Solidaridad* in Chile. Often these experiments face the contradiction of wanting to be alternative means of communication, closely linked to progressive social organizations, and having to act within a system and a market that limit their influence and circulation. As Juan Pablo Cárdenas, director of *Análisis,* puts it:

Because of the firm restrictions that exist in the country, it is very difficult to maintain relations systematically with our readers. Today in Chile, it is difficult to meet, to call assemblies of receivers, and in the same way it is difficult for people who work in the magazine to consult freely with the mass organizations that read us and follow us with interest. But we are trying to the extent that there has been some evolution in our country, to have a closer relationship to our readers. (Quoted in Richards, 1980)

Other efforts focus on content, giving preference to a certain sector of society. The magazine *La Bicicleta,* also published in Chile, represents a real advance. It tries to give an account of currents and alternative cultural expressions from various sectors of Chilean society that are seeking the recovery of a democratic way of living together: "We are alternative," says the director of *La Bicicleta,* "because we try to resituate people with regard to their own experience, their reality, their real aspirations, which go beyond the consumerist longings with which they are inculcated by their environment. We are alternative as a matter of cultural expression valuable to society at this moment, as a counterproposal to the one that is being diffused through the most official and traditional channels—the consumer culture, which ends up alienating and harming youth, young people who are being manipulated in their taste, motives, behavior, values" (quoted in Richards, 1980).

Experiments at this level are not confined to the written word. Various recording companies have emerged as an alternative within an industry at the heart of capitalist transnational development. Record Companies like Alerce in Chile, Foton and NCL in Mexico, and the Cooperativa de Acción Cultural in Portugal demonstrate the possibility of creating, at the national level, an alternative approach and alternative contents. Another exemplary field is constituted by radio stations like "La Voz de la Costa" in the province of Osorno, Chile, or "Radio Enriquillo" in the southern part of the Dominican Republic. The creativity of their programming and their content is born directly of their relations with local organizations and the demands of an audience anxious to develop links with the broadcaster. In spite of their local range, their alternative content has had a significant influence throughout each country.

Alternative Macromedia

Alternative macromedia emerge from the joining of regional and world forces with the aim of creating a discourse in opposition to the one created by the transnational system. This category comprises certain news agencies, audiovisual exchange systems, and publications that, in governmental and non-governmental organizations, promote an understanding of information and communication as a social responsibility rather than as a trade process. This approach allows the clarification of a certain confusion that has marked the analytic development of alternative communication, since the communication in force has sometimes been identified with macromedia and alternative communication with micromedia. So says José Ignacio Rey: "The preference for or exclusive use of micromedia does not in itself ensure a real alternative communication. On the other hand, it has never been shown that the great media of communication, in and of themselves, make genuine communication impossible; in most countries, factors external to the media make it impossible" (1980). At this level more than at any other, alternative communication is not necessarily defined by the instruments or media used to create it, but basically and principally by its contents and by the commitments of the social sectors that at the national and international levels are proposing a development characterized by sharing and solidarity.

An eloquent example is the news agency Inter-Press Service. This news agency was born in 1965 as a journalists' cooperative and has progressively evolved a commitment to the positions of Third World countries and to their demands for a new economic order and, at the same time, a new international information order. This latter demand rejects the news values imposed by the transnational system and fortifies the links between the sectors of the Third World and the North that are capable of searching together for a development free from the burdens of colonialism, neocolonialism, accelerated industrial development, and political and economic authoritarianism:

Alternative communication . . . constitutes information that can be classified in the following categories: analytical/systematic/contextual/non-elitist/relevant/oriented towards development.

Alternative information is *analytical* because it locates events, themes, processes, in the adequate historical, political, social, economic and cultural contexts. It is *systematic* because it does not focus on the exceptional but maintains regular and constant coverage of themes and geographic areas. It takes into account *processes* in that it recognizes that society is the result of various processes, which are fundamental for the daily life of all people, even when this is not very obvious. Alternative news is *not directed by the elites,* in the measure in which it tends to cover masses instead of people who have attained prominence and visibility through political, economic or other power. It is *relevant* because it tends to relate information being produced to the needs of the people involved. Finally, alternative information is *oriented towards development* because it focusses on successes and difficulties of the policies and actions adopted by various groups and nations which work in favor of social development. (Savio and Harris, 1980)

These approaches are not alien to other searches for alternative content. A case in point is the national news agency pool of the nonaligned countries.

This unique force tries to achieve a certain international influence for the perspective of decolonization. Another expression is constituted by forces like the Pan-African News Agency, which focuses on information about Africa. ALASEI is a project whose goal is to create a feature service to circulate alternative messages in the established press of Latin America, a novel and difficult task. Acción de Servicios Informativos Nacionales joins the forces of the official news services of ten Latin American countries. These exchange news daily and each may reuse the products of the others.

In the area of macroalternative forces, the fundamental requisite for the development of alternative communication is most evident: the creation of networks. Within the transnational system, interrelationships have created a fabric of power at the international and national levels. The transnational network atomizes society, while basing itself on a supposed new history constructed for the "mass society." Cultural diversity and the creativity of groups or individuals are deferred to the field of curiosities, anecdotes, and deviations from the normal. What remains is a transnational world of common references and symbols. Networks of information, of the production and exchange of radio and television programs, of alternative magazines, of videocassettes, of microcomputer and data-bank users, are challenges that herald the development of the alternative at a level of effective influence. It is here, finally, in the creation of networks, that micro, intermediate, and macro alternatives interweave. Diverse experiments and searches can find mutual support, united in a common desire for change at the level of local, national, and world relations.

The Basic Perspectives for Alternative Communication

How can alternative communication avoid the danger of being co-opted in one way or another by the dominant system?

First, one must affirm that alternative communication is a *process*. Consequently, in order to achieve the democratization of communication, it is its task to speak up for the present and future reality. As Dorfman says:

It is a question of exploring this everyday world: discovering that domination is not omnipotence, that its margin is reduced, that even though human communication is an area of conflict, very difficult, it is possible. Today we have a challenge: there is an imperial culture that tries to dominate all the corners of daily life. If we are not capable of understanding them in our science, in our daily action, the consequences will be very grave for our continent. (*Uno Más Uno,* 1980)

Openness to using everything makes possible the clarification of consciousness and the generation of social alliances to respond to the atomized model of society. This approach allows the reformulation of new technologies that emerge from the developed and developing countries. Technology itself does not constitute the response, the new communication. It is the consciousness of what needs to be said that enables those technologies to be recovered in the movement toward individual and social liberation.

The second important affirmation is that communication is not only a sending process, but also a receiving one. It is a dialogue that occurs where popular culture is living and growing. However, it is important to understand the necessity of stimulating, in an organized way, a process of critical consumption of the products of the dominant communication system. Ossandón, in an analysis of popular communication in Chile, says:

The people's construction as a historical subject presupposes the creation of the capacity to arrest the ideologizing and immobilizing effects of the mass media in popular sectors. The problem then becomes how to arrest that influence, how to diminish the effect of this manipulation, by ensuring the critical consumption and the autonomy of judgment, taste, and creation of the person who receives these messages day by day. It is understood too that this task is inseparable from the other, fundamental one: to ensure the creation of the people's own media and forms, designed to satisfy their need for education and expression, especially those that emanate from liberation struggles. (1981)

The organizational task required by this goal of critical consumption includes the need to stimulate the diverse forms of participation within the experience of alternative communication, whether these involve micromedia, the media of intermediate development, or alternative macromedia. *Participation* is the essential concept, the motivating principle behind the development of communication that is consistent with liberated and liberating structures. From this principle and its practice, the conditions can be created for an alternative relationship between communicator and receiver, between media and audiences, and the possibility of creating the space for active social participation in communication.

References

Aguirre Bianchi, C., and G. Hedebro (1980). "Another Development, Another Information: The Next Step After the MacBride Report." Paper presented to the IAMCR conference, Caracas.

Arrieta, M. (1980). "Sobre la Comunicación Alternativa." *Comunicación* (Caracas), 28–29.

Ascueta, M. (1981). "La Comunicación Popular: Participación en el Centro de Villa El Salvador." Paper presented to the Seminar on Comunicación y Movimiento Popular, sponsored by CELADEC, Lima, September.

Canclini, N. (1977). "Cine Documental, Histórico, de Ficción, de Entretenimiento: Caminos de un Cine Popular." *Arte, Sociedad, Ideología* (Mexico), 1, June.

Chapa, G., and M. Angel (1980). "Comunicación Alternativa, Comunicación del Oprimido." *Estudios del Tercer Mundo: Comunicación* (Mexico), 3, 3.

DESCO (1980). *Cultura y Clases Sociales.* Lima: DESCO.

Dupuy, J. P., and J. Robert (1979). *La Traición de la Opulencia.* Barcelona: GEDISA.

Eapen, E. (1980). "Popular Communication in India." *Media Development* (London), 28, 2.

"La Fotografía Como Arma Lucha" (1981). *Tiempo* (Maputo), April.

Hamelink, C. J. (1978). "The Cultural Synchronisation of the World." *WACC Journal* (London), 1.

Kaplún, M., and J. O'Sullivan (1978). "FORO-Cassette." Working paper. Caracas.

Marcuse, H., et al. (1968). *La Sociedad Industrial Contemporánea.* Mexico City: Siglo XXI.

Mattelart, A. (1981). *Comunicación y Transición al Socialismo: El Caso Mozambique.* Mexico City: Serie Popular Era.

Mattelart, A., and M. Mattelart (1981). *Los Medios de Comunicación en los Tiempos de Crisis.* Mexico City: Siglo XXI.

Morin, E. (1981). *Pour Sortir du Siecle 2000.* Paris: Ed. Seuil.

"La Nueva Canción en Costa Rica." *Aportes* (San José, Costa Rica), Oct.

Ossandón, F. (1981). "Comunicación Popular y Rearticulación del Movimiento Popular en Chile." Paper presented to the Seminar on Comunicación y Movimiento Popular, sponsored by CELADEC, Lima, September.

Prieto Castillo, D. (1980). *Discurso Autoritario y Comunicación Alternativa.* Mexico City: Edicol.

Rameda, M. (1980). "El Disco Alternativo." *Cuadernos del Tercer Mundo,* 38, June.

Rey, J. I. (1980). "Comunicación Alternativa y Comunicación Popular." *Comunicación* (Caracas), 28–29.

Richards, J. A. (1980). "La Prensa Alternativa en Chile: El Testimonio de Sus Protagonistas." *Comunicación* (Caracas), 28–29.

Savio, R., and P. Harris (1980). "IPS-Third World Agency and NIIO." *Media Development* (London), 28, 2.

Uno Más Uno (1980). Interview with Ariel Dorfman. Aug. 8.

Vidal Beneyto, J. (1979). *Alternativas Populares a la Comunicación de Masas.* Madrid: Centro de Investigaciones Sociológicas.

Index

Advertising: as language, 137–40; economic base of media, 81–84, 130–32; global marketing, 136–37; ideological, hegemonic function, 117–18, 147; product sales, 129, 132–37, 139; role in transnational capitalism, 81–84, 105, 14–15, 117–18, 127, socio-cultural impacts, 82–83, 132–41; United States (transnational) market domination, 82–84, 101, 105, 127, 131–32. *See also* Capitalism; National communication policy; Transnationalization
Aguirre Bianchi, Claudio, 184–85
ALASEI, 19, 66, 212. *See also* News
Allende, Salvador, 51, 55
Alternative communication: barriers to, 206–8; definitions of, 18–20, 38–40, 67–68, 85–86, 165–66, 169–78, 180–86, 190, 193, 204–13; and language, 200–201; links to liberation theology and comunidades de base, 67, 170, 183, 198; macro and micro means of communication, 36, 194, 199, 205–9; as resistance to cultural domination, 39–40, 57, 67–68, 80, 169–75, 194–99, 201–12; role of communication workers, 176, 207–8; role of researcher in, 18–22, 38–41, 60–61, 67–68, 181–86, 190–93, 212–13; role of state in, 166, 176n, 184–85; as social praxis, 20, 67–68, 178–83, 194–212; strategies for and examples of, 19–20, 57, 66, 85, 172, 180–86, 191–92, 195–212; theory of spiral communication flow, 202–5; vanguard theory, 172–79. *See also* Broadcast media; Democratic communication; Hispanic American critical research; Liberation; News; NIIO; Technology; Transnationalization

Alvaredo, Velazco, 184
Alvez, Luis Roberto, 183
Argentina: Malvinas crisis, 51; media development, 97–98; Peronism, 51; research from, 42, 97–98
Argumedo, Alcira, 181
Ascueta, Miguel, 209
Atwood, Rita, 3–4, 13
Audley, P., 33
Avila, L., 166

Barthes, Roland, 54
Bebeland, August, 173
Beltrán, Luis Ramiro, 12, 13, 18, 29, 31, 32, 48, 57–59, 61, 62, 67, 94
Blumler, Jay G., 16
Bolivia: miners' radio, 183, 202–3
Bourdieu, Pierre, 91
Braudel, F., 42
Brazil: alternative communication, 198, 206, 209–10; colonization of, 98–101; cultural history of, 98–102; export cultural products, 65, 105, 108–9; new technologies, 102–3; newspapers, 102–3, 106–7; Rede Globo television, 96, 102, 104–6; research from, 42, 85, 89–111; role of military, 103–6; transnationalization of economy and media, 100–110, 127, 129, 139
Bringas, Guillermina, 183
Broadcast media. *See also* Advertising, Education, Technology
—radio: as alternative media, 183, 199, 202–3; in Bolivia, 183, 202–3; in Brazil, 101; in Uruguay and Venezuela, 199
—television: audience effects, 149–60; content in Mexico, 148–49; as hegemonic cultural force, 101–5, 115–21, 147–49; industry structure, 145–46; Latin Ameri-

215

COMPOSED BY G & S TYPESETTERS, INC., AUSTIN, TEXAS
MANUFACTURED BY EDWARDS BROTHERS, INC., ANN ARBOR, MICHIGAN
TEXT AND DISPLAY LINES ARE SET IN TIMES ROMAN

Library of Congress Cataloging-in-Publication Data
Communication and Latin American society.
(Studies in communication and society)
Includes bibliographies and index.
Contents: Assessing critical mass communication
scholarship in the Americas / Rita Atwood—
Seminal ideas in Latin American critical communication
research / Emile G. McAnany—Hispanic American
critical communication research in its historical
context / Cristina Schwarz and Oscar Jaramillo—[etc.]
1. Communication—Research—Latin America.
2. Intercultural communication. I. Atwood, Rita.
II. McAnany, Emile G.   III. Series.
HM258.C5835   1986   302.2'098   86-40044
ISBN 0-299-10720-5